Maya® Studio Projects

Game Environments and Props

MICHAEL MCKINLEY

Wiley Publishing, Inc.

Acquisitions Editor: MARIANN BARSOLO
Development Editor: KIM WIMPSETT
Technical Editor: CAMPBELL STRONG
Production Editor: CHRISTINE O'CONNOR
Copy Editor: SARA WILSON
Editorial Manager: PETE GAUGHAN
Production Manager: TIM TATE
Vice President and Executive Group Publisher: RICHARD SWADLEY
Vice President and Publisher: NEIL EDDE
Assistant Project Manager: JENNY SWISHER
Associate Producer: DOUG KUHN
Quality Assurance: JOSH FRANK
Book Designers: CARYL GORSKA, MAUREEN FORYS, KATE KAMINSKI
Compositor: CHRIS GILLESPIE, HAPPENSTANCE TYPE-O-RAMA
Proofreader: NELSON KIM, WORD ONE NEW YORK
Indexer: ROBERT SWANSON
Project Coordinator, Cover: LYNSEY STANFORD
Cover Designer: RYAN SNEED
Cover Image: MICHAEL MCKINLEY

Copyright © 2010 by Wiley Publishing, Inc., Indianapolis, Indiana

Published simultaneously in Canada

ISBN: 978-0-470-52403-9

For general information on our other products and services or to obtain technical support, please contact our Customer Care Department within the U.S. at (877) 762-2974, outside the U.S. at (317) 572-3993 or fax (317) 572-4002.

Wiley also publishes its books in a variety of electronic formats. Some content that appears in print may not be available in electronic books.

Library of Congress Cataloging-in-Publication Data

McKinley, Michael (Michael T.)
  Maya studio projects : game environments and props / Michael McKinley. — 1st ed.
    p. cm.
  ISBN-13: 978-0-470-52403-9
  ISBN-10: 0-470-52403-0
  1. Computer Animation. 2. Computer games—Programming. 3. Digital video. 4. Computer graphics. 5. Maya (Computer file) 6. Simulation games. I. Title.
  TR897.7.M39525 2010
  006.6'96—dc22
                          2009043717

10 9 8 7 6 5 4 3 2 1

Dear Reader,

Thank you for choosing *Maya Studio Projects: Game Environments and Props.* This book is part of a family of premium-quality Sybex books, all of which are written by outstanding authors who combine practical experience with a gift for teaching.

Sybex was founded in 1976. More than 30 years later, we're still committed to producing consistently exceptional books. With each of our titles, we're working hard to set a new standard for the industry. From the paper we print on, to the authors we work with, our goal is to bring you the best books available.

I hope you see all that reflected in these pages. I'd be very interested to hear your comments and get your feedback on how we're doing. Feel free to let me know what you think about this or any other Sybex book by sending me an email at nedde@wiley.com. If you think you've found a technical error in this book, please visit http://sybex.custhelp.com. Customer feedback is critical to our efforts at Sybex.

Best regards,

Neil Edde
Vice President and Publisher
Sybex, an Imprint of Wiley

To my beautiful Ginger Rose.

Acknowledgments

This book would not have been possible without the encouragement, understanding, patience, and love of my wonderful wife Ginger. Without her, I'd be a lonely husk of a man and I am forever grateful for her companionship through the process of writing this book. She put up with a lot and I am so glad she was there through it all. Ginger, I love you with all my heart. ■ To my parents, who have always encouraged me to follow my own path and chase my dreams, thank you. I love you both very much. ■ And of course, there's no way this book would ever have gotten done without the invaluable help of those at Sybex who guided me in the process. Mariann Barsolo, Kim Wimpsett, Campbell Strong, Christine O'Connor, and I'm sure more that I haven't remembered or properly met. Thank you all for your help and guidance! ■ Philippians 4:13

About the Author

Michael McKinley is originally from southern Mississippi, where he grew up in a rural environment. Knowing from an early age that video games were his dream, he packed up after high school and set out to make his way in the world. He is now a senior environment artist working at Zombie Studios in Seattle, Washington. He has worked in the game industry for seven years on a variety of titles, including *NFL Street 3*, *Tomb Raider: Anniversary*, *Garden Defense*, and *SAW*. Not to mention a long list of titles that for whatever reason didn't make it to release!

Michael is the author of *The Game Artist's Guide to Maya* as well as *The Game Animator's Guide to Maya*. Back in the day, he was a teacher's assistant in Maya classes at Collins College in Tempe, Arizona. He can be found frequently working as an administrator at www.simplymaya.com and is always open to questions or comments about Maya or game development.

CONTENTS AT A GLANCE

Introduction ◼ **xi**

Chapter 1 ◼ Walls, Ceilings, and Floors **1**

Chapter 2 ◼ Foliage **37**

Chapter 3 ◼ Weapons **71**

Chapter 4 ◼ Vehicles **109**

Chapter 5 ◼ Buildings **143**

Chapter 6 ◼ Illuminators **183**

Chapter 7 ◼ Ambient Movement **203**

Chapter 8 ◼ Putting It All Together **217**

Chapter 9 ◼ Pro Tips **241**

Appendix A ◼ Image Gallery **249**

Appendix B ◼ About the Companion DVD **257**

Index ◼ **263**

Contents

Introduction   xii

Chapter 1 ▪ Walls, Ceilings, and Floors   **1**

Understanding Backgrounds   1

Project: Creating a Brick Wall   3

Information Overload   35

Chapter 2 ▪ Foliage   **37**

Understanding Foliage   37

Project: Creating Ivy   38

Project: Creating a Savannah Tree   53

The Illusion of Detail   69

Chapter 3 ▪ Weapons   **71**

Understanding Weapons   71

Project: Creating and Animating
a Western Revolver   72

Moving Right Along   106

Chapter 4 ▪ Vehicles   **109**

Understanding Vehicles   109

Project: Building a Dune Buggy   110

Where to Go from Here?   141

Chapter 5 ▪ Buildings   **143**

Understanding Buildings   143

Project: Building a Skyscraper   144

Let's Light It Up   181

Chapter 6 ▪ Illuminators   **183**

Understanding Illuminators   183

Project: Creating a Wall Sconce   185

In the Home Stretch!   201

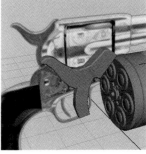

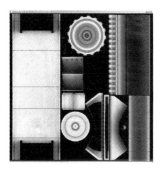

Chapter 7 ▦ Ambient Movement   **203**

    Understanding Movers   203

    Project: Creating an Industrial Fan   204

    Not Just a Level   215

Chapter 8 ▦ Putting It All Together   **217**

    Project: Creating a Sci-Fi Prop   217

    Project Complete!   239

Chapter 9 ▦ Pro Tips   **241**

    Using Mudbox or ZBrush   241

    Creating Level of Detail   241

    Mipmapping   243

    Using Multiple UV Channels   244

    Creating Collision Meshes   245

    Being Professional   246

    Have Fun!   247

Appendix A ▦ Image Gallery   **249**

Appendix B ▦ About the Companion DVD   **257**

    What You'll Find on the DVD   257

    System Requirements   258

    Using the DVD   260

    Troubleshooting   261

    Customer Care   261

Index   **263**

Introduction

My teaching style has always been about preparing a student for a job in the game industry. I always try to instruct based on the realities of the position and not an idealized fantasy. Game development is hard work for all those involved, from the artists to the programmers, and to prepare to be one of those artists, it helps to get the straight skinny from someone who has "been there and done that." I know getting such inside information from an industry veteran was a great help to me when I was first starting out. Although I may not be the most experienced old fogy in the biz, I do try to pass down what I have learned to the next generation, with only one request I ask in return— don't get so good that you take my job!

The projects in this book are based on projects a real game environment artist would be tasked with doing. And in completing the projects, I hope you get a grasp on the process of creating a game art asset that could potentially be used in a game. After following these lessons and reading over the information within, I believe the art asset development pipeline will be made more clear to you and give you a step up toward your own career in developing games!

Who Should Buy This Book

I am making certain assumptions about readers of this book:

- You are familiar with basic computer functions.
- You know basic Maya functions, such as camera navigation and manipulation tools.
- You have a grasp on basic modeling, how to apply a Bevel or Extrude, and how to manipulate vertices.
- You are familiar with basic Photoshop functions.
- You have a rudimentary understanding of layers and masks in Photoshop.

This book is intended for the artist who has learned the basics of creating something in Maya and now wants to steer those skills more acutely toward a career creating environmental art for games. You won't find tutorials about creating a cube or bouncing a rubber ball in this book. Or much of anything to do with NURBS! This book takes the projects that a professional game artist has done and recreates them here with step-by-step instruction. If you are completely new to Maya, I recommend using this book *in addition to* a beginner's guide to Maya.

Creating game art can be an extremely rewarding and fun experience, but just as with anything that is worth doing, it takes practice. Everyone starts somewhere, and that's usually at the beginning! Keep your eye on the prize, soak up as much knowledge as you can, and you will come out the other end well on your way toward your dream job. I hope you enjoy the ride!

What You Need

To follow along with all the examples in this book, you'll of course need Maya. The latest version of Maya as of this writing is Maya 2010, but you should be able to follow along with the steps even if you have a previous version of the software. You'll also need some kind of texture creation software, such as Adobe Photoshop or Corel Painter.

 When you see a DVD icon like this in the book, you'll know that the files being referenced in the tutorials are available on the book's companion DVD. These files will allow you to follow along with the book's step-by-step instruction. See Appendix B for more details on the DVD contents and how to access them.

What's Inside

Here is a peek at what each chapter covers:

Chapter 1: Walls, Ceilings, and Floors begins with the basics by creating the fundamental building blocks that make a room. Using Maya and Photoshop, you'll create tiling geometry and textures for background elements.

Chapter 2: Foliage dives into the creation of plants and vegetation. Using basic modeling, you'll create a vine of ivy and a tree. This chapter also introduces the usage of transparency maps.

Chapter 3: Weapons shows more complex modeling by creating a six-shooter revolver. This chapter goes over more complex UV mapping and texture baking.

Chapter 4: Vehicles covers the advanced creation of a desert dune buggy vehicle.

Chapter 5: Buildings introduces you to the concept of building modularly and takes you through the process of creating 10 modules that can be used to create a large variety of different buildings.

Chapter 6: Illuminators shows how to create an object that is used as a light source, introducing the concept of emissive textures.

Chapter 7: Ambient Movement covers the creation of an animated background prop, in this case, an industrial fan. Creating the model and the animation are both taught in this chapter.

Chapter 8: Putting It All Together takes everything that has been taught previously in the book and puts it together to create a science-fiction-style prop, complete with glowing effects!

Chapter 9: Pro Tips goes over extra information that any good environment artist should know.

Appendix A: Image Gallery displays a variety of examples of game environment work from several professional artists.

Appendix B: About the Companion DVD tells you all about the DVD that comes with this book.

> The companion DVD is home to all the project files, video supplements, and bonus resources mentioned in the book. See Appendix B for more details on the contents and how to access them.

How to Contact the Author

I try to always make myself available to anyone who has a question. Feel free to contact me through my website at www.mtmckinley.net. There I have my own personal portfolio as well as information about this and other products I have been involved in. You can also find me acting as an administrator at the website www.simplymaya.com and I am always happy to chat. I look forward to hearing from you!

If the need arises for updates or further information on the book, please go to www.sybex.com/mspgame.

CHAPTER 1

Walls, Ceilings, and Floors

A basic interior game environment consists of some combination of walls, ceilings, and floors. For the most part, the way you create any of these three surfaces will follow standard procedures, but they definitely have differences that you need to consider. These surfaces (and I'll refer to them as *backgrounds* from now on) will be forming the foundation from which you'll be building all other props and environmental visuals in your interior spaces. You definitely want to treat your backgrounds consistently and to the highest quality.

Understanding Backgrounds

In this chapter, the term *backgrounds* refers to 3D surfaces that serve the basic function of a wall, a ceiling, or a floor. The way a game handles such surfaces can differ depending on the game editor being used, if any. A game's editor is typically the program used to create the levels in a game. Assets from applications such as Maya are imported into the editor to be used. The level can then be exported from the editor into a format the game itself (or the game engine) can understand and run as a playable product. Many types of editors exist, and not all game engines use them in the same ways. Your art lead will fill you in on the specific idiosyncrasies of the project you are working on.

For instance, in *Tomb Raider: Anniversary* (published by Eidos), there wasn't an editor involved at all. All of the game environments were created directly in the 3D program and exported into a format the game could understand. In games created with the Unreal engine (developed by Epic Games and licensed to other game developers), developers used the Unreal Editor to create shapes and volumes of surfaces that can be textured to form background surfaces. Other editors have terrain generators that can create large expanses of ground or water volumes. And in some games, certain background surfaces aren't even needed. In *Diablo II* (famously developed by Blizzard Entertainment), the game's overhead, isometric perspective eliminated the need to create ceilings.

Most games, no matter what kind of editor they use or what type of backgrounds they need, will adhere to very specific rules for creating them. These can vary greatly between projects, but most do have two commonalities. They will have specific sizes and shapes and they will *tile*.

When something tiles, it means several assets (textures, models, and so on) can be laid end-to-end and there will be no gaps or visible seams between them. This applies to all background surfaces as well as textures. Walls need to tile from left to right, while ceilings and floors need to tile from all four directions. I'll go into much more detail about tiling later in the chapter.

You also need to regulate the specific sizes of background shapes you create. If environment artists were to create background pieces without such regulations, it would make the process of tiling them in a game level much more difficult and time-consuming. It can even change the way a game can be played. If it is specified that a game character can climb up onto platforms that are no higher than eight feet tall, then it's important that such platforms are created in that manner, as well as making sure areas that *shouldn't* be climbed are higher than eight feet. These different sizes can also vary between games, but whatever size conventions are used, they must be used consistently.

Background surfaces will typically be used throughout an entire game. The wall that is used in a castle in level one is actually the same wall being used in the dungeon in level two. It just has a different texture applied. The floor? Same thing. The floor that represents a marbled foyer is the same one for the hardwood floor in the forest cabin with different textures applied. And so on for ceilings. In this example, these would be in your game's set of "man-made" background elements.

The more varied in style the backgrounds a game has, the more sets of background pieces will need to be made. For example, you'd need a different set of background pieces for your cave environments or your sewer environments, and so on. But all the pieces within each set should tile together with others from the same set. A custom piece could then be created for the purpose of merging two sets. A cave entrance piece, for instance, could lead from one environment set into the cave environment set seamlessly.

Understanding this, you can see that it's actually the textures that are the most important part of making the background elements. While there are just a handful of different shaped wall segments, there can be dozens, if not hundreds, of textures that could be applied to drastically change how each wall looks. Start tiling the backgrounds end-to-end, placing floors and ceilings, adding props and lighting, and before you know it, you have a game environment on your hands!

But hold on. Don't put Maya away just yet! The path toward creating tiling textures for your backgrounds still requires some 3D work. You'll understand better when you start your first project. You'll start simple, with a grungy, dirty brick wall.

Project: Creating a Brick Wall

You'll use Maya to create a brick wall. Without worrying about polycounts, UVs, or any other game art restriction, you'll create a high-resolution wall of 3D bricks. Once that's completed, you'll then create your low-resolution wall. This low-resolution wall will be the actual piece that will go into your fictional game. Then, using your high-res geometry, you'll create your textures in a 2D image program, such as Adobe Photoshop. But I'm getting ahead of myself.

Creating a Brick

The first step of creating a simple brick wall is creating a simple brick. In this and in all of this book's projects, you'll be using polygons for both high- and low-resolution models. You'll also use this standard: one unit in Maya is equal to one foot (or 12 inches) in real-world space. A quick look into architecture will show you that a typical brick is $8 \times 4 \times 2.25$ inches. For your purposes, you don't have to be incredibly accurate. The only real criteria that most game artists have for their final results are as follows, unless of course something else is important to your game's play:

- Does it make sense?
- Does it look cool?
- Does it work in the game?

If those criteria are all met, for the most part, you've got a winner!

Before starting, make sure you set your project to your project directory by going to File → Project → Set.

Since you know the typical dimensions of a standard brick, you'll use that as your starting point and create a brick:

1. When first opening Maya, make sure your Menu Set is set to Polygons.
2. Select Create → Polygon Primitives → Cube → Options.
3. In the options, set Width to 8, Height to 4, and Depth to 2.25.
4. Click Close.
5. Hold the Shift key and click near the origin of your scene. This will create the cube with the entered dimensions rather than creating it interactively. A cube will be created using the set dimensions. Go ahead and hold the X key and move the cube to the origin. Holding the X key while moving an object enables Snap to Grid mode, which allows you to snap the cube to the origin.
6. Rotate the cube 90 degrees in the y-axis to make the forward-facing side of the brick point in the positive X direction in your scene. You can also move it up 2 units in the

Y direction to make it appear to set upon the grid like a shelf. This is mainly to make viewing your scene easier.

7. With the cube selected, select Edit Mesh → Bevel. This will apply a Bevel command to your geometry. In the Channel Box on the right side of the screen, under the Inputs list, select the new polyBevel1 item that has appeared, if it's not selected already.

8. Under polyBevel1 is a list of different settings that you can adjust for your new bevel. Change Offset to 0.15, Segments to 2, and Smoothing Angle to 90.

   You should have a box with rounded edges, like in Figure 1.1.

> Your grid spacing may vary from mine, depending on what your settings are. My settings (you can find yours under Display → Grid → Options) have Length and Width set to 12, Grid lines every 5 units, and Subdivisions every 5 units. In general, it shouldn't affect the project negatively if your settings are different.

9. Change to the Front viewport and select Edit Mesh → Cut Faces Tool. Holding the Shift key to make straight cuts, click and drag to the right, cutting four or five cuts into the front of the brick, dividing it roughly into equal slices along its entire height. Do it again vertically, dividing it lengthways in the same manner. In the Side view, do the same: Cut two or three vertical slices into the brick. You should end up with something like what you see in Figure 1.2.

10. Duplicate this brick two times, giving yourself three pristine bricks to start with.

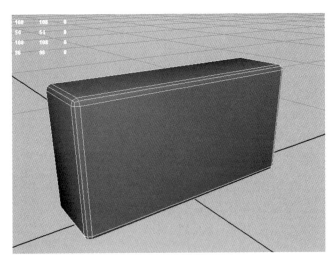

Figure 1.1
The brick so far

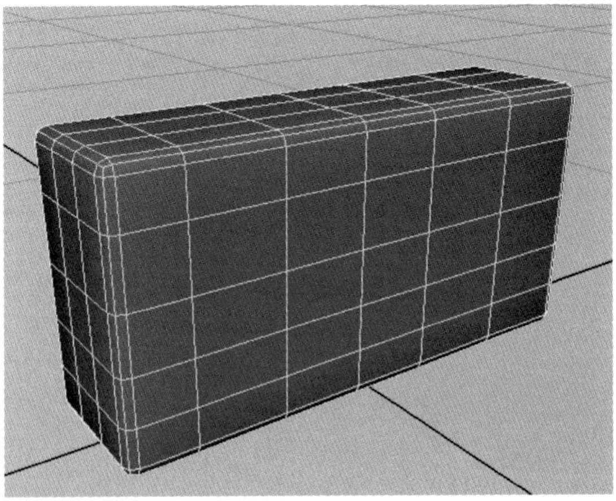

Figure 1.2
Sliced up

Adding Nooks and Crannies

Now that you have some very clean-looking brick shapes, you'll dirty them up a bit. You'll add some pockmarks, chipped-off chunks, and so on, so that your bricks look like they've been out in the elements for years and years.

1. Select Create → Polygon Primitives → Sphere. Create a small sphere next to your first brick.

2. In its Inputs, under the polySphere1 options, change both Subdivisions Axis and Subdivisions Height to 8.

3. With the right mouse button (RMB), hold on the sphere and choose Faces from the marking menu, turning on Face component mode.

4. Select and delete the faces that make up the lower half of the sphere.

5. Press F8 twice to return to Object mode. With the half sphere selected, select Mesh → Fill Hole. This will cap the hole that you left behind, creating a solid half sphere (Figure 1.3).

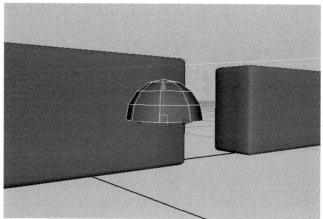

Figure 1.3
The halved sphere

The half sphere will become a negative-space object. It is going to be used to carve out pieces of your currently pristine bricks. You first need to knock it around a bit—mess the sphere up so that it looks more like a rock than a smooth round shape.

6. Make sure the Keep Faces Together setting is selected in the Edit Mesh menu. Entering Face component mode again, select the sphere's remaining faces (*not* selecting the cap face you just created with the Fill Hole command) and select Edit Mesh → Extrude. Pull these new faces out and scale them inward.

7. In the extrude face's Inputs in the Channel Box, adjust the Random attribute until you get a suitably randomized result without any faces sheering.

8. Back in Object mode, select Mesh → Triangulate (Figure 1.4).

The main goal of this step is to get an organic, natural-looking shape. The only thing you don't really want is to have sheer edges that are overlapping or intersecting each other. You'll go one step further in making the sphere look a bit more messed up to get a few more surface variations.

Figure 1.4
That sphere is messed up.

9. Select a clump of three or four faces on the top of the sphere and select Edit Mesh → Extrude to extrude them up. Scale them inward a bit. Do the same on another clump of three or four faces, extruding them up at a different height, scaling them inward slightly.

10. Duplicate your resulting rock-like object two more times. Leave the first as it is, but scale the second up to be tall and skinny. Scale the third down to be short and squat. You should have something like the objects in Figure 1.5.

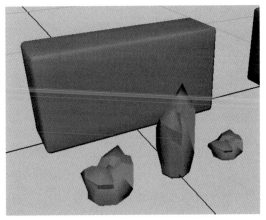

11. Start duplicating and positioning these rocky objects around your first brick, slightly intersecting. Rotate them so that the rocky tops are the sides that are intersecting into the brick shape. Think about where a brick would

Figure 1.5
Three negative-space objects to play with

be the most weathered. Focus on the corners and along the edges more than the flat surfaces. Don't be afraid to clump the rocks together, intersecting each other. You can also continue to scale the shapes further if necessary.

12. Do the same for the second brick, making certain to intersect the rocky shapes differently than you did for the first. Don't position them on the third brick at all.

Just remember, don't intersect them too deeply. You mainly want the bricks to look as if they have been chipped, not gouged out completely! When you're done, you should have something like Figure 1.6.

Figure 1.6
The bricks prepared
for chipping

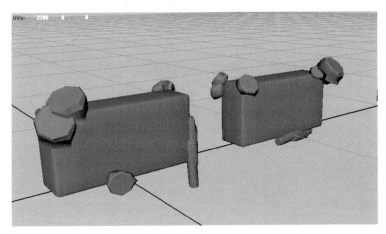

13. Now for the fun part! Select your first brick and Shift-select one of the intersecting rocks that are around it. Select Mesh → Booleans → Difference. The rock should disappear, carving out of the brick wherever the rock intersected the brick.

14. With the brick selected, Shift-select another rock and press the G key. (The G shortcut key will redo whatever action you last did.) Continue to carve out the remaining rocks from both bricks, making sure that the brick is selected first and then a rock is Shift-selected before pressing the G key.

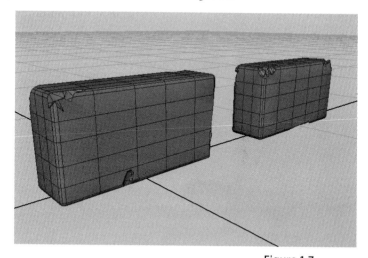

If, when you are done, you find that you would like more chipped-away parts or that some of your rocks were intersecting the bricks too deeply and too much brick has been carved away, undo (Z) and readjust them until you get a result you like. Eventually, you should get a result similar to Figure 1.7. With these three bricks, you'll have enough variation that your brick wall shouldn't look too repetitive or boring.

Figure 1.7
Two chipped bricks ready for placement

Laying Bricks

Now, you'll lay out your bricks to form your tileable wall, from which you will be able to create your brick wall textures. The important part is laying them out in a way that doesn't look too mechanical. The story you are trying to tell is that these bricks weren't laid out by a machine but by a flesh-and-blood masonry worker, in other words, someone who couldn't possibly align bricks next to each other perfectly.

1. First you'll get organized. Select all three bricks and make sure they have their pivots centered by going to Modify → Center Pivot.

2. Select the clean brick—the one without any nooks or crannies carved out of it. Select Edit → Group. This command places the brick within a group. Once you have a bunch of clean bricks lying around, it'll make it a lot easier to select them all if they are grouped. Name your new group `CleanBricks`.

3. Repeat this with the other two bricks. Name the first group `DirtyBricks1`. Name the second dirty brick's group `DirtyBricks2`.

4. Now, you'll create a surface to place the bricks against. Select Create → Polygon Primitives → Cube. Follow the onscreen instructions and lay out a cube. Once the cube is in place, click its polyCube1 Inputs in the Channel Box and set the following: Width: 10, Height: 100, Depth: 100.

   Reposition the cube to be set on the grid.

Figure 1.8

The first clean brick
laid at the corner of
the wall

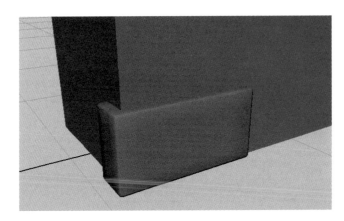

5. Grab your clean brick (don't select the CleanBricks group, just the brick itself). Position it at the bottom-left corner of the blank wall, approximately as in Figure 1.8.

6. Duplicate (shortcut Ctrl+D) the brick and move it to the right, leaving what would be about a 1-inch gap between the first brick and the second.

7. Immediately after placing the duplicate brick, you can press Shift+D. This is the shortcut for Edit → Duplicate With Transform, which will make a new duplicate and automatically move it the same distance as you moved the previous duplicate. Continue pressing Shift+D until you have a complete row of bricks that stretches across the entire blank wall.

8. Press Shift+D one more additional time to make an extra brick on the end of your line of laid bricks.

9. Select all of the bricks you have so far and press Ctrl+D to duplicate them all and raise them up, leaving about an inch gap between the two rows. Now, move the entire row of new bricks to the left until the left-most brick is extending about halfway beyond the blank wall's surface. The extra brick you made in step 8 is now filling in what would have been a gap on the far-right edge of your second line of bricks (Figure 1.9).

Figure 1.9

Two rows of
laid bricks

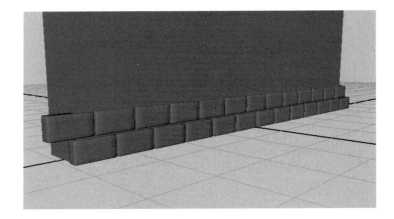

10. Select *both* rows of bricks now. Press Ctrl+D to duplicate both rows and move these new bricks up, also leaving about an inch gap between the old rows and the new ones.

11. Press Shift+D to Duplicate With Transform. Continue until you have filled the empty wall's space as in Figure 1.10.

Adding Chance

Well, you have a full brick wall now, but that was a little *too* easy, don't you think? And what about your dirty bricks? How do you fit them in? And how did your masonry worker set these bricks out so uniformly? You'll add some random dirty bricks and natural chance into your brick layout.

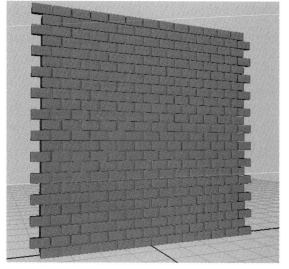

Figure 1.10

A full brick wall

1. Start selecting bricks at random, holding down the Shift key to add each additional brick to your selection. Try to *really* be random about it and don't let your selection fall into any sort of pattern. Try to select at least one or two bricks on each row. Keep selecting bricks until you have selected about 10 to 15 percent of them. If you see any of your selected bricks in an unintentional pattern, don't be afraid to deselect them and choose an alternative by Ctrl-clicking them. Once you have a selection of bricks that you are happy with, press Delete to get rid of them.

2. Go into the Side View and turn on Wireframe mode (by pressing the 4 key). In Wireframe mode, you can more easily see where your new gaps are in the brickwork. Select one of your dirty bricks (once again, only select the brick, not the DirtyBricks layer it belongs to). Move it into one of the vacant spots on the wall.

3. Press Ctrl+D to duplicate it and move it into another empty spot. Don't worry about lining it up perfectly with the bricks on either side, because the goal is imperfection. Don't fill *every* gap, but fill about half the available empty spots with duplicates of this brick.

4. Do the same with the second dirty brick, duplicating and repositioning it to fill in the rest of the empty spots.

   Now, you have a good random percentage of bricks that have some imperfections, nicks, scratches, and the like. However, they all are kind of the *same* nicks and scratches. You'll add another level of chance to your layout.

5. Select one of the clean bricks and press the up arrow on the keyboard. This will step up the brick's hierarchy to select the CleanBricks group. Press Ctrl+H (or Display→Hide→Hide Selection) to hide the clean bricks, leaving just the dirty bricks visible.

6. Now, select one of the remaining dirty bricks and press the up arrow as well, selecting its group (in my case, I selected DirtyBricks2). Select Window → Outliner. The
   Outliner is a window that simply displays everything that is currently in your scene.
   In the Outliner, scroll down until you see the group you have selected. Click the +
   symbol next to the group name to expand the group and to see all of the group's
   contents (in my case, all of the dirty bricks within the DirtyBricks2 group).

   Holding Ctrl, select every other brick in this list and rotate them all in the Y direction 180 degrees, flipping them completely around. The side of these bricks that was
   hidden from view is now revealed on the wall. Deselect them.

7. Holding Ctrl, select some of these bricks at random, whether or not you just flipped
   them around, and rotate them in the X direction 180 degrees, flipping them upside-
   down. Deselect them.

8. Lastly, make another random selection, whether or not you have made any change to
   them yet, and rotate these in both the X and Y directions by 180 degrees. Deselect them.

   What these last couple of steps did was take some of the dirty bricks from the
   DirtyBricks2 group and flip them around completely, some of them upside-
   down, some of them around and upside-down. Some bricks were left completely
   untouched. This gives you a randomized look, even though they are all the exact
   same brick.

9. Repeat steps 6–8 on the bricks in the other dirty brick group (in my case, DirtyBricks1).

10. If you look and see spots that, even after all those steps, still have a couple of identi-
    cal bricks right next to each other, go ahead and rotate one of them around, upside-
    down, or both to prevent that kind of pattern.

11. Press Ctrl+H (or Display → Show → Show Last Hidden) to unhide the clean bricks.

> If you've hidden other items or turned Maya off since you last hid the CleanBricks group so
> that it is no longer the "last hidden" item, you can display it by going to Display → Show →
> Show Geometry → Polygon Surfaces.

You Can Never Get Enough Chance

What else can you do to add interest and chance to your brick wall? So far, you have a
nice smattering of bricks that aren't pristine in your wall, but they are still very regularly
spaced and placed. Except for your dirty bricks, which you intentionally didn't align
perfectly, the rest of them are perfect and pristine in how they are placed in relation with
each other. You'll change that now.

1. Return to the Side View and once again hold Shift as you select a random selection
   of both clean and dirty bricks. Go ahead and choose about 15 to 20 percent of them,

trying not to pick them with any sort of pattern. If you select any brick that extends beyond the left or right edge of the wall, make sure you also grab the one on the opposite edge of the wall to make sure your final result tiles properly.

2. Move these bricks outward, making them protrude from the wall slightly more than the rest. Then, deselect them.

3. Select another random 20 percent, making sure that you again select the brick on both sides if you select one that extends beyond the edge of the wall, and move these slightly down and to the left. Then, deselect them.

4. Repeat the selection process, ensuring no pattern and not worrying about whether or not you have already selected any brick more than once. Move these bricks inward slightly, so they don't protrude outward as much as the rest.

5. Select another set of bricks randomly, and move these slightly up and to the right.

6. Take a look at the results. If you see any bricks that are intersecting or touching, fix that by moving them apart.

7. Now, select just a few bricks. No more than 10. Rotate these very slightly, tilting them to the right.

8. Repeat this, selecting no more than 10 bricks randomly, and rotating them slightly to the left and slightly tilting downward. You can move these bricks outward some as well if you'd like, but not cartoonishly so. They shouldn't look as if they are about to fall out of the mortar.

9. Double-check to make certain no brick is protruding too far out, is too close to any of its neighbors, or is intersecting, and reposition any offending brick(s) if necessary. Also double-check to make certain that any bricks that are extending beyond the wall on the left or right edge match the position of their counterpart brick on the opposite edge. If they are different, it will mess up your brick wall's ability to tile correctly.

Now that's a wall! With this, you can create a good representation of a real-world wall, with all of the imperfections, age, and interest that will make your game environment feel true and alive (Figure 1.11).

Figure 1.11
A much older, dirtier, left-to-chance kind of wall

Generating Texture Sources

Unfortunately, no magical button exists that will spit out a perfect texture. You will need to do some work first. You'll need three kinds of textures (or maps) for your brick wall project: diffuse, normal, and specular. See the "Diffuse, Normal, and Specular Maps" sidebar for more information regarding these texture types.

DIFFUSE, NORMAL, AND SPECULAR MAPS

The first texture types you'll be using in this book are Diffuse, Normal, and Specular textures. In the game industry, textures are most commonly referred to as *maps*. Each map type serves a very specific purpose and is applied in a specific way.

A *diffuse map* is simply the texture that contains the surface's color information. A diffuse map of a metal oil drum will contain metal, rust, scratches, paint flakes, stains, and so on. A diffuse map of a human character will have skin, wrinkles, hair, eyes, denim jeans, cotton shirt, glasses, hat, and so on. To put it as simply as I can, the diffuse map looks like the thing to which it will be applied. To get a diffuse map to function in Maya, you apply it to the Color attribute of any material. In nearly all cases, everything in a game has to have, at the very least, a diffuse map applied.

A *normal map* contains spatial information for how far any part of an object's surface extrudes or intrudes and how a light reacts to that surface direction. For example, in your brick wall project, the bricks extrude outward from the surface of the wall and the mortar that is in between each brick. The normal map will provide that sort of information to a game engine to make certain light reacts appropriately. To get a normal map to be viewed in real time in Maya, follow these steps:

1. First, apply the normal map to the Bump Mapping attribute of any material, just as you would with any type of texture.

2. In the bump2d node that is created, change the Use As setting from the default Bump to Tangent Space Normals. This tells Maya that rather than a standard bump map, you're using its much cooler big brother, the normal map.

3. After your normal map is applied, when you toggle High Quality Rendering mode in any of your viewports, the normal map will become enabled. Put a light in your scene and move it around to get the full effect.

A *specular map* contains the surface's shininess information. For example, a matte piece of paper wouldn't have any specular applied to it, while a shiny trophy would be *very* specular. These two examples describe two extremes of specular levels. Some objects have very little specular, but it's still there. To represent any level of specular information, a specular map is required. To get a specular map to function in Maya, you apply it to the Specular Color attribute of any material that contains specular attributes, most commonly a Blinn material.

You can create textures using several methods. The method I use with the most success is to generate my basic texture sources in Maya and then manipulate these sources in a 2D image program such as Adobe Photoshop to get my finished results. There are plug-ins and applications that can automatically generate texture sources, but I find them to be either too slow or too imprecise. This is all a matter of preference, of course, and with these tools your mileage may vary. Although most methods have their valid uses, for this book, you'll be following this method.

You'll now focus on each of your three texture sources, one at a time. Once you have your finished texture maps, you'll apply them to a low-poly mesh that will represent a finished wall in a game.

Generating a Diffuse Source

You'll first create a simple source for your wall's diffuse map. This source will act as a starting point for your final diffuse texture later.

1. Select all of your bricks (not selecting the background cube) and select Mesh → Combine. This will combine all of the bricks into one object. Name your combined brick object `Hi_Bricks`. You can also name the background cube simply `Background`.

> Now is a good time to perform some housekeeping on your scene by deleting the unnecessary history that your objects may have. To do this, simply select everything and select Edit → Delete By Type → History. I tend to make a Shelf shortcut for this common command by holding down Ctrl+Shift and selecting it from the previously mentioned menu path. It will then appear on your Shelf for easier access.

2. With Hi_Bricks selected, hold down the right mouse button and, from the marking menu that appears, choose Assign New Material → Lambert. The Attribute Editor for your new material should automatically open. If not, open the Attribute Editor by pressing Ctrl+A, and then click the Lambert2 tab near the top-right of the window that opens to access the new Lambert material's attributes.

3. With the attributes of Lambert2 displayed, change the color to white by simply dragging the Color attribute's slider all the way to the right. Feel free to rename this Lambert to something more appropriate (perhaps `brickColor`?) by typing a new name in the text field near the top of the Attribute Editor, next to where it reads "Lambert."

4. Select the Background cube and repeat step 2, assigning a new Lambert material. This time, change this Lambert's color to black by dragging the Color attribute's slider all the way to the left. Again, you can rename this Lambert material to something more appropriate if you like, such as `mortarColor`.

5. In the Side View, select Create → Polygon Primitives → Plane. Drag from the top-left corner to the bottom-right corner of the brick wall. A new plane is created.

6. With the plane selected, now select its creation options under the Inputs section of the Channel Box on the right and set the following:

Width	100
Height	100
Subdivisions Width	1
Subdivisions Height	1
Create UVs	Normalization Off

7. Rename the plane **Low_Poly_Wall**. Center it on the high resolution wall geometry and have it "set" on the grid just as the wall does.

   By turning off UV Normalization, you've prevented problems in the future. Specifically, with Normalization on, the plane doesn't use 100 percent of the UV space available for its textures. For tiling textures, it's important to use the entire UV space. If you don't, you'll have large gaps in your textures when they tile.

   UVs are texture coordinates. Think of it this way—as you probably know, 3D geometric space is represented by three coordinate directions, width, height, and depth, which are represented as X, Y, and Z. Texture space in Maya is represented with two coordinate directions, width and height, which are represented as U and V. That's how you get the common shorthand term: *UVs*.

8. Push the Low_Poly_Wall plane back so that it is embedded into the brick wall you have created so far. You'll want to move it into the wall so that you do not see the plane between the bricks anymore. Deselect everything.

9. On the status line in the upper-left corner's drop-down box, switch your menu set from Polygons to Rendering. There are lots of useful new menu commands here, but there's only one that you're interested in right now.

10. Select Lighting/Shading→Transfer Maps. The Transfer Maps dialog box will open. There are lots of settings and options in here that you will be making extensive use of throughout this book. Move the window to the side so you can easily see it and your scene.

11. Select the Low_Poly_Wall (use the Outliner if you have difficulty selecting it while it is inside the wall). In the Transfer Maps window, under the Target Meshes section, click the Add Selected button. The Low_Poly_Wall will be added to the Target Meshes section.

12. Select the Hi_Bricks and Background objects that make up the high-resolution mesh. Under the Source Meshes section, click the Add Selected button. Likewise, the selected high-res models are added to the Source Meshes section.

13. Under the Output Maps section, click once on the Diffuse button, indicated by the four-color circle in the row of icons. Beneath it, you should see a Diffuse color map check box appear, along with several settings.

    In these settings, click the folder icon next to the Diffuse color map setting and browse to a good location to save your generated source textures. Save it as a Targa (tga) file and call it `brickwall_diffuse_source.tga`.

    Before moving on, make sure the check box next to the Diffuse color map section title is checked if it isn't already.

14. Under Connect Output Maps, uncheck Connect maps to shader if it isn't already.

15. Lastly, under the Maya Common Output section, make sure the following are set:

Map Width	1024
Map Height	1024
Keep Aspect Ratio	Yes
Sampling Quality	Medium (4×4)

    This will generate a 1024×1024 texture with a medium quality. You don't need anything to be super high quality at this stage. The higher the quality you set, the longer it takes to finish generating your textures.

16. Back up at the top, under Target Meshes, change the Display drop-down menu to Both and slide the Search Envelope (%) slider to the right until the red plane in your scene extends in front of the bricks. In my scene, I extended it by about 3.0 percent.

    The Search Envelope tells Maya how far out from your plane's original position you want it to look to generate your texture. You don't want it to look too far, so that you save processing time, especially in cases where there is other geometry in the scene that could interfere with the textures being generated.

Figure 1.12

Our diffuse texture source, generated from Maya

17. Click the Bake button.

    This may take a few minutes, but when done, you should have a black-and-white image of your brick wall, like in Figure 1.12.

Adding a Little Color

Black and white is OK, but it's a bit boring. Just to help out a little, you'll add some color to your source image before moving on.

> For this project and all other projects in this book, I'll be using Adobe Photoshop for textures. Other 2D image programs, such as GIMP (GNU Image Manipulation Program) or Corel Painter are also viable but will obviously have their own commands and shortcuts to do the same tasks I'll be doing in this book. They should be similar enough, though, that you won't have too much trouble following along.

1. In Photoshop, with your `brickwall_diffuse_source.tga` open, select the entire image (Ctrl+A) and copy it (Ctrl+C).

2. Open the Channels tab (next to the Layers tab). Click the Alpha 1 channel to select it and paste (Ctrl+V). You now have a copy of your black-and-white brick image in your Alpha channel.

3. Deselect all (Ctrl+D). Click the RGB channel to get out of the Alpha channel.

4. Ctrl+click the Alpha 1 thumbnail next to its channel to load that channel as your selection. This means that you've selected the white area of the bricks and not the black area of the mortar between the bricks. Return to the Layers tab without deselecting.

5. At the bottom of the Layer palette, click the New Layer button to create a new layer above your original layer. Double-click it to rename it `Bricks`.

6. Change your foreground color to white and fill your selection with white by pressing Alt+Delete. Deselect all.

7. Select the Background layer (your original layer) and fill it with black. Now, you've recreated your original image, but with your two layers separated you can manipulate the bricks and the mortar separately! Before continuing, select the Bricks layer to make it the active layer.

8. Click the New Layer button to make an empty layer above the Bricks layer and fill this layer with a red color. Rename this layer `Color`.

9. Hold down the Alt key on your keyboard and put your cursor *between* the Bricks layer and the new Color layer. Your cursor should change to what looks like two intersecting circles. Click here and the Color layer will indent above the Bricks layer.

By nesting the Color layer over your Bricks layer, the color will appear only where your bricks layer is visible, allowing the black background layer to show through. You'll be doing something similar to this later when you start making the final textures for your brick wall.

Save this file as `brickwall_diffuse.tga` and a copy of the Photoshop file as `brickwall_diffuse_master.psd`. If you like, go ahead and apply `brickwall_diffuse.tga` to your Low_Poly_Wall plane to see what it looks like. It should look similar to Figure 1.13.

Generating a Normal Source

The next step will be to generate a starting point for your normal map. You'll again use the Transfer Maps tool in Maya. I'll also show you an alternative method that can be useful for certain situations. But first, you'll get a little organized.

1. You'll create a couple of layers to make things a bit more manageable, so if the Layer Editor isn't already visible, toggle its button above the Channel Box to enable it.

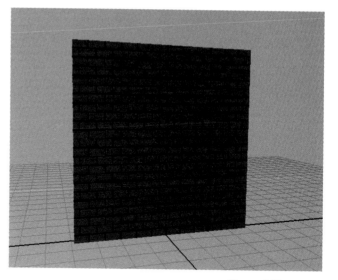

Figure 1.13
The red brick wall so far

   The three available Channel Box displays show the Channel Box, the Layer Editor, or both the Channel Box and Layer Editor together. Choose either the second or third option to toggle the Layer Editor as useable.

2. Click the Create a New Layer button twice. Double-click Layer 1 and in the dialog box that opens, rename it **high**. Do the same for Layer 2, renaming it **low**.

3. Select both the Background and Hi_Bricks objects, right-click and hold on the high layer, and from the menu that appears, choose Add Selected Objects.

4. Select the Low_Poly_Wall object, RMB and hold on the low layer and choose Add Selected Objects.

   Now, you can toggle the visibility of the two layers to make it easier to select what you need. With that done, you can focus on generating your normal map source. It's done in much the same way as the diffuse map source was generated, with the Transfer Maps set of commands.

5. Hide the high layer so only the Low_Poly_Wall is visible. Select it and select Lighting/Shading → Transfer Maps. By having selected the wall before opening the Transfer Maps window, it automatically loaded it into the Target Meshes section.

6. Unhide the high layer, select the Hi_Bricks and Background objects and, under Source Meshes, click the Add Selected button.

7. Under Output Maps, if the Diffuse color map section is still there, you can click the Remove Map button next to it to remove it from the output list, or simply uncheck it to deactivate it.

8. Click the Normal icon to add a Normal map check box. Within the Normal map section, make the following changes (if they aren't already made by default): set File Format to Targa (tga), and set Map Space to Tangent Space.

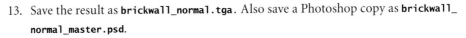

Object-space normals can be used in limited circumstances, but they aren't used nearly as often as Tangent-space normals in most games. Object-space normals can be used (if the game engine supports them) on objects that are not going to be rotated, deformed, animated, and so on. Otherwise, the shading would change and make it incorrect to the viewer. Tangent-space normals are more flexible, allowing limitless deformation and rotation.

You'll want to use all the same settings that you did for your diffuse map in the Transfer Maps options.

9. Click the folder icon next to the Normal map option and browse to the folder where you saved your diffuse textures. Name it `brickwall_normal_source.tga`.

10. Click the Bake button and wait as the normal map gets generated and saved. This can take a while, depending on the complexity of your objects. For this brick wall, though, it shouldn't take too long.

11. Open Photoshop and open `brickwall_normal_source.tga`. In the Layer palette, located in the middle of the buttons that run along the bottom, click the Create New Fill or Adjustment Layer button and choose Brightness/Contrast from the list that appears.

12. Set Brightness to +10 and Contrast to +30. Then click OK.

13. Save the result as `brickwall_normal.tga`. Also save a Photoshop copy as `brickwall_normal_master.psd`.

Figure 1.14

The generated normal map

This helps your normal map "pop" a little, getting rid of some of the washed-out look that the generating process sometimes can give you. Figure 1.14 shows my resulting normal map.

You can go ahead and assign the normal map to your material's bump map attribute to see what it looks like. You would have to turn on High Quality Rendering mode and maybe create a light source to get the full effect (as mentioned earlier).

Using an Alternative Method: The Light Array

What you just did is the process of creating a normal map source that you'll use for 99 percent of every model you make in your career. However, this brick wall project is presenting you with that exceptional 1 percent scenario—you are creating a texture using a flat, square plane of modeled source details. This allows you to use the light array method. This alternative method works only with these sorts of projects, but it can give you quicker, more accurate results.

1. Hide your low layer and unhide the high layer. You can turn off High Quality Rendering mode if you haven't done so already.

2. Select the Background and Hi_Bricks models and apply a new Lambert material by right-clicking and choosing Assign New Material → Lambert from the marking menu that appears.

3. In this Lambert material's attributes, change the Color to white and slide the Diffuse attribute all the way up to 1.0. You can then close the Attribute Editor.

4. Select Create → Lights → Directional Light. Scale it up larger if needed to make it easier to see and manage. Facing the brick wall, move the light to the right and rotate it 180 degrees in the X direction so that it is pointing to the left, in my case, along the positive z-axis.

5. In the Persp viewport menus, select Lighting → Use Selected Lights. In the following steps, only the selected light will be active in the scene. As you can see right now, a white light is currently hitting the wall from the right side.

6. With the light still selected, hit Ctrl+A to open its Attributes. Click the white box next to the Color attribute to open the Color Chooser dialog box.

7. Under the Sliders section of the Color Chooser, change the drop-down menu from using HSV (which stand for Hue, Saturation, and Value) values to instead use RGB (which stands for Red, Green, and Blue) values. Also make sure that the drop-down menu on the right is set to 0 to 1.

8. For the R, G, and B sliders, input the following: `R 1.0`, `G 0`, `B 0`. This makes your light 100 percent red. Click Accept to close the Color Chooser and minimize the Attribute Editor. In the scene, you now have a red light coming from the right side.

9. Duplicate (Ctrl+D) the red light and move it to the left of the brick wall and rotate it 180 degrees to face the right, along the negative z-axis, pointing back toward the first light. Open the second light's Attributes and, keeping it red, change the Intensity value from 1.0 to −1.0.

10. Select both lights and you can see you have the red light on the right and the negative red light on the left (displaying as black). Duplicate the first light and rotate it 90 degrees to point it down and move it above the brick wall. Change its color from 100 percent Red (1, 0, 0) to 100 percent Green (0, 1, 0). Make sure this light's intensity is a positive 1.0.

11. Duplicate this green light, rotate it 180 degrees to point up, and move it below the brick wall. Make its Intensity value −1.0.

12. Duplicate the first light once more and rotate it 90 degrees in the Z direction to point this light at the front of the brick wall. Move it to a position in front of the wall. Change its color to 100 percent Blue (0, 0, 1) and 1.0 Intensity.

13. You're almost done with the lighting setup. Select Create → Lights → Ambient Light. Move the new ambient light in front of the brick wall as well. Set Ambient Shade to 0, and make these changes to Color:

Color	R	0.5
	G	0.5
	B	0.5

14. In the viewport menus, select Lighting → Use All Lights (or press the 7 shortcut key) and your resulting lighting should look something like Figure 1.15.

So, what was the point of all that? If you go to your Side View camera angle and render an image, you get what looks like a complete normal map! Check out the side-by-side comparison in Figure 1.16. The normal map on the left was generated using the Transfer Maps method while the one on the right was rendered with the light array method. The one on the right is just a bit crisper and more vibrant. It's up to you to decide which method you prefer, but remember, this alternative *only* works when dealing with a block of detail geometry that can be rendered from one direction like this.

It doesn't have to be that limited, though. For example, you could render a normal map of a grid formation and *add* it to another normal map in Photoshop. This way, you can add details with different models. I'll go over how to combine normal map details together later in this chapter in the "Mixing Normals" section. Be creative and you can come up with all sorts of uses for both normal map generating methods.

Figure 1.15

Our final lighting setup

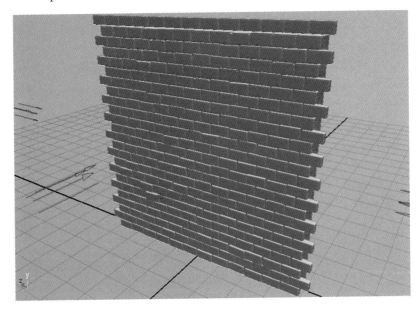

Figure 1.16

Left: Generating from Maya's Transfer Maps options. Right: Rendering from the light array.

Generating an Ambient Occlusion

The last source texture you'll generate is known as an Ambient Occlusion map, or an AO map. It will be used to help create your final diffuse map. Once again you'll use the Transfer Maps commands to do this. An ambient occlusion is used as an adjustment layer. It's not a map that you'll use all on its own, but rather it's an image that you'll add to your final diffuse map to give additional details. In the next section, I'll go over that process. But for now, just worry about actually making it.

1. Select the Low_Poly_Wall object and open the Transfer Maps window, automatically adding it to the Target Meshes section.

2. Add the Background and Hi_Bricks objects to the Source Meshes section as you did earlier in the chapter.

3. Click the Ambient icon under the Output Maps section to add an ambient occlusion map check box with options. Deselect the normal map check box if it's still checked from a previous step. Here, you want to keep the default settings. Click the folder icon to browse to your texture locations and name the ambient occlusion map `brickwall_AO.tga`.

4. Unlike the diffuse map and normal map, which used the Maya Common Output settings, the ambient occlusion will use the mental ray Common Output settings. Here, set the following:

Map Width	1024
Map Height	1024
Keep Aspect Ratio	Yes
UV Range	Normal (0 to 1)

Otherwise, keep default settings. All you did here was make certain the resulting texture will be 1024×1024, just like your previous generated textures.

To generate an ambient occlusion map, make sure you have mental ray turned on. To do this, select Window → Settings/Preferences → Plug-in Manager. In the list of available plug-ins, check the Loaded and Auto load check boxes next to the Mayatomr.mll plug-in. All of the mental ray options should now be available.

5. Click Bake. This can take a few minutes. Eventually, you should have something like what you see in Figure 1.17.

Figure 1.17

Our AO map

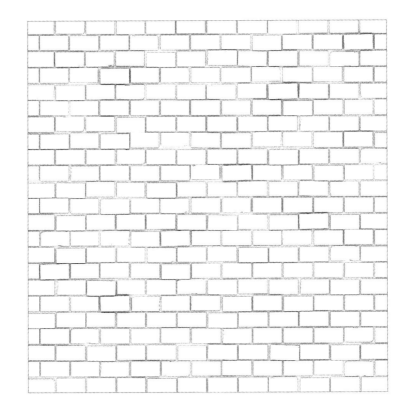

Creating the Final Textures

You're now ready to create your final textures. Texture creation is one of the most important steps in any game asset's pipeline. You can have a fantastic 3D model, but if the texture isn't good, the model won't look good. On the flip side, even a mediocre 3D model can look amazing with a great texture!

Texture creation is also a very experimental step in an asset's pipeline. If you're following along with me on the DVD video supplement, you may notice I try a few things before settling on a result I like. Here in this written instruction, I'll be showing you the steps I decide to use for my final textures.

1. Browse on the DVD to the Brick Wall project and open `Brickwall_Start.psd` in Photoshop. In this file, I have the generated normal map in its own Normal folder set to invisible. In the Diffuse folder, I have the previously generated AO map as well as the white and black masking layers from the `brickwall_diffuse_master.psd` file. This will be your starting point.

> It's a good idea to keep a library of texture resources handy. Rock, wood, foliage, brick, skin, metal—the more photographic reference material and source material you have, the more flexibility you'll have in your textures. One good online resource for these kinds of source files is `www.cgtextures.com`.

2. Open a good concrete source image from `www.cgtextures.com` or from your own personal texture source library. The one I've chosen can be found on the DVD as `ConcreteBare0145_1_M.jpg`. Drag it into your brick wall file in Photoshop to add it as its own layer above the black background layer near the bottom of the layer stack. Double-click the new concrete layer's name and rename it `Mortar`.

3. Double-click the AO layer. This opens the Layer Style window where you can do all sorts of layer adjustments. Right now, you just want to adjust the AO layer's Blend Mode. There are lots of different blending modes to choose from and you should take some time to look into them to see how they react with different color values and such in future projects.

   From the drop-down list, choose the Multiply blend mode. This makes all white pixels become transparent and all black pixels remain opaque.

4. Select the Mortar layer and create a new adjustment layer (from the button at the bottom of the layer window); choose Brightness/Contrast and set Brightness to `+23` and Contrast to `+40`.

   This gave your mortar layer a bit more contrast and brightness without adjusting the layer itself. Only layers below an adjustment layer are affected by them.

5. Drag the Mortar layer to the Create a New Layer button at the bottom right of the layer window to create a copy of the Mortar layer. Rename this layer `Brick` and drag it to be above the Brick_Mask layer.

6. Hold the Alt key and click in between the Brick and Brick_Mask layers to nest the Brick layer in the mask layer. This way, the mortar below the brick layers will show.

7. With the Brick layer selected, create a new Brightness/Contrast adjustment layer and set Brightness to `-35` and Contrast to `+35`.

    For my concrete sample, this will increase the contrast while darkening the brighter areas of the texture to serve as a good base for my brick.

8. If you're using the same concrete texture source that I am, select the Brick layer and click Ctrl+T to turn on Free Transform mode. You may need to zoom out (Ctrl+-) a bit to see the full extents of the Free Transform handles. Pull these in to be flush with the sides of your texture. Press Enter to finalize the adjustment.

9. With the Brick layer still selected, create another adjustment layer. This time choose Hue/Saturation. Input these values: Hue `-72`, Saturation `-37`. This will shift the brick layer's color toward the cool side of the spectrum, adding a more blue/purplish hue.

10. Hold the Alt key and click between the Brick layer and the Hue/Saturation adjustment layer. Do the same between the Hue/Saturation and Brightness/Contrast adjustment layer. This nests both adjustment layers within the Brick_Mask layer, keeping the Mortar layer beneath unaffected by the adjustment layer's effects.

    At this point, you should have something like Figure 1.18.

Figure 1.18

Our brick texture in progress

11. Create a new layer above the Brightness/Contrast adjustment layer and Alt-click between them to nest this new layer within the same group as the Brick_Mask. Rename this layer `Color`.

12. Fill (Alt+Delete) this layer with a dark red color. I chose a color with the RGB Values as follows: R `102`, G `54`, B `54`.

13. Change the Color layer's Blend Mode to Overlay. This mixes the Red layer's color in with the color of the layers below it, giving you a good base red color for what will be a red-brick wall.

14. Take the Color layer's Opacity down to about 90 percent to lessen its impact a tad.

Adding Color Variation

In real life, hardly anything is just one hue. Things usually have some kind of color variation, splotches of dust or grime, scratches, and so on. You'll add a layer of that to your brick texture.

1. Get a new concrete-like source image, one with more splotches of dark and light hues. It doesn't really matter what color it is. The one I found can be located on the DVD called `br013.jpg`. Drag it into your file and nest the new layer below the Color layer, keeping the group of layers nested with the Brick_Mask layer as before. Rename the layer `Color Variation`.

2. Change the Color Variation layer's Blend Mode to Overlay and take its Opacity down to about 55 percent.

3. This new color variation layer overpowers the general look of the brick a little too much, so you'll try something new. Double-click the Color Variation layer to open the Layer Style window. Toward the bottom are two sliders—one labeled This Layer and the other labeled Underlying Layer.

   Using the Underlying Layer slider, slide the black handle about halfway to the right. You should notice that the Color Variation layer starts to "melt" away, showing more of the layers beneath it. See Figure 1.19 for an illustration of what I mean.

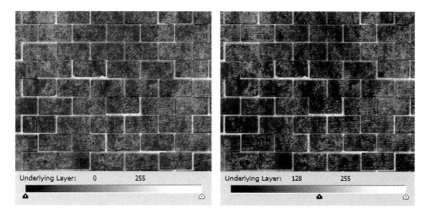

Figure 1.19

The result of the Underlying Layer adjustment

You can continue to adjust the sliders to get a look that you are satisfied with. But to be honest, no matter how I adjust these sliders, they tend to result in a very grainy, speckled look. In a game especially, that kind of thing can lead to strange mosaic patterns developing when a grainy texture is viewed from a distance. Let's smooth the blend transition.

4. Looking back at the Underlying Layer slider, hold down the Alt key and click and drag the black handle to the left. You'll see the handle actually *split in half*, creating a smoothing effect on the blending! Take a look at Figure 1.20 to see the results of this kind of adjustment. It's subtle, but it helps prevent speckling and graininess.

Figure 1.20

The result of the new Underlying Layer adjustment.

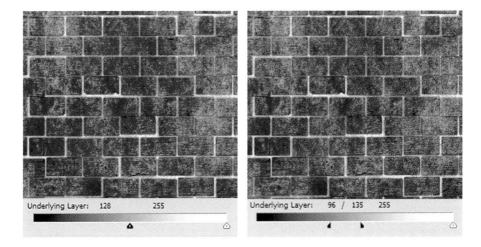

5. You'll add a gradient to the texture so that it is darker toward the base of the brick wall, representing years of dirt and grime that accumulates at street level. Create a new layer and place it above the Color layer. Don't worry about nesting this one. Rename it `Grime`.

6. Click the Gradient Tool (G) and you'll have a new set of options along the top of Photoshop's interface, giving you several different gradient types to choose from. Make sure Linear Gradient is the active option.

   Hold the Shift key and click and drag upward, making a gradient that runs upward black-to-white. Move the layer down so that the blackness only covers about 20 percent of the lower side of the texture.

7. Change the Grime layer's Blending Mode to Multiply and lower the Opacity to about 35 percent.

8. Select the topmost AO layer. With the Rectangular Marquee Tool (M), select an area around an individual brick. Create a new Brightness/Contrast adjustment layer. With

the brick selected, it automatically loaded the selection into the adjustment layer's mask so *only* the selected area is being affected. Set Brightness to –**26** and Contrast to –**10**.

Continue to select random, individual bricks and within the mask fill your selection with white to add it to the adjustment layer's mask. Do about 10 bricks.

9. Do it again, selecting an individual brick and creating a new Brightness/Contrast adjustment layer. This time, set Brightness to +**26** and Contrast to +**10**. Add about ten random bricks to this adjustment layer's mask.

    These last few steps added some random discoloration throughout the wall, giving much more of a worn, aged look and feeling, which is always important for such environments. At this point, your Diffuse texture is nearly done. You can do one last thing to finalize it and make it ready for your wall.

10. Select all (Ctrl+A) and press Ctrl+Shift+C to Copy Merged. This command copies every visible layer, not just the selected layer. Press Ctrl+V to paste, making a new layer. Move the layer to the top of the stack if it's not already there and name it `Final`.

11. With the Final layer selected, select Filter→ Sharpen→Unsharp Mask. Make the following adjustments:

Amount	50%
Radius	1.5 pixels
Threshold	5 levels

    The Unsharp Mask filter will help sharpen up the details of the texture, allowing them to stand out, and remove any unwanted smudging.

12. Save the .psd file so you can make any future adjustments that may be necessary and save it as `Brickwall_Diffuse.tga`. Apply the new texture to your wall to see how it looks so far (Figure 1.21).

Figure 1.21
The final Diffuse texture on the wall plane

Creating the Final Normal Map

Now, you will take your Normal map source and modify and improve it to create a final normal map texture you can use for your wall. As mentioned, in the `Brickwall_Start.psd` file, I've provided you with a Normal folder that includes the normal map images you would have created thus far. You are free to replace these with the ones you have generated yourself if you prefer.

With the source that you generated, you already have the basic forms that make up the individual bricks and the grooves in between them for the mortar. However, other than those large details, there aren't any smaller details in the normal map source, such as scratches, granularity, grooves, and so on. These small details are what you will add now.

1. First, you'll take a source image from your diffuse texture layers. Hide the Final layer as well as the AO layers and Brightness/Contrast layers until all that remains is the red-rock brick and white mortar. Click Ctrl+Shift+C to Copy Merged.

2. Open the Normal folder and select the Brightness/Contrast layer here. Ctrl+V to paste the copied brick layer. Rename this layer `BrickNormal`.

3. Select Image → Adjustments → Desaturate to desaturate the brick image, removing the color information and leaving a grayscale version.

4. Back under the Diffuse folder, Ctrl+click the Brick_Mask layer to load it as a selection. You'll notice that you have the bricks selected and not the mortar.

5. Select the Select → Inverse menu to invert the selection. Now, you're selecting the mortar pixels instead of the bricks. If it's not still selected, select the BrickNormal layer back in the Normal folder.

6. Select Image → Adjustments → Levels to open the Levels dialog box. Lower the Output Levels values near the bottom from the default of 0, 255 to **0**, **49** to make the mortar area black rather than white.

   When converting a grayscale image into a normal map, the range from white to black plays an important role in determining height. Where pixels are dark, a normal map will be indented or recessed. Where pixels are light, a normal map will be bumped up or raised. So, if you wanted to accurately represent a brick wall's depth in your grayscale image, you needed to make the mortar much darker. Otherwise, the mortar would look like it was sticking far out of the wall.

   Now that you have your grayscale image more accurately represented, you can convert it from height information into normal information for use in a normal map. Several widely used Photoshop plug-ins exist that can do this for you. I like to use xNormal, which you can download for free at `www.xnormal.net/Downloads.aspx`. Another popular one is the nVidia Normal Map filter (`http://developer.nvidia.com/object/photoshop_dds_plugins.html`). For this book's instruction, I'll be using xNormal commands, because I like the quality of its results better than most other alternatives.

7. Now you'll convert your grayscale height map into a normal map. With the Brick-Normal layer still selected, select Filter → xNormal → Height2Normals. In the dialog box that opens, the default is typically fine, but feel free to play with the settings to get the results you are after. Press Continue; your grayscale image will be converted into a normal map.

NORMAL MAP COLORS

As you may already know, a normal map's colors represent 3D space. Just as XYZ in Maya is represented by red, green, and blue (or RGB), those same directions are represented by those same colors in a normal map. Green represents distance in the Y direction, or height. Red represents distance in the X direction, or width. The prevalent Blue color represents distance in the Z direction, or depth.

What you may not know is that while width and height (the red and green colors, representing X and Y) in a normal map may have negative values, depth (the blue color, representing Z) in a normal map can only be positive. You can't have negative depth in a normal map. It always has a baseline of 0.

If you want to mix your BrickNormal layer with your original Normal_Source layer you have to take this into account. You could just lower the transparency of the new normalized details so that the layer below is visible, but that would result in muddy details and a washed-out original. What you want is accurate normals with excellent quality. To mix the two normal maps effectively, you need to follow the next steps. I'll explain what is happening as you go.

8. Select and drag the BrickNormal layer to the New Layer button to effectively make a duplicate layer above the original.

9. Rename the new layer `NormalAdd`. Rename the BrickNormal layer `NormalSubtract`. So, now you have the NormalAdd layer above the NormalSubtract layer in the Layer palette.

Mixing Normals

The next steps will mix the normalized details of your new layers with the Normal_Source layer by using the NormalAdd layer to remove negative values and the NormalSubtract layer to remove the positive values. It sounds complicated, but as you go through it, you'll pick up on what each step is doing.

1. Select the NormalAdd layer and select Image → Levels. Make the following changes, changing Channel first:

CHANNEL	RED	GREEN	BLUE
Input Levels	128, 1.00, 255	128, 1.00, 255	
Output Levels	128, 255	128, 255	0, 0

In the NormalAdd layer, you've removed all negative values, leaving only the positive values. You'll work on the NormalSubtract layer next. You can hide the NormalAdd layer by clicking the eyeball icon next to it in the Layer palette.

2. Select the NormalSubtract layer and select Image→Levels. Make the following changes, changing Channel first:

CHANNEL	RED	GREEN
Input Levels	0, 1.00, 127	0, 1.00, 127
Output Levels	0, 127	0, 127

3. Leave the Blue channel as it is.

   Similar to removing the negative values from the NormalAdd layer, here you've removed the positive values from the NormalSubtract layer. Next, you're going to convert these two layers into offsetting positive and negative values which can then be blended with the Normal_Source layer.

4. With the NormalSubtract layer still active, select Image→Adjustments→Channel Mixer. Change the Output Channel to Red and set Red to **–100** and Constant to **50**.

5. Change the Output Channel to Green and set Green to **–100** and Constant to **50**.

6. Change the Output Channel to Blue and set Blue to **–100** and Constant to **100**. Click OK.

7. Unhide and select the NormalAdd layer. Open the Channel Mixer once more, set Output Channel to Red, and set Constant to **–50**.

8. Change the Output Channel to Green and make its Constant value **–50** as well. Make no changes to the Blue channel.

   The NormalAdd layer now contains offsetting positive values while the NormalSubtract layer contains offsetting negative values. You'll adjust their Blending Mode to finally mix the values with the original Normal_Source layer.

9. Select the NormalAdd layer if it isn't selected already and change its Blending Mode setting to Linear Dodge. The linear dodge blending mode takes the base colors and brightens them with the blend colors, enhancing their affect on the base normal information rather than overpowering it.

10. Select the NormalSubtract layer and change its Blending Mode to Difference. The difference blending mode is the function that actually causes the color subtraction to take place.

Voilà! The normals are mixed (Figure 1.22)! You may want to adjust the intensity of your new normal information by decreasing the opacity of *both* Add and Subtract layers. I typically might reduce them both by 50 percent, but in this particular case, leaving them at their full intensity looks pretty good. Make sure that you make any changes to both layers to keep their offsetting values in sync.

Figure 1.22

The results of mixing normals on the right

Save your Photoshop file and save your normal map as `brickwall_normal.tga`. Feel free to take a look at your handiwork in Maya if you like. Remember that High Quality Rendering mode must be active to view a normal map in Maya in real time.

PRODUCING NORMAL MAPS FOR UNREAL

In the Unreal Engine (`www.unrealtechnology.com`), which is very prominent in the game industry, the normal maps that you generate from Maya need to be flipped in the Y direction. (This may be true for other engines as well; make sure you consult your art director to be certain.) You can easily flip the normal maps using Photoshop or most other image-editing applications:

1. Open any normal map generated from Maya as it has been described in this chapter.

2. Open the Channels palette (if it's not at its default tab next to the Layer palette, you can find it by going to Window → Channels).

3. Select the Green channel. If you recall, the color green controls the Y direction in normal maps.

4. Press Ctrl+I to Invert (or select Image → Adjustments → Invert) to invert the channel.

5. Select the RGB channel to return to the image and save it.

Creating the Final Specular Map

The final step in your texture creation process for this project is to create a specular map. Unlike the normal map or diffuse map, you don't need to generate anything from Maya to have a source. Instead, you'll be using Photoshop to make one from scratch.

Specular maps can be grayscale images, where black represents areas with no specular and white represent areas with maximum specular values. They can also include color information. If they do have color, the color is seen in the hue of the specular shine on the model.

Realistically, only metallic objects should have colored specular maps. However, including some color in a specular map on nonmetallic objects can help pump up their visual presentation, which can add a bit of pizzazz to the look of an object. It'd really be up to the art direction of each particular project and how realistic you were trying to be. In general, the main concern is that your art looks good. Looking good usually trumps looking realistic. After all, realism can be boring!

So let's get started!

Make sure you don't confuse reflection with specularity. If my plastic spoon is shiny and reflective enough, I can see myself in it and see that my reflected image is obviously in full color. But the spoon's specular highlights are themselves always white. A metallic surface's colored specularity will reflect my own coloring as well as the coloring of its surface, tinting my reflection a different color.

1. First you'll take a source image from your diffuse texture layers, just as you did when you began your final normal map. Hide the Normal folder. Then, hide the Final layer as well as the AO layers and Brightness/Contrast layers until all that remains is the red brick and white mortar. Press Ctrl+Shift+C to Copy Merged.

2. Select the Final layer and press Ctrl+V to paste the copied brick layer. Rename this layer **Spec_Base**. Move this layer so that it's between the Diffuse or Normal folders. You're going to make a new folder for it.

3. With the Spec_Base layer selected, select Layer → New → Group From Layers. In the dialog box that opens, name the new folder **Specular**. You should now have a new folder named Specular between the Normal and Diffuse folders. Within the Specular folder is your Spec_Base layer.

Because you're dealing with a brick wall, your final specular map will be mostly grayscale. As mentioned previously, it's primarily metallic objects that will have a colored specularity. However, because of what brick is made of, there are tiny rocks and metallic particles within it. To convey this, you'll add just a hint of color to your specular map.

4. Select Image → Adjustments → Desaturate to desaturate the brick image, removing the color information and leaving a grayscale version.

5. Create a Brightness/Contrast adjustment layer and set Brightness to -42 and Contrast to -42. This will darken the image. If you left the whitest pixels as bright as they were, your specular would be incredibly bright and hot. You'll want to be a little more subtle.

6. Create a Levels adjustment layer and make the following changes:

Input Levels	0, 0.77, 162
Output Levels	0, 186

7. Above the two adjustment layers you've made, create a New Layer and name it `Color`.

8. Click the Foreground color swatch on the Tools palette (usually on the left side of the Photoshop interface) to bring up the Color Picker. Select a deep red color and click OK.

9. Click the Background color swatch and choose white and click OK.

10. With the new Color layer selected, select Filter → Render → Clouds. This command will fill the image with a cloudy pattern using the two colors you've selected.

11. Change the Color layer's Blending Mode to Soft Light, adding a tint of the red color to the specular map.

12. Lower the Color layer's Opacity to about 50 percent to reduce the impact of the coloring.

13. Save your Photoshop file and save your specular map as `Brickwall_specular.tga`.

In Figure 1.23, you can see the final specular map. You can view the end result in Maya by assigning the specular map to the Specular Color attribute of a Blinn material on your wall. To see a more accurate view of the specular map in real time, you'll need High Quality Rendering mode turned on.

With the final diffuse, normal, and specular maps completed and applied, your brick wall is complete (Figure 1.24)! You can apply the textures you've created to a modular wall mesh system to create an interlocking series of walls in a final game world. And you can create textures for ceilings and floors in the same fashion as you have for this wall. In the next project, you'll get off the walls and start making some scenery.

Figure 1.23

The final
specular map

Figure 1.24

The finished,
textured wall

Information Overload

It may seem as if I've introduced an enormous amount of new information to you in just this first chapter. Don't be too concerned if you feel a case of information overload. Such a feeling is common when starting a new job in the game industry as well! All it takes is time and practice to develop a familiarity with each of these methods.

The concepts introduced in this first chapter will be gone over again in later chapters to help give each task additional information and context, and to allow you, the artist, more practice in using them as well as learning new concepts that are introduced as the book progresses.

CHAPTER 2

Foliage

When creating any sort of exteriors, rural and urban alike, you'll usually have some sort of foliage. Trees, vines, grass, flowers, weeds, corn stalks, lily pads, fungi, river reeds, seaweed, etc. The list can stretch on potentially forever. Not to mention the possibility of completely fictional plant life that can be created for fantasy or science-fiction games. But even with the current game consoles and high-powered PCs, there are still concessions that must be made to realize those details in any lush digital environment.

Understanding Foliage

Practically every game requires some kind of plant life. For example, Rockstar Games' *Grand Theft Auto IV* takes place in an intricately detailed metropolis, filled with high-ways, streets, overpasses, sidewalks, skyscrapers, warehouses—in other words, complete urban sprawl. Yet there are trees, potted plants, grass, and other types of realistic foliage scattered around in parks and gardens, flower beds, and front lawns. Another example is Blizzard's *World of Warcraft*. Each area of this massive, online role-playing game is covered in unique types of trees and plants, a large portion of which are complete fantasy. Even an arena-based sports game like Electronic Arts' *Madden NFL '09* has trees and bushes lining the exteriors and interiors of several stadiums, not to mention the grass and turf football fields themselves.

But all of these different game environments share one particular detail in common: *opacity maps*. In Chapter 1, "Walls, Floors, and Ceilings," you learned about the three major texture types—diffuse maps, specular maps, and normal maps. Opacity maps are a fourth texture type, and you'll learn how to use them in this chapter. Opacity maps, as you may gather from the name, control the *opacity* (or transparency) of a model. And if there's any type of environment prop that heavily relies on opacity maps in games, it's foliage.

Think of all those leaves! Each and every one of them. If you modeled a tree with every single leaf in place, how many polygons do you think that would take? For *one* tree? What about a dozen trees? Or a hundred? And then let's say you want them to *sway* in the breeze. Imagine a game like *World of Warcraft*, for instance, that has a forested area.

If every single leaf and branch were modeled and present, the amount of calculations and animations involved in such a simple thing as tree branches swaying with the breeze would be staggering, never mind trying to have an actual game running in there somewhere. Frame rates would chug to a crawl, and the game would be completely unplayable.

So, what's a tree-loving game artist to do? That's where opacity maps come in. Using different sized sheets of geometry and a well-crafted opacity map, you can create the illusion of heavy details (like thousands of leaves). In the first project of this chapter, you'll come to a better understanding of how you can create such foliage models and opacity maps.

Project: Creating Ivy

Imagine an ivy vine crawling up a tree or a swath of ivy covering an old church and you'll realize ivy is a great plant to start with when learning how to create foliage. Ivy is almost completely made up of leaves, with a few vines thrown in for structural stability's sake. Taking a look around my neighborhood, I came upon several different examples of ivy that you can use as inspiration in this project (Figure 2.1).

> Before starting, make sure you set your project to your project directory by going to File → Project → Set.

1. Browse on the DVD to Projects → Chapter2→ Ivy and open Ivy01_Start.ma. This file contains a preset scene to begin creating the ivy.

2. In the Side view, you can see the reference image of an ivy leaf in full profile. Start by going to Mesh → Create Polygon Tool.

Figure 2.1

Examples of ivy
photo reference

Using this tool, begin placing points along the profile of the leaf, tracing its image, starting from the base of the leaf (where it would meet a stem) and ending halfway around the leaf at its tip. Press Enter to finalize the tool's action.

3. With half of the leaf filled in, select Mesh → Mirror Geometry → Options. Make sure that the Mirror Direction is set to +Z (or whatever direction is applicable to your scene, if you aren't following along exactly), and that Merge With the Original and Merge Vertices are both selected. The half of leaf you have created so far should now be mirrored and connected on its opposite side.

4. If the tip or the base of the leaf isn't merged together, select the two vertices at these points and select Edit Polygons → Merge to merge them together.

5. After merging the two sides, select the edge that runs down the center and delete it.

6. Back in the Side view, you can tweak the vertices of the new side of the leaf to more closely match the image reference you have. If you need to add vertices, you can use the Split Polygon tool found under the Edit Mesh menu. With the tool active, simply click once on an edge where you want a new vertex and press Enter. At this point, you should have something similar to Figure 2.2.

Figure 2.2

The leaf so far in Perspective View

7. Once you have your leaf profile the way you like, select the face that makes up the entire leaf and select Edit Mesh → Extrude. Pull out the extrusion a small amount to give the leaf some thickness.

8. Select the front face again and select Edit Mesh → Bevel. Adjust the Offset to be about 0.32. You can delete the face on the back of the leaf.

9. Select the edge loops that run along the tips of the leaf's pointy ends and the indentions between leaf fronds (as indicated in Figure 2.3) and apply a new Bevel. Adjust this bevel's Offset to be around 0.34.

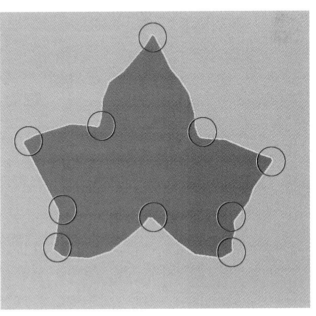

Figure 2.3

Edges that need beveling

Adding Veins

The next step is to add detail by cutting in geometry to represent the details that make up the veins of the leaf. You'll do this primarily with the Split Polygon tool. You'll want this leaf to be able to fold later, so while you're working, you can cut in the necessary geometry for that to work as well.

1. Using the Split Polygon tool, start cutting in geometry in the path and shape of the leaf veins. You can also cut in geometry to help with bending later. Figure 2.4 demonstrates what I mean.

2. Once you are finished cutting, you can select the faces that make up the veins of the leaf, but deselect the faces that are on the very ends of the veins where they merge into the tips of the leaf. Apply an extrude command and pull the veins out slightly.

   The reason for not extruding the faces at the tips of the veins is that you want the vein geometry to blend back into the main leaf mesh. You can do this easily at the ends of the veins in the next step.

3. Select and delete the two faces on the end of each extruded vein. Then, use Edit Mesh → Append to Polygon Tool to close the gaps between them, as portrayed in Figure 2.5. You can also reference the video supplement on the DVD for more details regarding this step.

4. When all of the veins are sufficiently blended, select the edges of each vein and apply a Bevel to them with an Offset of approximately 0.6.

   The Select Edge Loop tool, which you can find in the Select menu, can help select the vein's edges quickly. With the tool active, simply double-click an edge, and the entire loop of edges will be added to your selection.

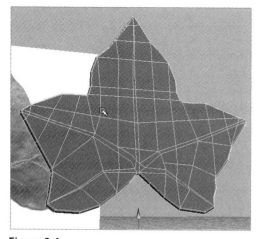

Figure 2.4

Cutting in the veins and folding detail

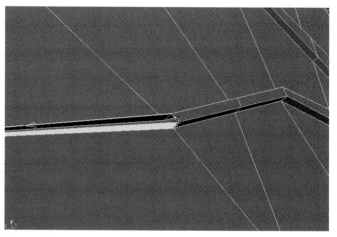

Figure 2.5

Blending the veins into the leaf geometry

5. Now you'll bend the leaf geometry to make it not so cardboard-rigid and straight. First change your menu sets from Polygons to Animation (either through the interface or by using the F2 shortcut key). Deformers are under the Animation menu set.

6. With the leaf mesh selected, select Create Deformers → Lattice. You'll see a wire box appear around your leaf.

    The lattice deformer simply modifies a large number of points using a cage of fewer points. This helps by making large changes to a high-resolution mesh much easier to manage.

7. After applying the lattice, in the Channel Box on the right, change the following settings, which are found under the Shape node named ffd1LatticeShape: S Divisions: **2**; T Divisions: **4**; U Divisions: **5**. This gives you a better density of lattice points to work with based on the shape of the leaf.

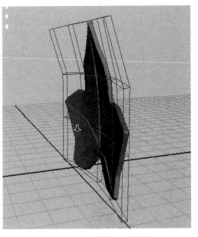

8. Right-click the lattice and select Lattice Point from the marking menu that appears to activate component mode and gain access to the lattice's points. Manipulate the lattice points to bend the leaf into a concave shape like in Figure 2.6.

9. Delete the history of the leaf (Edit → Delete by Type → History in case you have forgotten). Deleting the history removes and bakes in the changes made to the leaf by the lattice deformer (as well as all previous modeling operations, if you haven't deleted the history before now).

Figure 2.6

Deforming the leaf into a concave shape

10. With the leaf still selected, return to the Polygons menu set (F3) and select Normals → Soften Edge. If your leaf is like mine, you'll probably notice it become covered in dark splotchy colors. This is because you need to adjust just *how* soft you want the leaf's normals to be.

11. After applying the Soften Edge command, click the polySoftEdge1 Input in the Channel Box to access the Soften Edge command's options. Change the Angle setting to about 80 degrees, or whatever value works best on your model. The goal is to remove the majority of the splotches, yet avoid obvious hard edges in your model.

12. Rename your model `HiLeaf`.

Generating Texture Sources

Just as you did with the brick wall in Chapter 1, you'll follow many of the same steps to create your texture sources for the ivy leaf. You'll start by creating your low-resolution mesh to bake your texture sources to.

All operations and commands in this book assume the default options are set. You may need to reset the options of tools and commands to follow along most accurately.

1. Create a polygon plane by going to Create → Polygon Primitives → Plane. Switch to the Side view to view the leaf head-on and left-click and drag to create the plane surrounding the area the leaf is within (Figure 2.7).

2. In the Perspective view, move the plane forward until it is completely in front of the leaf, with none of the leaf's parts intersecting it. In my case, I moved it forward about 8.1 units. Rename the plane **Leaf**.

3. Click the polyPlane Input options in the Channel Box and make sure that the Create UVs setting is set to Normalization Off.

4. You also will want to ensure that the plane's surface normal is pointing to the front, or *away* from the HiLeaf mesh. You can check this by selecting the Leaf plane and going to Display → Polygons → Face Normals. This will make the green line that represents the normal direction of the plane's face appear.

   If it's pointing the opposite direction, select Normals → Reverse. Otherwise, click the Face Normals display command again to turn it off.

5. Now you're ready to start generating some texture sources. Switch your menu set from Polygons to Rendering. Then, with the Leaf plane selected, select Lighting/ Shading → Transfer Maps.

6. In the Transfer Maps dialog box that opens, make sure that you slide your Search envelope percentage down to 0, if it's not already.

7. Select the HiLeaf mesh and load it into Source Meshes. You'll notice that your Leaf plane is automatically loaded into Target Meshes since it was selected when the Transfer Maps options were opened.

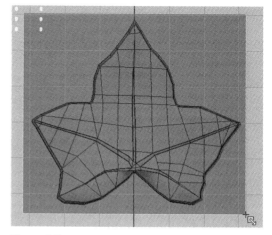

   You can follow the same steps from Chapter 1 with regard to the settings for an Ambient Occlusion (or AO) and normal map. This time, you can choose to bake more than one map at once because you now have a better idea of how to do it. Go ahead

Figure 2.7
Creating a plane surrounding the leaf

and bake two 1024×1024 texture sources—
a normal map called `Leaf_Normal_source.tga`
and an AO map called `Leaf_AO.tga`.

Once the baking finishes, feel free to
apply your new maps to check out how
they look so far. Don't forget that you need
High Quality Rendering turned on for a
normal map to render correctly in real
time. Figure 2.8 shows how mine looks
so far.

You may notice that the normal map
results are a bit harsh. You could probably
stand to clean that up a bit. Let's open up
Photoshop.

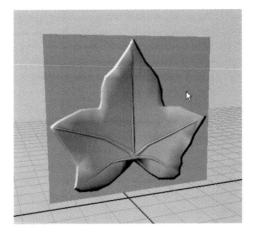

Figure 2.8

The AO and
Normal source
maps applied

As I mentioned in Chapter 1, I'll be using Adobe Photoshop for textures. Other 2D image
programs, such as GIMP or Corel Painter, are also viable but obviously will have their own
commands and shortcuts to do the same tasks I'll be doing in this book. They should be similar enough, though, that you wouldn't have too much trouble following along.

Making Normal Map Adjustments

The resulting normal map isn't too bad, especially the outer edges of the leaf. The irregular smoothing that I normally would attempt to fix doesn't look too bad on what should
be a rather irregular shape such as a leaf. You'll just want to smooth out some of those
harsh edges and angles.

1. In Photoshop, open your `Leaf_Normal_source.tga` file. Copy its background layer by
   dragging it onto the Create New Layer button at the bottom-right side of the Layer
   palette. Rename this copied layer `SmoothDetails`.

2. With this new layer selected, select Filter → Blur → Gaussian Blur.

3. Adjust the Gaussian Blur settings to blur the layer by 4.5 pixels. Now the normal is
   definitely softened, but maybe a bit too much in most areas. Why not make the blur
   effect take effect only where it's needed rather than all over the whole thing?

4. With the SmoothDetails layer still selected, click the Add Layer Mask button on the
   bottom row of buttons on the Layer palette.

   A *layer mask* is a grayscale image that is associated with a particular layer in
   Photoshop and acts as an opacity map: Where a layer mask is colored black, the
   layer is invisible; where a layer mask is colored white, the layer is visible. To apply

white or black coloring to a layer mask, you have to make sure you select the mask, represented on the layer as a second preview thumbnail.

5. Select the layer mask and fill it with black, making it entirely invisible.

6. Then, with the mask still selected, start painting in white over areas that need to be softened. Make sure you are using a soft-edged brush. You want to remove unnatural hard edges that are visible in the normal map.

> To quickly scale your brush size larger and smaller in Photoshop, use the [and] keyboard shortcuts.

7. To soften the blend between the harder edges of the leaf's vein into the surface of the leaf, you'll change the opacity of your brush's painting strength. With the paintbrush tool still selected, at the top of the Photoshop interface, change the Opacity value from its default 100 percent to 50 percent.

8. First, paint over *all* of the veins with white using the 50 percent opacity brush. This will make the veins have a softer appearance once the normal map is applied in Maya.

9. Change your color to black and paint over the ends of the veins, softly blending them into the main surface of the leaf. In Figure 2.9, you can see my final layer mask and resulting normal map.

Figure 2.9

The layer mask applied and painted to soften the normal map's harder details

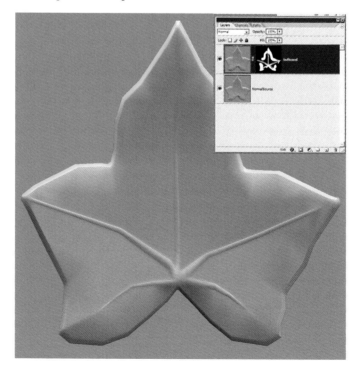

Creating an Opacity Map

Now that you have a good source map for both your diffuse and normal maps, you need to make the opacity map to get rid of the excess geometry that you can see surrounding the leaf. After all, you want your leaves to look like leaves, not big squares with pictures of leaves on them! Creating the opacity map for this particular project is actually quite easy.

1. Open the `Normal_Source.tga` file again, if you don't still have it open from the previous step.

2. Select the Magic Wand tool (you can press W on the keyboard). With the tool active, at the top of the screen, change the Tolerance value to 0.

3. Select the original normal source layer (not the softened one) and click anywhere outside the leaf.

   The Magic Wand tool selects pixels of similar hue values. The Tolerance setting adjusts how exact the hue value has to be for it to be selected. With the tolerance set to 0, you're telling it to select *only* the specific color of the pixels you click. In this case, the tool will select the entire area outside of the leaf on the normal map. This is the perfect selection with which to create your opacity map.

4. With the region outside the leaf selected, create a new layer and fill the selection with black. Press Ctrl+D to deselect.

5. Create a new layer and fill the entire layer with white. Move this new layer to be beneath the previous one. Select the black layer and press Ctrl+E to Merge Down with the white layer beneath it. The result gives you a new layer that contains a white silhouette of the leaf with a black background. This is your opacity map!

6. Save the resulting black and white image as **Leaf_Opacity_source.tga**.

At this point, it really depends on your project's guidelines as to whether your opacity map is truly finished. Saving it as a separate file like you have done here is a common practice in certain editors and game engines, but there is another method (the one used by Maya) that many other editors use as well. This method utilizes alpha channels.

You may remember that I briefly used an alpha channel in Chapter 1 as a selection mask when creating a diffuse map source. While that is a valid way an alpha channel can be used, the way they are used in a game engine is entirely different.

Many games use alpha channels as a way of essentially "storing" an extra channel of information. For example, you can have the black and white data that represents a specular map within the alpha channel of a diffuse map that is read by the game engine—two maps in one file. The same thing can be done with opacity maps, and this is how Maya in particular uses them, so that's what you'll do here. Don't forget to consult your art director about how alpha channels are used in your own real-life projects.

Using an Alpha Channel

It is very simple to include a texture in the alpha channel of a file. The main criterion is that it must be grayscale only. No colored maps can be included in an alpha channel since colors (Red, Green, and Blue) take up their own channels. So, although a grayscale specular map can be included in an alpha channel, a colored one could not and would have to be done a different way. But now you'll focus on putting your opacity map into your diffuse map's alpha channel.

1. Open your `Leaf_Opacity_source.tga` file, if it isn't already open.

2. Select All (Ctrl+A).

3. Copy Merged (Ctrl+Shift+C).

4. Open your `Leaf_AO.tga` file. Next to the Layers palette tab is the Channels tab. Click it to open the Channels palette and select the alpha channel.

5. Paste (Ctrl+V) to paste your copied opacity map into the alpha channel.

> If your file does not have an alpha channel already, you can easily create one by clicking the Create New Channel button (in the same place as the Create New Layer button normally would be). The new channel will automatically be called Alpha 1 and will be considered your active alpha channel.

6. Save your file using the Save As command (or by pressing Ctrl+Shift+S) and save your file as **`Leaf _AO_Opacity.tga`**. This time, in the Targa Options box that opens, make certain you choose 32 bits/pixel. Click OK.

Differentiating Between 24 Bits/Pixel and 32 Bits/Pixel

I'll take a moment to talk about the difference between 24 bits/pixel and 32 bits/pixel. If you notice in the Channels palette, you have three channels by default, not counting any alpha channel—Red, Green, and Blue (the RGB channel is simply a combination of the other three and not counted as a channel on its own). Each channel requires 8 bits/pixel. So typically, if you don't have an alpha channel, you can save your image as a 24 bits/pixel image: Three channels at 8 bits each equals 24 bits total. Therefore, if you *do* want an alpha channel, you'd need to add the 8 additional bits, making it 32 bits/pixel.

Make sure that, when you save a `.tga` file without an alpha channel, you don't save it with 32 bits/pixel because it will create an empty alpha channel for you in most game engines. This wastes texture memory, which, by the time a project is coming to its last few months, becomes a precious commodity!

Creating the Ivy Vine

Let's get back to Maya. Apply your new Leaf_A0_Opacity.tga file to your leaf plane's mate-rial's Color attribute. You should get a result like Figure 2.10. Only the leaf part of the plane is visible!

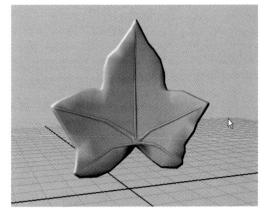

Figure 2.10
The opacity alpha channel at work

You'll finish up the textures later. For now, you'll create the rest of the ivy.

1. Select the leaf plane and press the Insert key on your key-board. This toggles Edit Pivot mode. Move the plane's pivot point to about where you would expect the leaf to meet a vine—where all of the veins converge in the middle. Press Insert again to exit Edit Pivot mode.

   With the pivot moved to where the leaf would meet its vine, you can more easily position and rotate the leaf when you have the vine mesh completed.

2. In the Side view, select Create → CV Curve Tool. By left-clicking, create a curve that will represent the path of your vine. You can see mine in Figure 2.11.

3. Shrink your leaf to be a correct shape next to the curve, as if the curve was the vine the leaf had grown from. I shrunk mine down about 0.2 percent from its original shape, but the amount you scale it will depend on how big your leaf originally was compared to how big your curve is.

4. Curve snap (hold the C key and middle mouse button, and click and drag on the curve) the leaf to the curve. Because your pivot point was moved to be at its connection point, the leaf will run along the curve at the correct position to represent the idea that it had grown from the vine.

5. Duplicate the leaf and position the new leaf on the vine. Rotate the leaves to point downward and to point in different directions so they aren't all uniform. Scale the leaves so that they begin larger near the top of the vine and shrink to be much smaller near the vine's tip.

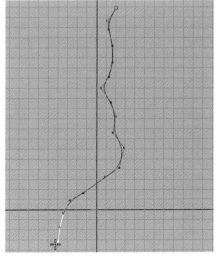

Figure 2.11
The path of my vine

6. Create another curve and curve snap the first point to the first curve before creating the rest of it. This way, the new curve looks like it is a branch growing off the vine.

   Continue placing ivy leaves on both curves. Eventually, you should have something like Figure 2.12.

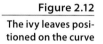
Figure 2.12

The ivy leaves positioned on the curve

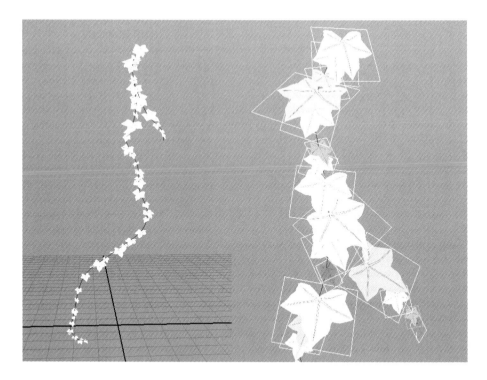

7. Select Create → NURBS Primitives → Circle. Click and drag to draw a small circle approximately the diameter of the vine you want. Mine had a radius of about 0.75.

8. Under the makeNurbCircle1 Inputs in the Channel Box, change the number of Sections to 4.

9. Select the circle and Shift+select the main curve that makes up the long vine. Change your menu set to Surfaces. The Surfaces menu set contains menu commands that mostly relate to working with curves and NURBS surfaces. Select Surfaces → Extrude → Options.

10. Make the following changes:

Result position:	At path
Pivot:	Component
Output geometry:	Polygons
Type:	Quads
Tessellation method:	General
U type and V type:	Per span # of iso params
Number U and V	1

11. Click the Extrude button. A polygon tube should be created, running along the pathway of the curve you had drawn. Repeat the extrude step for the smaller vine's curve, creating a tube for it as well. You should have a result similar to Figure 2.13.

Project: Creating Ivy ▨ 49

12. Take the opportunity to adjust the vines' shape by manipulating the Curve Points on your vine curves. When you're happy with the shapes, select both pieces of vine geometry and delete their history.

13. Go back to the Polygons menu set. Select the vertices at the tip of one of the vine meshes and select Edit Mesh → Merge To Center. This will combine and collapse the vertices together to make the end of the vine into a point. Do the same for the tip of the other vine section.

14. Select the row of vertices next to the tip on one of the vines and scale them in. Select the next row and scale them in slightly less. Select the next row of vertices and scale them in even less. Continue until you have tapered the ends of both vines, making them look like they are thick near the top and become thinner as the vine grows near its tip. You can make the top, or base, of the vine thicker if you need to.

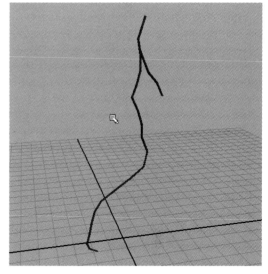

Figure 2.13
The vine geometry

15. At this point, your leaves may need to be repositioned to more closely match the new vine meshes you've created. Go through and position them so that they are accurately attached to the vine.

When all of the leaves are in place, your vine model is complete. Now it's time for the final texture work.

Creating Ivy Textures

The main challenge of creating the ivy textures will be avoiding a repeating pattern. You want all of these leaves to be clumped together naturally, but there's nothing more unnatural than being able to easily recognize that every leaf looks exactly the same. Of course they're going to, but there are ways to ensure that it's not *obvious.* By avoiding large details that can be easily seen from a moderate distance, you can prevent this pattern recognition.

1. Browse to the Ivy project folder on the DVD and open the Ivy_Start.psd file. This Photoshop file contains a diffuse, a normal, and an opacity folder with the base textures I have created inside.

2. Open a good leaf source image. The one I used is called Leaves0051_S.jpg from www.cgtextures.com. It shows a nice amount of detail in the leaf's surface as well as some good vein detail that you can use. I'm going to grab the vein detail to use for my own leaf.

3. Click the Polygonal Lasso tool and at the top of the screen, make the Feather value 5 pixels (px).

4. If you're following along with me, select the main vein down the center of the leaf with the lasso tool until you have the entire vein selected.

5. With the Move tool, click within the selected area and drag from your source image into your Photoshop file. This will drop the selected leaf vein into your file. Reposition and rescale it with the Select Transform tool to make it fit along the middle of the leaf.

6. Repeat these steps, selecting source pixels from the leaf image and moving and positioning them on your texture to create the vein details.

7. Select an area of leaf surface detail and move it into your texture underneath your vein details. If your selected detail contains any veins, remove them by using the Clone Stamp tool. Copy the leaf detail around until it covers the surface of your leaf. Merge all of the surface detail layers together into one layer.

> To use the Clone Stamp tool to hide surface details, hold the Alt key and click your image where you want to copy pixels *from*. Let go of Alt and left-click to paint pixels from where you Alt-clicked to the new area, effectively covering up the details you want to hide.

8. Create a Brightness/Contrast adjustment layer on top of all of your new leaf details and make the Brightness **-11** and Contrast **+25**. These (and all such future adjustments) will be entirely dependent on what your source image is. If you're using a different image than me, then your adjustments will vary.

9. Create a Hue/Saturation adjustment layer and increase the Lightness to **+20**. Rename it `Highlights`. Fill the mask with black and, using a soft white brush, paint in the mask to apply the adjustment layer's effect. Paint along the edges and veins of the leaf. Once done, you should have something like what you see in Figure 2.14.

10. Create a new Hue/Saturation adjustment layer and adjust this one's Lightness to **-25**. Rename it `Lowlights`. Fill the mask with black and then, using a soft white brush, paint in the mask to apply the adjustment layer's effect. You want to paint around where the leaf merges to its stem and also around the leaf's surface between the veins to add some color variation.

11. Find an interesting "grime" image from your texture sources. I chose the speckled grime image that's on the DVD called `dira002.jpg`. Using my example, I copied the image into my Photoshop file and adjusted its blend mode to Multiply. Scale and position the grime the way you like it. Rename the layer `Grime`.

12. Lower the Grime layer's opacity to about 50 percent.

Figure 2.14

The leaf's diffuse texture so far

13. You'll add a little color to the leaf so it's not just green. In a real project, you'd prob-ably want several different leaf textures: some with color variation, some just green. This way you can have variety in your foliage in the game's presentation.

    Choose an interesting color for your foreground color and green for your background color. I chose a red hue. Apply the gradient so that the color you've chosen is visible toward the tip of the leaf. Rename the layer `Color`.

14. Change the layer's Blend Mode to be Soft Light and lower the Opacity down to about 50 percent. I chose the Soft Light blend mode simply because I liked the way it looked. If you prefer a different look, feel free to choose a different style.

15. Save your file as a 32-bit targa file and name it `Leaf_Diffuse.tga`. Save your Photoshop source file too.

    Right now, the leaf texture is 1024 ×1024. This is *huge* for a leaf's texture! The level of detail that you actually need for this leaf is much smaller. Think of it this way—even with an HDTV, the largest resolution on your television screen is 1,080 pixels wide. So to have a 1,024 pixel-wide leaf texture would mean that the leaf would need to fill the TV screen to make the most of that texture's resolution. I think it's safe to say that in *most* cases, you don't need your ivy to be focused on that closely. So, at most, you can probably imagine the leaf will be at least a character's arm's width away.

16. With that in mind, open the Leaf_Diffuse.tga file you've just made and select Image → Image Size. Decrease the width and height to 128 × 128. This will blur your texture significantly.

17. Select Filter → Sharpen → Unsharp Mask. Make the Amount about 50 percent and the Radius about 1.0. Click OK.

The Unsharp mask filter was able to sharpen the details on a per-pixel basis, bringing all those details you spent so much time on back into focus, even at such a small resolution. In Figure 2.15 and Figure 2.16, you can see the final diffuse texture and how it applied in Maya onto the leaf meshes.

Figure 2.15

The final diffuse texture, at original and resized resolutions

Now, after you create a simple diffuse texture for the vine, it'll essentially be completed. The vine is a very thin piece that's not meant to draw too much attention. It merely needs to keep the leaves together in a logical way. The leaves are the main focus and the main thing needed for believability, but if the vine weren't there, you'd instantly notice the floating leaves and wonder where it was. I've prepared a final scene as an example on the DVD called Ivy04_Vine.ma. You'll now move on to the chapter's next project and expand on the practice of using opacity maps by creating a tree.

Figure 2.16

The diffuse texture applied in Maya

Project: Creating a Savannah Tree

Trees can be such a hassle in games—so much so that there are several tools and software plug-ins that are used for the express purpose of creating trees and plants to take a lot of the burdens off the artists. But whether they are generated procedurally or individually by hand, trees are a necessary object in most games, and in many cases, games need lots of them. Being on tree duty can be pretty boring and repetitive. (Don't get me started on being on *rock* duty!) For this project, you'll learn how to create one that isn't your typical oak or pine tree but instead a more interesting and stylized version of an African acacia tree, such as the ones found in these reference images (Figure 2.17).

Before you begin, it's important to know ahead of time how a tree will be used. For example, will the player be able to stand next to it? Or will it only be seen from a distance? Will the player's experience only be on the ground and therefore, will the player only look up at the tree? Or will they be able to fly and look down on it? How will it be placed in the scene? Standing upright like a normal tree? Or will it be on its side, as if it had been cut down? There can be many factors involved. For your tree, assume that the game doesn't allow flight and that the players will be able to see the tree only from the ground, looking up at it.

Figure 2.17

Two reference photos of acacia trees

The reason knowing this is important at the outset is because it dictates how you will construct the tree. You can focus all of your time ensuring that the tree will look good from the player's only vantage point and not be too concerned if it looks odd from above.

A good example of this is the extremely popular game *World of Warcraft.* As this game was first released, when players started out they were only able to walk, run, swim, and ride a horse (or some other animal). Occasionally, a player could hop a ride on a zeppelin or take a ride on a winged animal to get from point A to point B, but these flight paths were fixed, and the player couldn't control the flight's direction or elevation. After a year or two, the game released an update that allowed players to enter another world where they could obtain *flying* mounts, which allowed them to fly anywhere they wanted! This was very fun for players in this new world; however, the game designers decided that these new, winged mounts could not be used in the original game world. They were only allowed in the new area that had been expressly designed for this kind of gameplay.

The reason for limiting this new mode of travel was because the original game world was not designed with player-controlled flight in mind. There were entire cities that would completely look ridiculous if the player could see them from the air!

Before starting, make sure you set your project to your project directory by going to File → Project → Set.

With this in mind, don't be surprised if your tree in this project looks rather ridiculous from above. Luckily, the players in your fictional game won't ever see that. All they will see are great-looking trees from the vantage point they were designed to be seen from.

1. Begin with a new Maya scene and create a polygon cylinder. Position it as if it were set on the grid, and under the polyCylinder1 Inputs in the Channel Box, set the Subdivisions Axis to 12, Subdivisions Height to 6, and the Subdivisions Caps to 0. Scale the cylinder up to be a tall trunk for your tree. This will be the starting point.

2. Press the F2 shortcut key to switch the current menu set to the Animation menu set, if it isn't already. With your object selected, select Create Deformers → Lattice. Adjust the lattice points to shape the trunk so that it tapers from the base to the tip of the trunk (Figure 2.18).

3. Continue to adjust the lattice points to insert some bend into the trunk and some flaring in the trunk's base. The idea is to get rid of the straightness and add in some natural-looking curves. Once you have the trunk to your liking, you can delete the mesh's history to bake in the lattice's changes and remove the lattice.

4. In the Front or Side view, use the CV Curve tool (found under the Create menu) to create a curve from the top of the trunk to the tip of your tree's main branch like in Figure 2.19.

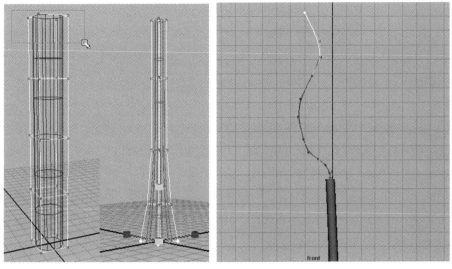

Figure 2.18
Using the lattice to shape the trunk

Figure 2.19
Creating a curve for the main branch

5. Position the curve so that its end is centered on the end-face of your trunk and rotate it so that it isn't straight up and down but flowing in the same direction the trunk is, so that when you attach them in the next steps, they'll merge together smoothly.

6. Return to the Polygons menu set, if you haven't already, by pressing the F3 shortcut key. Enter Component Select mode and select the face on the end of your trunk. Hold Shift and select the curve. You should now have the face *and* the curve selected at the same time. With the selection still active, select Edit Mesh → Extrude. You'll notice right away that a new section of trunk has extended off the face and stretched across to the end of the curve. But that's not exactly what you want.

7. Under the polyExtrudeFace1 Input in the Channel Box, scroll down toward the bottom of the available settings and increase the Divisions setting to 14 and the Taper setting to 0.2. If you like, you can also add some slight Twist to the branch as well. After applying settings you like, you should have something like Figure 2.20.

8. The tip of the branch is a bit too straight in my example. To add a few divisions, I'll use Edit Mesh → Insert Edge Loop Tool. With this tool, you can click an edge and have a new loop of

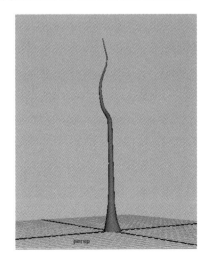

Figure 2.20

The main branch attached to the trunk

edges be inserted into the mesh. Do this a couple of times to add a few edge loops anywhere the branch or trunk look too straight. You can then move these new points to add more curvature.

9. Select the face on the end of the branch and select Edit Mesh → Merge To Center. This will collapse the face down into one point. Select the rings of vertices leading up to the point and scale them to make the branch taper gradually to the end.

10. Let's create another branch. Use the CV Curve tool in the Side or Front view to create the path of another branch off the trunk, as in Figure 2.21.

11. Create a NURBS circle and scale it down to about the diameter of the branch you want. Select it and then hold Shift and select the branch's path curve to add it to your selection.

12. Open the Surfaces menu set. Select Surfaces → Extrude → Options. Use the same settings you used before for the ivy vine, except this time, you'll increase the Number V value to 2. Keep the Number U value at 1 as before. Click Extrude to apply the command.

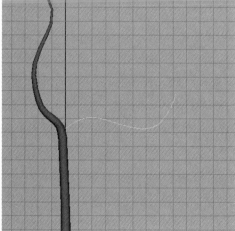

Figure 2.21
The path of the next branch

13. With history still active, you can select the branch's path curve (not the mesh) and reposition it on your trunk to perfect its location if needed. You can also scale the circle if your diameter is a little off from what you wanted. When you have your position and diameter as you like, you can delete the mesh's history.

14. Select the vertices at the tip of the new branch and use the Merge To Center command again to sharpen the tip to a single point.

15. Select the adjacent rings of vertices and scale them to create a tapering look to the branch. You can scale the base of the branch out some if you want to flare it, but don't have it extend beyond the shape of the trunk.

16. If any additional edge loops are needed to improve the branch's curvature, you can add them now as well. Eventually, you should get something like Figure 2.22.

17. You can duplicate, reposition, and scale the existing branch to make new ones, or you can repeat the previous steps to make new branches from scratch. Whichever method you choose, make about three or four more large branches and position them on the tree to make an interesting shape. Mine turned out like Figure 2.23.

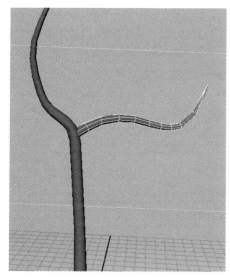

Figure 2.22
The new branch in place

Figure 2.23
The main branches completed

Creating Secondary Branches

Adding smaller, secondary branches growing from the main branch system is pretty much the same process. The only real difference is that the branches are smaller. These branches will help fill out the rest of the tree's structure as well as provide a base that your future leaves can be attached to.

1. As before, in the Front or Side view, draw out a curve using the CV Curve tool coming off of one of your main branches. Once you get a nice curved shape using around 4 to 5 points, position it in the Perspective view so that it's accurately positioned on the tree branch.

2. Duplicate this curve and position it around the tree. Scale them up and down slightly to ensure they aren't all identical. I placed about seven branches (Figure 2.24).

3. Just as before, create a small Nurbs circle to use as an extrusion profile.

Figure 2.24
Secondary branch curves placed around the tree

Figure 2.25

Secondary
branches in place

Perform extrude commands for each branch curve and adjust their shapes to create a tapered affect from their base to their tip. When complete, you should have something like Figure 2.25.

Creating Tertiary Branches

With the ivy, each plane you created was an individual leaf. For a vine of ivy with a few dozen leaves on it, it's not too big of a hit to a game engine or to your time to place them each by hand. A tree, on the other hand, is a different story. You really can't place each individual leaf in the same way. Not only would it be extremely time-consuming, but it would result in a polycount far exceeding what most games would probably be able to budget to a simple tree.

With that in mind, you'll now create a couple of textures that contain a large number of leaves that you'll use to populate your tree. Rather than the relatively realistic style you've used so far in the brick wall and ivy vine, you'll try a more cartoony style, similar to what was used in Nintendo's *The Legend of Zelda: The Wind Waker.* Such a texture style doesn't require as many different maps as the realistic styles do, but you'll still need a diffuse map and, of course, your trusty opacity maps. You'll start with a texture base, as usual. This time, you'll render your leaf texture sources directly from Maya's native renderer.

1. First, hide your tree geometry while you work on your leaves. Select your entire tree. In the Layer Bar (found under the Channel Box) create a new layer and name it **Tree**. With the tree still selected, right-click the layer and choose the Add Selected Objects option. Click the V icon next to the layer to toggle its visibility off, thereby hiding the tree from view.

2. In the Top view, create a small branch with leaves growing off it. First, draw out a curve that is mostly straight with some slight curvature to give it a natural look. Extrude a Nurbs circle along it and taper the ends just as you have done for the other branches you've made.

3. Select Mesh → Create Polygon Tool. Using your left mouse button, drop points into the shape of a leaf, similar to Figure 2.26. Press Enter when you're done to finalize the action and create the polygonal object.

4. Press the Insert key to toggle Edit Pivot mode and move the leaf's pivot to the base of the leaf, where it will most likely meet the branch.

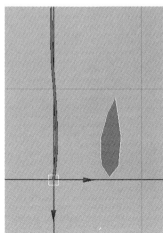

Figure 2.26

Creating a simple leaf shape

5. Move, scale, and rotate the leaf to place it on the branch. Duplicate and repeat this process until the branch is covered in leaves to your liking. Scale them in such a way that, as the leaves approach the tip of the branch, they get smaller and thinner. Toward the base of the branch, the leaves are thicker and larger. Mine ended up like Figure 2.27.

Think of these as your tertiary branches. Rather than spending precious geometry on them, you'll give them a 2-polygon plane to give the illusion of more detail.

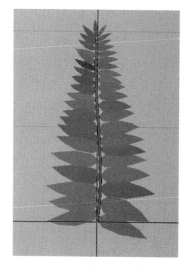

Figure 2.27
Positioned leaves on the branch

6. Apply a new Lambert material to the leaves and give it a forest green color. Apply another Lambert to the branch and give it a brown color.

7. Now you'll render an image of the branch to use as a texture for your tree. Select Window → Rendering Editors → Render Settings. These settings control how Maya renders an animation or a still image. Under the Common tab near the top, scroll down to the Image Size section and change the width and height to 256×512.

8. Under the Maya Software tab, near the top, change the Anti-aliasing Quality setting to Contrast Sensitive Production. Under the Multi-pixel Filtering section, make sure to deselect the Use Multi-pixel Filter check box.

The multi-pixel filter tends to blur your textures, especially if your textures are dealing with any kind of text or small details. I generally just turn multi-pixel filtering off as a rule.

9. Back in the top view, in the panel view menus select View → Camera Settings → Resolution Gate. Also check the Vertical option rather than the default Horizontal, if it's not already. You should see a box appear. Position your camera as best you can so that the branch is within the box. When you have it positioned, you can render it by clicking the Render Current Frame button at the far right of the Status Line (Figure 2.28).

10. Save the render as `branch.tga`.

11. Create a new layer and call it `branch_source` and put the branch geometry into it and hide its visibility. Unhide the Tree layer.

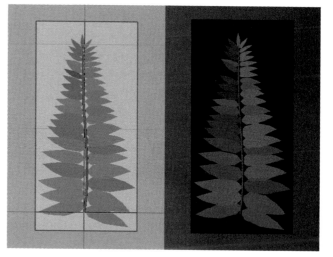

Figure 2.28
The Resolution Gate centered and the rendered result

12. Create a polygon plane with a width of 25.6 and a height of 51.2. Make sure the Normalization option is off. By creating the plane with these dimensions, you've maintained the size ratio of your 256×512 texture, so once it's applied, it won't be distorted.

13. After applying your branch texture to the plane, press the Insert key on the keyboard to edit the plane's pivot point. Move the pivot to the base of the branch where it would attach to the tree.

14. Select Edit Mesh → Insert Edge Loop Tool and drag a new edge down the middle of the plane. Select the two long edges of the plane and move them either back or forth a bit. This will give the branch a bit of depth rather than it just being a simple plane. This wedge shape can more easily be seen from multiple directions and is more pleasing to the eye as an organic shape.

15. Position the tertiary branch onto the ends of one of your preexisting branches. Duplicate and position more branches around your tree. Focus on placing one at the tip of each main branch and have a couple more branches spaced around to fill the tree out (Figure 2.29). Don't forget, these are simply your third round of branches. You will make some new leaves to act as "filler" in the next steps.

Figure 2.29
The tertiary branches in place

Creating Filler Leaves

The next texture will be the filler leaves for the tree. These will be the leaves that make up the majority of what is seen in the tree's canopy. Unlike the branch texture, this texture won't have any sort of "attach point" that obviously gives a position where it should meet the tree. These sorts of filler details are designed to literally fit pretty much anywhere and be scaled, rotated, and even intersected to give the illusion of depth and abundance of detail where there isn't any.

1. Hide your tree (be sure to add your new branch planes to the tree's layer) and unhide your branch_source layer. Move your branch geometry to the side.

2. Grab one branch of leaves, duplicate it, and move it over to a clear spot to work with. Use your CV Curve tool to draw out short lines that would represent small branches and position them in a clumping pattern. You'll probably need to adjust them later, but it's good to get a starting foundation.

3. Start duplicating and positioning your leaves around the clump of curves (representing branches), scaling and rotating them (to diminish their uniformity), with the intention of creating a scattered leaf/branch combination of details, similar to Figure 2.30.

4. Extrude a Nurbs circle along the branch curves as you have done before. Don't worry about tapering the ends or anything. Select the entire leaf cluster and delete all of its history. You can then group the leaves all together with Ctrl+G. Duplicate the group to make a new clump of leaves and position them below the first group and rotate and scale it so that it's not positioned exactly the same as the first group.

5. Depending on how dense your leaf cluster is, you may want to duplicate a third copy. Assign your green leaf and brown branch materials accordingly. With these duplicates, I have this result from the Top View camera (Figure 2.31).

Figure 2.30

The initial clump of leaves and twigs

6. Now, you'll render an image to use as a texture just as you did with the branch. Use the same settings as before, except this time, make the width and height values equal 512, resulting in a 512×512 texture. Save it as `treeleaf.tga`.

7. Assign the cluster geometry to the branch_source layer and hide it. Unhide your tree layer.

8. Create a square polygon plane and apply your leaf texture to it. Because it is just a flat plane, it doesn't really help us fill the tree with natural-looking leaves. Let's add another dimension to it.

Figure 2.31

The finished leaf cluster with rendered result

9. Select the leaf plane and select Edit Mesh → Poke Face. This will insert a vertex in the center of the plane. Raise the vertex up so that the plane becomes a pyramid shape.

10. Begin placing, duplicating, scaling, and rotating the leaf planes around your tree, creating an interesting-looking canopy. Don't be afraid to intersect them and extend beyond the strict boundaries of the 3D branches. My result looks like Figure 2.32.

Figure 2.32

Final leafy canopy in place

Creating Stylized Bark

The bark of your tree should match the cartoony look that you've created with the leaves and branches. There aren't really any photo sources you can find to get those kinds of results. It'll have to be done with actual painting by hand. As with any kind of art, painting takes practice. I know as a professional 3D artist, I tend to neglect the 2D aspects of my talent and don't draw or paint nearly enough. It's a pretty common thing in this industry. Try to always reserve time for you to practice drawing and painting. Only through practice will you be able to maximize your potential and your talent.

But even if you feel you aren't a good texture painter, you'll probably be able to do this cartoony bark texture justice. If your first texture doesn't come out quite like you want, don't be afraid to try again. Learning from your prior mistakes is one of the best ways to improve your skills.

1. In Photoshop, create a new file that is 512×1024, making a tall, vertical image file.

2. Fill the background with a similar brown color as you did with your branches previously.

3. Make a new layer. Name it Grooves. Take a soft brush and choose a darker hue of your brown color. Draw two relatively (but not completely) straight lines from the bottom of the image to the top using a small diameter brush, dividing your image into thirds. My brush is about 20 pixels wide (Figure 2.33).

4. Right-click the Grooves layer and open the Blending Options. Check the Outer Glow style check box. Change the color from the default pale yellow to a darker brown hue. Continue by making the following changes:

Blend Mode: Multiply
Opacity: 35%
Noise: 8%
Spread: 9%
Size: 68 px

You should get a "shadowing" effect around your two groove lines, making the grooves look as if they are intruding into the surface.

5. Create a Brightness/Contrast adjustment layer over the Grooves layer and change the Brightness to +21 and the Contrast to +15. Select the mask (the white box on the layer) to make it active and fill it with black, thereby hiding the adjustment layer's effects. Take a black brush and paint over the areas *between* the groove lines, making that space lighter and giving the illusion of height.

6. Drag the adjustment layer to the New Layer button to make a copy of it. Select the copy's mask and press Ctrl+I to invert the mask.

7. Double-click the new adjustment layer to access its settings and change the Brightness to +3 and the Contrast to +25. You should have something like Figure 2.34.

    Feel free to continue to adjust the bark's colors and settings until you get something you are happy with.

8. Now that you have some basic shapes, you'll want to make sure that it properly tiles, because you'll

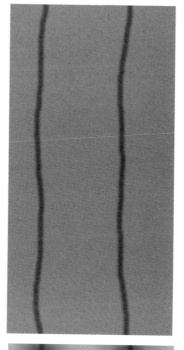

Figure 2.33
Starting your cartoony bark texture

Figure 2.34
The bark texture so far

want this texture to wrap around the tree's trunk and repeat as it extends up the trunk's length. Press Ctrl+A to select the entire canvas and press Ctrl+Shift+C to Copy Merged. Finally, press Ctrl+V to paste the copied image of the bark into its own layer. Name this layer **BaseBark**.

9. With this layer selected, select Filter → Other → Offset. The Offset dialog box will open with two main sliders to adjust. Type 256 into the Horizontal slider. This offsets the texture 256 pixels horizontally (or *half* of your image's total width of 512 pixels).

   In my case, it turned out that my texture looked good already tiling in that direction, but if you see any harsh lines running down the center of your image, get rid of them and apply the Offset filter again to put the image back to its original position.

10. Once again apply the Offset filter and remove the 256 from the horizontal slider (making it 0) and type 512 into the Vertical slider, inputting half of the height of your image. This offset result gave me an obvious seam that I'll need to fix in the next steps (Figure 2.35).

11. Apply the Offset filter once again to return to the image's original position. Select the Rectangular Marquee tool (or press M) and at the top of the screen, change the Feather option to 5 pixels.

12. Select a box around the middle of your image. You'll notice that the corners of your selection box are rounded, indicating that the selection is feathered. This is what you want, but you want the feathering to apply only to the top and bottom of the box, not the left and right edges.

13. With the selection still active, choose Select → Transform Selection. The Transform Selection tool allows you to interactively manipulate the selection boundary you have already drawn without manipulating the image within it. Hold down the Alt key and click and drag on the left or right handle of the Transform tool to widen the selection box to extend beyond the boundary of the image. Now the feathered edge will not feather the tiling border of your selection.

14. Press Ctrl+J to copy the selected area into its own layer. Name this layer **Patch**.

15. Select the BaseBark layer again and apply the offset filter, offsetting it 512 pixels vertically. You'll notice the Patch layer is overlaid on top of the seam you had before, although in my case, it hasn't perfectly fixed it right off the bat. I still need to make some adjustments.

16. In my particular image's case, I need to move the Patch layer around a little bit to best fit along the grooves I had drawn earlier. Then, I make a few strokes of the eraser to remove some trouble spots, and I am good to go. Here are my before and after results in Figure 2.36.

Figure 2.35

An ugly seam in
need of fixing

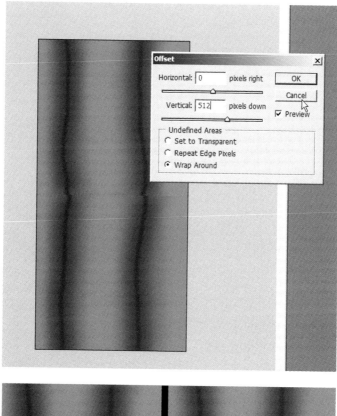

Figure 2.36

The bark texture
fully tileable

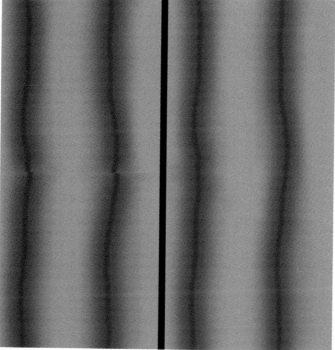

17. To add a little texture to your colors, you'll use an overlay image. From your texture library or from this book's DVD, pick out an image that provides some splotchy details. I chose a metal texture source. Add it to your Photoshop file as a separate layer and name it `Details`. Change its Blending Mode to Overlay.

18. Using the Free Transform tool (Ctrl+T), move and scale the image to lay on top of your bark texture in an interesting way. You may need to lower the Opacity of the layer, depending on how much contrast it has. I lowered my Details layer's opacity to about 36 percent.

19. Feel free to adjust the colors and remove any seams that the new Details layer may have added and save your finished bark texture as `bark.tga` (Figure 2.37).

UV Mapping the Tree

Back in Maya, if you apply your new bark texture to the tree's trunk, you'll probably notice that it doesn't quite look like you expected it would. Maybe

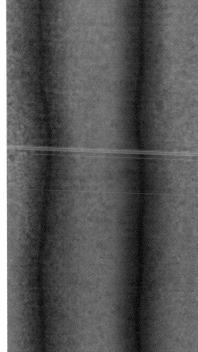

Figure 2.37
The final bark texture

it's all stretched out or has really ugly seams crisscrossing throughout the mesh. This is because the mesh needs to be UV mapped. *UV mapping* is the process of laying out your geometry's UVs to fit the textures you make for them. To get started, you'll open the UV Texture Editor from the Window menu.

1. You'll first get the hard part out of the way and begin with the tree's trunk. Select the faces that make up the straighter part of the trunk, starting from the base and ending right before the trunk begins to bend.

2. Under the Polygons menu set, select Create UVs → Cylindrical Mapping. A cylinder-shaped manipulator will appear around the tree trunk and the selected faces will appear in the UV Texture Editor window. You should see something like Figure 2.38.

3. If your results are like mine, you may notice that in the upper left and right of the UV shell that is currently active there is a face hanging by itself along with a gap where it should be on the opposite side. To fix this, you'll need to do some manual UV adjustment.

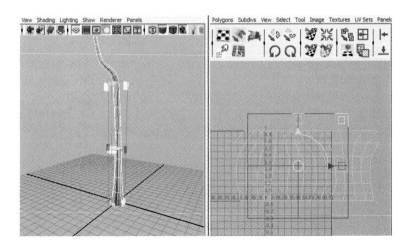

Figure 2.38

The lower trunk's UVs cylindrically mapped

4. Right-click *in the UV Texture Editor window* and choose UVs from the marking menu that appears. This will allow you to manipulate the UVs in the editor. Select the UVs of the trunk that you just mapped and move them to the side so that the rest of the UVs won't interfere with your work.

5. Right-click in the UV Editor and this time choose Edge component mode. Select the edge that connects the hanging face to the rest of the UV shell and in the editor's menus select Polygons → Cut UV Edges (or click the "cutting scissors" button on the toolbar). This will separate the face from the rest of the UV shell.

6. Now, select the two edges on the other side of the UV shell that border the gap that you want the hanging face to attach to. You'll notice that this also selects the corresponding edges on the hanging face. That's because the two edges you've selected are the same edges on the geometry. With these two edges selected, select Polygons → Move And Sew UV Edges. The hanging face should move to the other side and merge into the shell where the gap previously was.

7. Now that you've cleaned up any hanging faces, you'll want to position these UVs in a clean grid. The easiest way to do that is to select each individual column of UVs and use the Align command.

   On the UV Editor toolbar, you should see four buttons with arrows pointing in all four directions. These are the align buttons. Depending on which directional button you click, the current UV that you have selected that is the furthest in the selected direction will be the UV that the rest of your selection aligns to.

   Look at Figure 2.39 to see what I mean. In the first image, I have a column of UVs selected that are not aligned. The UV at the bottom of the column is the farthest UV to the left out of those I have selected. So when I click the button with the left-pointing arrow, all of the selected UVs line up as in the second image. Do this with each column of UVs to straighten them all out.

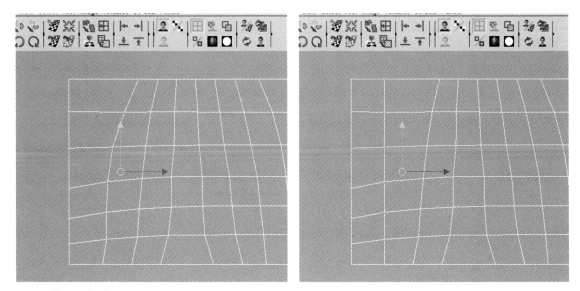

Figure 2.39

Aligning
columns of UVs

8. When your UV shell is straightened out, you can start positioning it within the Editor to get the results you want on the tree. Scale, position, and if applicable rotate your UVs as you watch the result on your tree geometry. When you have a layout that you like, you can move on to UV mapping the rest of the trunk in the same way. Mine turned out like Figure 2.40.

Figure 2.40

The trunk's UVs laid out to fit the texture onto the geometry

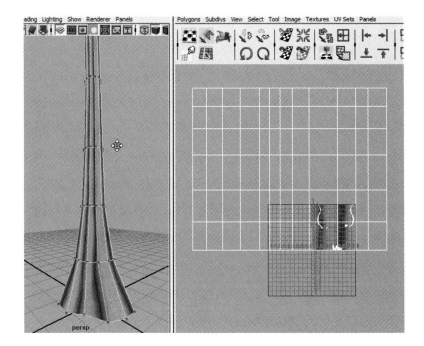

9. For the rest of the trunk, continue to select sections of faces and UV map them. Then go in manually to tweak and clean up the results.

10. Do the same for each of the branches until finally your entire tree—trunk, branches, and leaves—is UV mapped. Position each shell of UVs in the editor to get the kind of look you want. Mine ended up like Figure 2.41.

The final tree came out to about 1,800 polygons, which is a very conservative number in this current generation of game consoles. You could have several varieties of trees of this polycount range without too much of a problem.

The Illusion of Detail

As you can see from both the ivy and the tree, when it comes to vegetation, smart usage of opacity maps can make all the difference in creating the illusion of the details you strive for. And it works well for both realistic and stylized genres. Plants, flowers, grass, and more can all be made using the methods described in this chapter. In the next chapter, you'll tackle something man-made.

Figure 2.41
The final tree

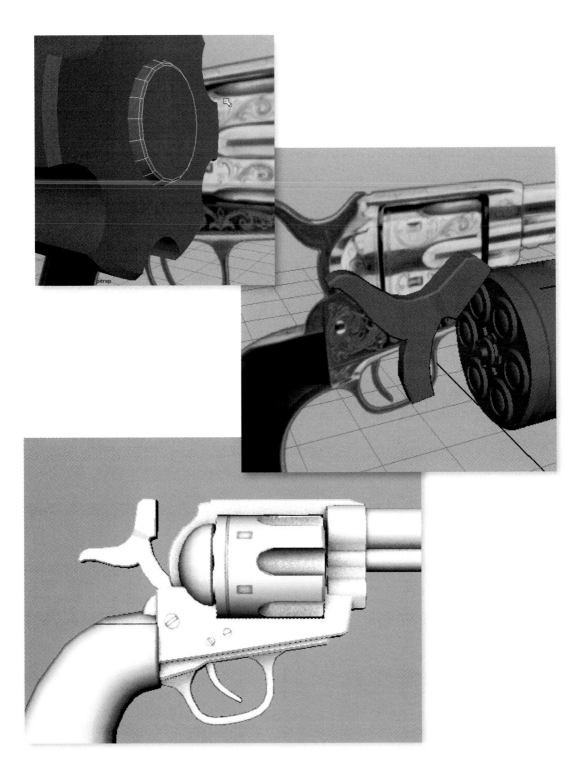

CHAPTER 3

Weapons

Although not in every game, combat appears in a large percentage of games. Whether it is guns, swords, or lightsabers, in combat-heavy games weapons play a major role. Especially in a game that requires switching weapons frequently, you may need to create a large variety of weapons. In fact, some role-playing games have arsenals of hundreds of unique weapon art assets for players to draw from. In this chapter, you'll focus on modeling in greater depth by going over some of the common modeling tools and commands that every game artist should know.

Understanding Weapons

Weapons in video games can come in all sorts of themes. In Microsoft's *Halo* series, the weapons are science-fictional and alien, firing lasers, plasma bolts, and other sorts of fantastical, otherworldly ammunition. In Rockstar's *Grand Theft Auto* series, the weapons are more realistic—machine guns, rifles, grenades, missile launchers, and so on. Medieval themes also are commonly used in role-playing games like Square Enix's *Final Fantasy* series, in which swords, magic staves, and crossbows are the norm.

All that is to say that a weapon can look like nearly anything and can be almost anything. Even a baseball bat with some nails driven into it can be a powerful weapon, such as in Konami's *SAW* video game based on the popular horror movie franchise.

Depending on the type of game you work on, weapons may need to be created in multiple levels of detail. For instance, in a first-person shooter, the weapon the player wields is seen extremely close-up. Being able to scrutinize the model so closely means it needs to be highly detailed and polished. After all, players will always develop favorite weapons that they will literally see all the time, and you want those weapons to look good. On the other hand, the weapon that the player finds in the world (whether set on the floor, hanging from the wall, hidden in a treasure chest, or so forth) will be seen from a farther vantage point. Because that version of the weapon is seen from a relative distance, it can be far less detailed.

Some melee-type weapons require damage systems. In *SAW*, the melee weapons the player finds will become damaged as they are used until they break. Each different state of damage the weapon has is a separate model that needs to be created and swapped in by the programmers.

For this project, you'll be going to the Old West and creating an old-fashioned revolver. Creating such a weapon will bring you to a new level of complexity that I've yet to cover—*animation*. By animating the revolver, you can create several different animation sequences that a game can use during the course of play. Firing, reloading, jamming, and so on, all require that different parts of the weapon move. Such techniques would be used for any weapon that was composed of moving parts, from guns to chainsaws. You'll explore how in this chapter.

Project: Creating and Animating a Western Revolver

Before you can jump straight into animation, you of course must first focus on creating the art for the weapon. You can probably find a ton of references online, but I've gone ahead and done the dirty work for you. On the DVD, open the `pistol_start.ma` file from the Chapter 3 project directory to begin. You'll first create a high-resolution mesh that you will use to bake your source textures from, as you have done in the previous chapters.

Before starting, make sure you set your project to your project directory by going to File → Project → Set.

1. In the scene, I have a reference image already set up and in its own Reference layer. To create the revolver's cylinder, the aptly named rotating cylindrical casing that holds the weapon's bullets, select Create → Polygon Primitives → Cylinder and draw the shape of a simple cylinder.

2. Rotate it 90 degrees on the z-axis to flip the cylinder to lie horizontally.

3. Change to the Front view and position scale and position the geometry to line up with the cylinder in the reference image like in Figure 3.1.

Figure 3.1

The cylinders lined up with each other

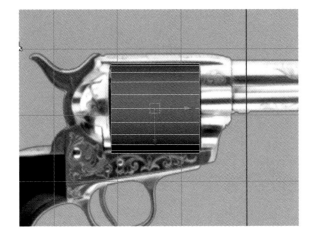

4. To make using the reference image easier, you can adjust the geometry's transparency. You could do this by turning on XRay mode in our viewport, but this makes *everything* transparent, reference image included. What you want is to make only your geometry transparent while maintaining the opaqueness of the reference image.

    To do this, you can simply apply a new Lambert material onto it and adjust the material's Transparency slider up a tad. Now, your reference image maintains its opaqueness and you can see it through the geometry you're working with. Do this now to the cylinder to see whether it helps you when placing it. As you need to throughout this lesson, raise and lower the transparency of this material to help you match the reference image.

5. Once you have the cylinder's scale and position like you want it, return to the Perspective view and, under the polyCylinder1 Inputs in the Channel Box, reduce the Subdivisions Caps value to 0 and increase the Subdivisions Axis value to 40. This will make the cylinder much rounder, giving you a far smoother shape to work with.

6. Select both caps of the cylinder and apply a Bevel (Edit Mesh → Bevel). In the polyBevel1 Inputs in the Channel Box, you can adjust its Offset value from its default 0.5 (which is way too large) to something more like 0.05 to give it a nice beveled edge.

7. Now, create a polygon sphere. Lower its Subdivisions Height value to be about 12 (while keeping the Subdivisions Axis at the default value of 20) to make its mesh less dense. Rotate it 90 degrees so that the sphere's poles are facing to the left and right of the reference image. Go into Face component mode and delete either the left or right half of the sphere.

8. Select the resulting border edge loop around the sphere's open end and extrude the edges (Edit Mesh → Extrude) approximately 3.5 units, thus creating a long, nearly bullet-like shape.

9. Select Mesh → Fill Hole to cap the open end of the shape.

    You're not actually going to use this to make a bullet, but rather to make the distinctive rounded indentations you can see within the pistol's fluted cylinder casing. To do this, you're going to use a Boolean operation, similar to what you did with the bricks in Chapter 1. See the "Boolean Operations" sidebar for more in-depth information about Booleans.

10. Return to the Front view. Position and scale the "bullet" on your cylinder geometry, matching the position of the reference cylinder's indentations. Apply the transparency material you made earlier and adjust its opacity a bit to help if needed (Figure 3.2).

Figure 3.2
Scaling the Boolean object

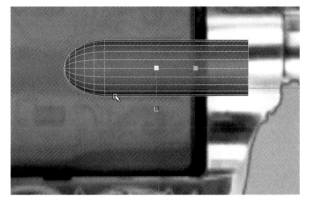

You can easily scale an object on two axes at the same time. With the Scale tool active, Ctrl-click and drag on the scale handle that you *don't* want to scale. The *other* two directions will scale normally and the Ctrl-clicked direction will remain locked in place.

BOOLEAN OPERATIONS

Boolean operations can be a source of great time savings. What could be a lengthy process of detailed modeling (such as creating pock marks in the face of a brick in Chapter 1) becomes much easier and faster with the use of Booleans.

But what is a Boolean anyway? The term refers to a system of logic developed in the 19th century by George Boole. This system has been brought forward into the computer age and is used in binary code and even Internet search engines. It's simply the use of the words *and* and *or* to come to a logical end result. At the risk of oversimplification, in 3D terms, Boolean logic has been used to give us three commands, which are all found under Mesh → Booleans:

- A *Union* Boolean operation will fuse two intersecting objects together. This is different than the Combine command (which combines two objects together) in that the Union command will delete the intersecting geometry of the two objects so that one object's surface will blend into the surface of the other.

- A *Difference* Boolean operation will take one object and subtract its shape from another. This is what you did in Chapter 1 to carve out grooves and pock marks into the bricks for your Brick Wall project. When performing a Difference, you must make sure that the first object you select is the object you want to keep. Then Shift-select the object you wish to use as a carving shape (or negative space object).

- And lastly, an *Intersection* Boolean operation will do the opposite of a Union operation. Where the Union command deleted the intersecting geometry of two shapes, the Intersection command will preserve the intersecting geometry but delete the nonintersecting geometry of two intersecting shapes.

Booleans can be very fun and can help create some very complex surfaces with little effort. However, a word of caution: They don't always work. Whether it is a problem with the math involved or something else, I've never found out. But whatever the case, trying to use a Boolean operation can sometimes simply cause all of the objects to disappear. I haven't found any satisfactory solution to this problem (feel free to contact me if you know of one!). I typically end up either remaking the piece, or if that isn't feasible, creating the detail I need in another file, and importing it back into the old one. But in any case, don't let their limited consistency stop you from making great use of Booleans!

For this project, creating the indentations and grooves that are so prevalent in the reference weapon's designs would be an immense undertaking without the use of Booleans. Otherwise, you could expect to be modeling each groove individually, which would take an enormous amount of time.

11. Once you have the shape matched to the reference, you can move the negative space object to intersect with the cylinder where the indentation should go. Take a look at Figure 3.3 to see an example.

As in the figure, position the Boolean object so that it intersects the cylinder just below its center edge. By ensuring that this edge isn't too close to the cylinder, you've prevented having a dirty geometric result after the Boolean takes place.

Figure 3.3

Lining up the Boolean object

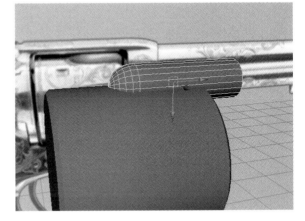

12. Double-click the Move tool in the Toolbox (on the far left of the interface) to open the Move tool's settings. Make sure that the Move Axis option is set to World, if it isn't already.

13. With the bullet-shaped Boolean object selected, press the Insert key (on the keyboard near the Delete key usually) to enter Edit Pivot mode. You want the pivot of the Boolean object to align with the center of the cylinder. You'll do this by holding the V key to enable Snap To Point. At the same time you are holding V, left-click and drag on the green y-axis handle and drag your cursor to a point on the edge of the cylinder that lines up with the cylinder's center. Take a look at Figure 3.4 to see this step illustrated.

You'll notice that instead of following your cursor, the pivot will instead align on the y-axis with whatever point your cursor hovers on.

14. Your revolver will be a six-shooter, so you will need six indentations positioned around the cylinder equidistantly apart. Since the cylinder is 360 degrees around, you can divide that by 6 to get the result of 60 degrees.

Figure 3.4

Aligning the pivot to the center of the cylinder while holding the V key

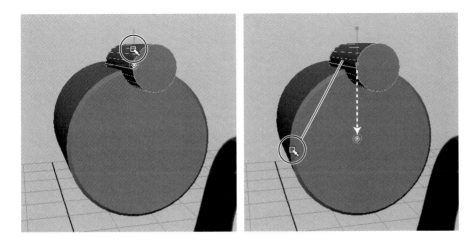

Duplicate the Boolean object and rotate the duplicate 60 degrees around the cylinder. You'll notice that with the pivot placed at the cylinder's center point, its position is placed perfectly aligned as the first one was. Do the same operation four more times to create six evenly spaced duplicates.

15. Select the six Boolean objects and select Mesh → Combine to combine them all together. This way you can do one Boolean operation rather than six, decreasing the chances of it failing (as was described briefly in the sidebar).

16. Deselect everything. Select the cylinder first and Shift-select the combined Boolean object second. Select Mesh → Booleans → Difference. You should get a result like Figure 3.5.

Figure 3.5

The cylinder is coming together nicely.

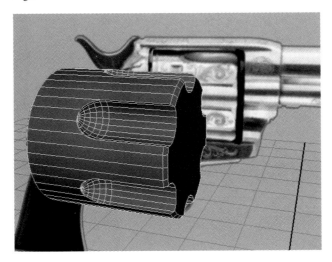

17. Select the Front view. You'll next add an indented channel into the surface, which will be seen later in the normal map that you generate. Enable the Cut Faces tool (under the Edit Mesh menu).

    With this tool, you can cut straight loops of edges through geometry based on your camera's view. If you hold the Shift key while doing it, the cut will align vertically or horizontally, depending on which direction you click and drag. On the left end of the cylinder (from the Front view perspective), hold Shift and drag down with the Cut Faces tool to cut a straight vertical edge loop into the cylinder.

18. Return to the Perspective view. Select one of the edges we just added and select the Select → Select Contiguous Edges menu item. This will select the entire edge loop.

19. Apply a Bevel to the loop and adjust the Offset to about 0.2, shrinking the new loop to fit the surface seam you'll add here.

20. Select the Select → Select Edge Ring Tool menu item, and double-click one of the horizontal edges within the new loop of faces, selecting all of the edges within the loop. Press Ctrl+F11. This is the shortcut for the Convert Selection To Faces command. Your selection of edges will convert to a corresponding selection of faces.

    Sometimes it's quicker to select an edge loop or ring like this and convert the selection to faces rather than selecting each face you want along the same path.

21. With the ring of faces still selected, extrude them inward, creating a groove running around the cylinder (Figure 3.6).

22. Center a small cylinder with a beveled end cap on the grooved side of the revolver's cylinder. This small detail will serve as the cylinder's axis for later when you animate it spinning (Figure 3.7).

23. Now, add one more detail before calling the outer surface of the weapon's cylinder complete and you switch your focus to another area. Create a small rectangular cube that's approximately $0.25 \times 0.25 \times 0.15$ units in size and center it above the cylinder.

24. Bevel the bottom-facing side (keeping the default offset) and then bevel the side edges, adjusting this offset to be approximately 0.4.

25. Lower the cube, intersecting it into the cylinder so that the beveled downward facing end is entirely submerged into the surface. Repeat the steps you did with the previous Boolean object:

    a. Edit the pivot point to be aligned with the cylinder's center point.

    b. Duplicate the cube and rotate it 60 degrees.

    c. Repeat until you have six cubes positioned around the cylinder at equal distances.

    d. Combine the cubes together.

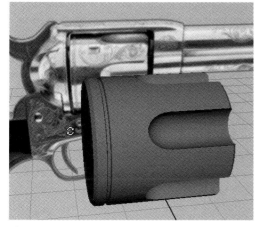

Figure 3.6

A surface groove running around the cylinder

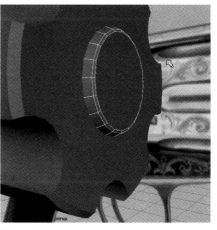

Figure 3.7

The cylinder's axis

Figure 3.8

Additional surface
detail carved into
the cylinder

26. Rotate the combined cubes 30 degrees so that they are positioned *between* the fluted indentations you made previously.

27. Making sure to select the cylinder first, perform another Difference Boolean operation to carve out the cubes from the cylinder. Figure 3.8 shows the result.

Adding Details and Components

Now that you have the basic form of the weapon's cylinder casing created, you can start adding details and components that are associated with this part. For instance, in the following steps, you'll add the tiny ratchet that will rotate the cylinder casing when the trigger is pulled, and you'll create the bullet caps that will rotate around the cylinder:

1. Create a new polygonal cylinder and center it with the cylinder casing on the end facing where the weapon's grip will be. Scale it down to be similar in scale to the axis you made in step 22 in the previous section.

2. Under the polyCylinder Inputs in the Channel Box, change the Subdivisions Axis value to 18. This will give you the number of faces you want for the next step.

3. To make the cylinder more ratchet-like, you're going to extrude teeth from the side of the cylinder. You want six teeth to coincide with the six bullet chambers that you'll eventually make. Select every third face on the side of the cylinder, giving you six total selected faces (you gave it 18 faces around the axis in the previous step because 18 ÷ 3 = 6).

   With the six faces selected, extrude them outward by about 0.04 units. Press the G key to redo your last action and extrude again by about 0.04 and taper the end slightly.

4. For this particular ratchet, the teeth have small hooks on the ends. You'll simulate this by selecting the left-side face of the last extrusion on each tooth and extruding them outward by about 0.02, tapering the ends and moving them down a bit to straighten it if needed.

5. Select the circular front face of the ratchet and perform another Extrude. Scale inward a small amount (with no outward distance extruded). Extrude again, this time pulling outward by about 0.02 and tapering the end. Extrude a third time, scaling this one in by about two thirds of diameter of the circle. Extrude a *fourth* time, pulling outward by 0.055 and again tapering the end.

6. Lastly, bevel the tip of this new face, adjusting the offset to be about 0.27. You can see the end result of these steps in Figure 3.9. These last several steps used a series of Extrudes and Bevels to create lots of shape detail in a small space. These details will all serve you well when you bake your normal map later on.

7. Next, you'll create the illusion of bullets loaded into the cylinder's chambers. Create a new cylinder and position it on the cylinder where the bullets would be visible, between the fluted indentations. Under the Inputs, lower the Subdivisions Caps to 0 to give you clean circular faces on each end.

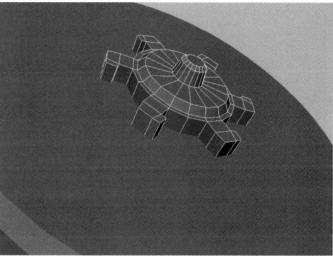

Figure 3.9
The toothed ratchet

8. Select the outward face and bevel it with an Offset of about 0.2 to give it a rounded edge.

9. Select the end cap face and perform an Extrude. Scale in the extrusion about one third of the cylinder's diameter and extrude again. Indent this extrusion into the cylinder very slightly, around 0.01 units deep.

10. Extrude this face again and scale inward a bit. Extrude once again, pulling this face back out and tapering it slightly. Apply a new Bevel with an Offset of 0.02 to give the edge a slight amount of rounding. With that series of Extrude and Bevel operations, you should get a result similar to Figure 3.10.

   This shape will act as the cap of the bullet that is loaded into the weapon. You don't need to actually see the entire bullet, just the cap to properly give the illusion of a full bullet resting in the weapon's chamber.

11. Duplicate six bullet caps around the cylinder and the ratchet in the same way you have done before with other things. Remember that you want to keep the bullets between the fluted indentations of the cylinder, as that is where there is room to accommodate them.

Figure 3.10
The bullet caps arranged around the cylinder

Creating the Barrel

With the cylinder and some details created, it's now time to move on to the revolver's barrel. The barrel is basically composed of a couple of cylinders, along with some additional details for the gun site and such.

1. Create a cylinder in the Front view, and match it to the reference image in length and diameter. Use your transparency-controlled material if you need to. Reduce the cylinder's Subdivisions Caps to 0 to remove those edges. Rename it `Barrel`.

2. Duplicate the barrel and lower it down and match the length and diameter to the ejector rod (the barrel-like cylinder beneath the actual barrel). It's OK if the two cylinders intersect. Rename it `Ejector`.

3. Select the face on the barrel-end of the ejector cylinder and apply a Bevel command. In the polyBevel Inputs in the Channel Box, increase the Segments to 3 and decrease the Offset to about 0.36. Increasing the Segments gives the Bevel a more rounded edge.

4. In the Front view, create a cylinder that matches the diameter of the gun site at the end of the barrel. Enter Face component mode and select the lower half of the cylinder's faces and delete them.

5. Return to the Perspective view and scale the width of the cylinder to more closely accommodate the barrel and how a gun site would actually be positioned. See Figure 3.11 for an example image.

6. Back in the Front view, adjust the profile of the gun site cylinder to more closely match the reference image, giving it a more sloped forward side.

7. Delete the remaining cap edges. Select the two bare faces that result and bevel them, decreasing the Offset to about 0.25. Adjust the gun site's scale as you see fit and rename it `GunSite`.

8. Back to the barrel, you'll perform a series of Bevels and Extrusions to create the barrel's opening. Select the face on the "business end" of the barrel and give it a slight bevel, decreasing the Offset to about 0.1.

9. With the end cap face still selected, perform an Extrude and scale the result about a fourth of the face's radius. Perform a second Extrude and move it into the barrel slightly, tapering the end. Extrude again and move it farther into the barrel. If you were to think of it in real distance, move in about an inch.

10. Do another extrusion and scale it inward slightly. Do one last extrusion and this time move the face all the way back into the rear of the barrel. When you're done, you should have something like Figure 3.12.

Figure 3.11

The gun site cylinder in place

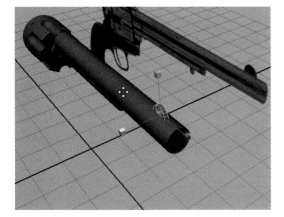

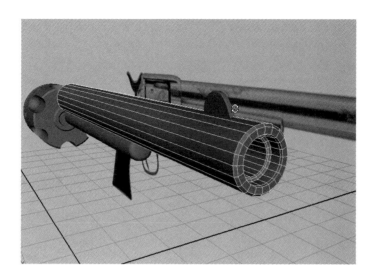

Figure 3.12
The barrel's modeled opening

Creating the Hammer

The hammer is the lever that the weapon's owner would pull back to arm the gun before pulling the trigger to fire it. When the trigger is pulled, the hammer would then slam down on the back end of a bullet, firing it from the barrel. This crucial piece of the gun is the next piece you will create.

1. In the Front view, select Mesh → Create Polygon Tool. Using your reference image as your guide, click points down to create a profile shape of the hammer.

   You'll have to use your own instincts and any supplemental reference you may be able to find to create the shape of the parts that are hidden in the provided reference. I added on a mallet-like head that I would assume such a piece would have. You can see how mine turned out in Figure 3.13.

2. In the Perspective view, select the hammer's profile and extrude it out, giving it some thickness. Rename it `Hammer`.

   When the profile was drawn in the Front view, it was drawn on the origin line. Extruding it extruded it *from* the origin, resulting in the hammer's center no longer being aligned with the origin, or more importantly, with the gun.

3. With the hammer selected, select Modify → Center Pivot. Then, hold the X key to enable Snap To Grid mode. Move it back to the center grid line, centering it with the revolver parts you've created so far.

Figure 3.13
The hammer's profile in the Front View

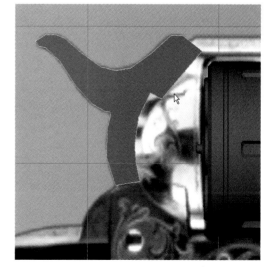

4. Select both of the hammer's profile faces and bevel them, adjusting the Offset to be about 0.8.

5. The hammer's "head" should be wider than the rest of its "body," so use the Split Polygon tool (from the Edit Mesh menu) and cut in a couple of edges to separate the head from the rest of the shape. Do so on both sides of the hammer.

6. With these cuts in place, you can adjust the head of the hammer's vertices, widening it. You should have something like in Figure 3.14. You'll return to the head later, but for now, you can move on to the grip.

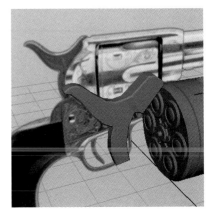

Figure 3.14
The hammer's head widened and in position

Creating the Grip

In this section, you'll focus on modeling the weapon's grip, the handle that will be held by a character in the game. It can be important ahead of time to know how the weapon will be seen in the game before spending too much time detailing the area of a weapon that is covered by the hand of a character model. If the player will never see the weapon grip, there's not much reason to spend too much time on it. However, if the model that the player holds is the same model that is found in the game's world, such as in a gun case, then the time spent detailing is worth it since the gun's handle will be seen.

Make certain the communication between you and your art director is detailed and clear. Many games will have a highly detailed model for the weapon the player holds and a less detailed model for the weapon the player finds within the world. Knowing which one you are working on can save you a lot of unnecessary work, or can save you from lacking the detail that is needed in your weapon's grip. For your project in this book, you can give the grip all the details you want!

1. Select the Front view. Create a new cylinder, remove its Subdivisions Caps, and position it where the grip meets the pistol as in the reference image. Rename it `Grip`.

2. Draw out a curve from the cylinder through the center of the reference grip to the base, as in Figure 3.15.

3. In the Perspective view, make certain the Grip cylinder and the curve you've just drawn are both centered at the origin line with the rest of the revolver geometry before continuing.

4. Just like you did with the tree trunk in Chapter 2, select the face of the cylinder that is touching the curve, hold Shift, and select the curve. You should now have both the face and the curve selected at once.

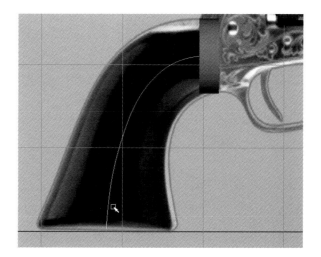

Figure 3.15
The curve drawn
through the center
of the reference grip

Perform an Extrude and the extrusion will stretch down to the base of the curve. In the Channel Box, under the polyExtrudeFace settings that are available, scroll down to the bottom and increase the Divisions to around 6, depending on how many points your curve is made of (or whatever looks best in your own scene if it's different from mine).

5. Back in the Front view, adjust each row of edges on the grip, rotating them for a smoother flow and scaling them up to more closely match the width of the grip in the reference image. You can see my result in Figure 3.16.

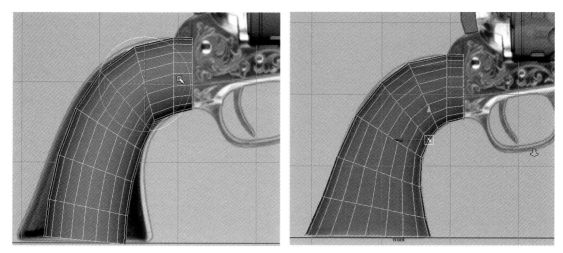

Figure 3.16
The revolver grip before and after adjustment

6. Returning to the Perspective view, it's obvious that the scaling you just did caused the grip to flare out comically toward the base. That's all right; you can fix that now. Selecting each row of vertices in turn, scale them in the x-axis (assuming your revolver's geometry is oriented the same as mine) making the geometry thinner. Do so for each row, allowing it to flare outward toward the base.

7. Feel free to touch up any vertices to help smooth the curvature of the grip and improve the flow of the surface geometry.

8. Once you have the grip's shape as you like it, select the bottom face of the grip and apply a Bevel, adjusting the Offset to be approximately 0.2 and giving it a rounded lip at its base.

Creating the Trigger

The next step is to model the trigger and trigger guard, a very distinctive area of the gun. Once again, like the grip, the trigger is an area that may or may not receive much scrutiny in an actual game. In fact, many games won't even animate the trigger being pulled since it's so infeasible and the player will never see it. The shower of sparks and smoke that come out of the end of the barrel is usually enough to convince any player that, yes, the gun was fired! For the purposes of this book's lessons, however, all aspects of this weapon will be created with the idea that it will be looked at, even if not very closely.

1. In the Front view, create a small cube and place it where the trigger guard meets the pistol on the side nearest the grip. In vertex mode, adjust the cube's profile to match the reference like in Figure 3.17.

2. Select the bottom face of the cube and extrude it down about 0.07 units and scale it in the x-axis to match the width of the trigger guard reference.

Figure 3.17

The adjusted cube used to begin creating the trigger guard

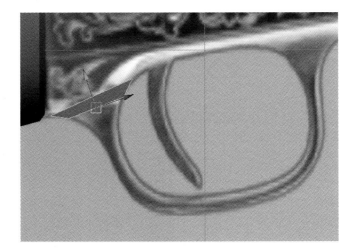

3. Extrude again approximately the same distance and scale it in to match the trigger guard reference's width. Repeat this step again, continuing the trigger guard mesh along the reference.

Figure 3.18
Your curve for the trigger guard

4. You could continue to extrude and scale, extrude and scale, along the entire trigger guard if you'd like, or you can use the curve extrude method again. Draw a curve from the last extruded face around to the other side, like in Figure 3.18.

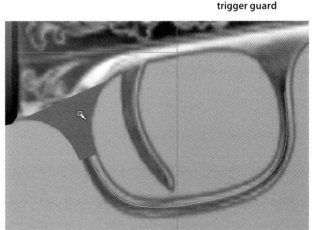

5. Select the bottom face (the last extruded face from before), hold Shift, and select the curve. With both the face and the curve selected, perform an Extrude. Increase the extrusion's Divisions to about 10 or so, depending on how many points your curve was made of.

6. Extrude the new end of the trigger guard a few times to match its opposite end.

7. In the Perspective view, scale up the rows of vertices where the trigger guard meets the body of the pistol so that it appears to blend into the future surface of the gun at both ends. You can see how mine looks in Figure 3.19.

8. Back in the Front view, create a small cube at the base of the trigger reference. You'll use the curve extrude method again here as well. Draw out a CV Curve from the bottom of the cube through the length of the trigger in the reference image.

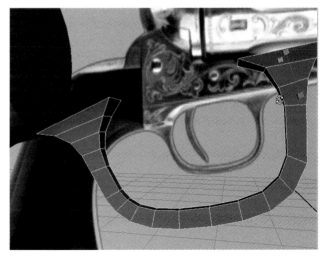

9. Just as before, select the bottom face of the cube, hold Shift, and select the curve. Perform the extrusion and increase the divisions to approximately 5 (depending on how dense your curve is) and increase the taper to 0.6 to make the extrusion smaller as it gets nearer to the tip of the trigger.

Figure 3.19
The trigger guard's end scaled up to blend into the pistol

10. Using the Select Edge Loop tool, select the four long edge loops of the trigger guard and bevel them, adjusting their Offset to approximately 0.4.

11. Do the same for the trigger, beveling the long edge loops to get rid of the hard edges.

12. Select the bottommost face and bevel it as well to round off the tip of the trigger. Make any vertex adjustments to the trigger guard and the trigger to get them positioned and shaped to your liking.

Creating the Trigger Frame

At this point, you've created the main focal shapes that make up the revolver's overall shape: the barrel, cylinder, grip, trigger and trigger guard, and the hammer. Now you'll focus on the center frame that holds all of these parts together. It's a rather complex shape and will require a bit more modeling finesse than the basic shapes you've created so far. To make things a little more digestible, I'll split the frame into two main parts: the cylinder frame and the trigger frame. You'll start with the trigger frame—the part of the frame that the trigger guard attaches to and that fits into the grip.

> Because the modeling of the frame *is* rather complex, you may find it useful to follow along with the video supplement that is found in the DVD's Video directory as you read the steps to help you understand each step's instruction better.

1. To help with your focus, create a new layer in the layer bar and name it `HighRes`. Select all of the pieces of your revolver, right-click the HighRes layer, and choose the Add Selected Objects option from the marking menu that opens.

2. With all of the existing geometry included, click once on the middle box next to the layer. A **T** will appear in the box and the geometry will become locked and in Wireframe mode.

   This is called Template mode and it allows you to see the geometry without accidently moving or adjusting it. Also, because it is in Wireframe mode, you are able to see through it and do not have the geometry blocking your view.

Figure 3.20

The trigger frame's profile using the Create Polygon tool

3. In the Front view, use the Create Polygon tool from the Mesh menu and create a profile of the trigger frame using your image as a reference. You can see an example in Figure 3.20. Don't concern yourself with the revolver's cylinder. You'll accommodate it in a much later step. Press Enter once you have completed your profile to finalize the Create Polygon action.

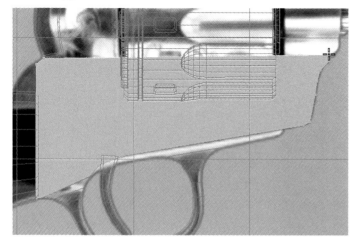

Notice in the figure that the bottom of the trigger guard profile doesn't include the extension that is present in the reference where the right arm of the trigger guard meets the frame. This will be added shortly, starting with step 9.

4. In the Perspective view, you will see the profile in the center of the pistol at the origin. Click on the HighRes layer's T to toggle it to an **R**. The pistol's geometry comes back into view, but it is still locked.

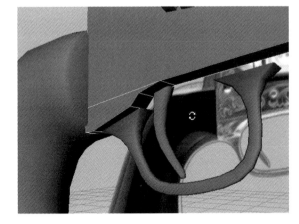

   This is Reference mode, which is identical to Template mode except for the obvious fact that instead of wireframe, the geometry is rendered normally. This is useful if you want to keep the geometry locked but need to see it more clearly.

5. Extrude the trigger frame profile out about 0.2 units, or until it's a few centimeters past the trigger guard. Rename this object `TriggerFrame`.

6. Delete the back face of the frame.

7. Using the Split Polygon tool, cut an edge as in Figure 3.21, directly across from where the frame extends down to the left arm of the trigger guard to the back of the frame where it meets the grip.

8. With this edge in place, you can now select the face without selecting that lower section and extrude again approximately 0.3, or until it begins to poke out of the grip where they intersect.

9. Using your reference, cut in another edge toward the front of the trigger frame where the lower extension (that we didn't use when drawing out the frame in step 3) meets the frame.

10. Select the two faces shown in Figure 3.22 and extrude them about 0.08 or until they meet the right arm of the trigger guard. Delete the backside faces this created.

11. This creates a rather obvious gash in the geometry near the trigger. This can be fixed easily by deleting the two faces of the gap and then merging the vertices together to stitch the gap closed.

12. Select the front edge of this extended piece of geometry and bevel it, giving it a rounded corner.

13. Select the large face on the side of the frame and bevel it, rounding the edges all around it. Also, bevel the edge loop that runs along the extension below the frame (Figure 3.23).

Figure 3.23

Bevels added to the frame and extension below

14. Make any vertex adjustments you like before continuing. When you're ready, Select the TriggerFrame and duplicate it (Ctrl+D). With the duplicate selected, scale it -1 in the z-axis, mirroring it to the other side of the gun.

15. Select both halves of the trigger frame and combine them together (Mesh → Combine). With the two halves combined together, select all of the vertices and select Edit Mesh → Merge → Options. In the options, input a low number, such as 0.001, as the Threshold value and press the Merge button. This will merge all of the duplicated vertices running up the middle of the frame together, giving you a clean mesh. You can then delete the center edge loop.

16. As you can see in the reference, there's a rounded object at the back of the trigger frame that merges into the grip. You can add this in with a simple cylinder with beveled caps inserted into the geometry, as in Figure 3.24.

Figure 3.24

Adding the round backing to the trigger frame near the grip

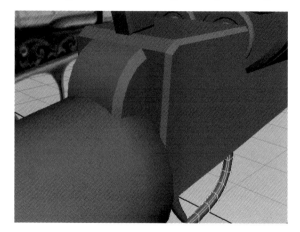

Creating the Cylinder Frame

Now that you have the main part of the trigger frame complete, you can move on to the cylinder frame, the part that holds the barrel, cylinder, and hammer together and attaches to the trigger frame. Once again, the shape is rather complex and will require a bit of work to achieve the results you want, so pay attention and study the figure images and the supplemental video to help you follow along.

Figure 3.25

The quarter sphere positioned on the cylinder

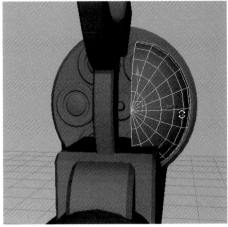

1. You'll start with the rounded part of the frame that supports the cylinder. Create a sphere and center it on the revolver. Lower its Subdivisions Height to 12 and, in the Front view, position and scale it to match the reference image.

2. Delete the front-facing half of the sphere and, in the Perspective view, delete half the sphere again, leaving a quarter sphere behind.

3. Position it as in Figure 3.25, so that it matches the general proportions of the cylinder. You may need to stretch it upward some.

4. Once you have it positioned the way you want, duplicate it to the other side. There will be a large gap between them. Select both quarter spheres and Combine them together. Then, select the edges that face each other on both halves and select Edit Mesh → Bridge. This will fill in the gap between the two halves, making an elongated shape. You can then use the Fill Hole command (under the Mesh menu) to cap off the open end facing the cylinder.

5. Next, create two new cylinders that are aligned with the two barrel cylinders but slightly wider in diameter. Position them on the ends of the barrel facing the cylinder and fill the gap between them. Don't worry about them intersecting. You'll fix that later.

Figure 3.26

Three cylinders positioned at the end of the barrel

6. Position a third cylinder below these (intersecting is OK here as well). On this one, manipulate its vertices to elongate it, as in Figure 3.26. Make sure all three cylinders are aligned together.

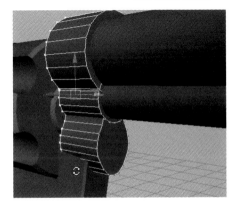

7. Return your focus to the rounded part of the frame near the hammer. Select the faces running down the rounded hammer side (that you created with the Bridge command earlier). Deselect any that were accidently selected or that are hidden from view. With the visible faces selected, select the Front view and extrude them outward until they match the depth of the reference image. Edit the extruded faces' vertices to more closely match the roundedness of the reference as in Figure 3.27.

Note in the image, the flattened topmost face is pointing up. This will be where the rest of the frame gets extruded from in the next steps.

8. Select that top face and extrude it up, matching the height in the reference image. Bevel the upper-left corner to round it off and get rid of the hard edge.

9. Using the Cut Faces tool (still in the Front view), cut through the upper-right corner of the extrusion, which allow you to lift up on the upper corner like in Figure 3.28 and more closely match the shape in the reference image.

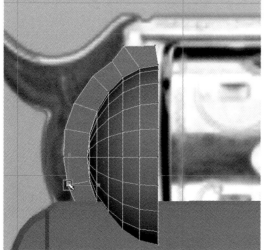

Figure 3.27
The extruded faces adjusted to match the reference

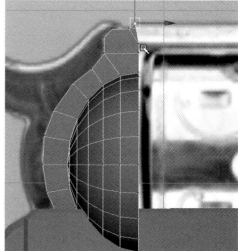

Figure 3.28
Using the Cut Faces tool to add detail

10. Use the Split Polygon tool to continue the edge loops into the surface facing the cylinder.

11. Now, selecting all of the forward-facing faces running down the middle, extrude them all the way to the right, aligning them with the forward edge of the three cylinders we created earlier (Figure 3.29).

12. Use the Insert Edge Loop tool, to insert an edge loop in this large extrusion directly in front of where it intersects with the three cylinders. Bevel the top forward edge to round the corner.

Figure 3.29
The result of step 11's Extrude

13. Now, you'll do a little bit more beveling to get rid of some more of these hard edges. Select both faces of the rounded parts of the frame (from the original quarter spheres you placed) and bevel them, rounding their edges. Then select the two long edge loops that run along the back and top of the entire frame and bevel them as well to round their edges.

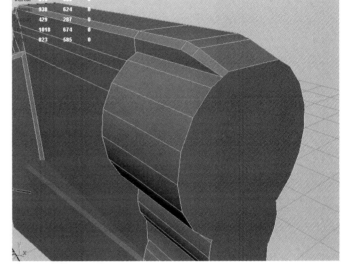

Figure 3.30
The rounded top of the combined frame

14. You can now start to do a bit of cleanup. Look back at the three cylinders near the barrel end of the cylinder frame. Select the top cylinder and Shift-select the middle one. Select Mesh → Booleans → Union. This will fuse the two cylinders together, removing the geometry that was intersecting between them. Delete this new object's history and unite it with the third cylinder below it by using another Union. Once again, delete the history.

15. Next, select the cylinder frame, Shift-select the fused cylinders, and perform another Union Boolean operation. This will merge this entire geometry group together.
Rename this fused object `CylinderFrame`. You may notice some miscellaneous edges sticking out here and there. Delete them and fix any hanging vertices.

16. Clean up the top of the CylinderFrame, removing the remains of the intersecting that was originally there and replace it with a smoother surface, as in Figure 3.30.

17. Select the front face of the frame, which is shaped like a deformed figure eight, and bevel it to round off the surrounding edges.

18. Make any geometry cleanup or adjustments to the shape that you want. When you're done, you should have something like Figure 3.31.

Figure 3.31
The revolver so far

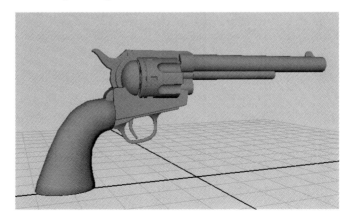

Adding Details

At this point, you have the major forms of the revolver complete. The next step is to add any details and additional components that you haven't gotten to yet to make it look even more realistic.

1. If you take a look at the reference image, the only major component that you've not made yet is the protrusion coming from the bottom of the ejector rod. This can be made with a simple beveled cube, adjusted to fit the shape and position seen in the reference.

2. You may also notice a few small screws: one on the ejector rod and a few on the side of the trigger frame. You can create a simple screw head by creating a sphere and deleting half from pole to pole.

3. Flatten down the half sphere so it's not so rounded. Select a rectangle of faces from the side of the screw and extrude them inward like in Figure 3.32.

4. Using the reference as your guide, position three duplicates of the screw head on the side of the TriggerFrame. Position the original on the underside of the barrel's ejector rod.

5. Because of the rounded surface of the ejector rod, you'll need to create a hole for the screw to be placed into. First, use the Insert Edge Loop tool to insert a loop of edges near the end of the rod, where you will be placing the screw. This will keep the hole detail localized to this area of the mesh and prevent it from creating any surface abnormalities along the entire length of the rod.

6. Create a cylinder and intersect it into the rod where the screw will be. Deselect everything. Select the ejector rod mesh, Shift-select the cylinder, and perform a Boolean Difference operation to carve out a hole in the rod where the cylinder was. Insert the screw head and you're good to go (Figure 3.33).

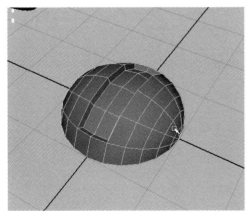

Figure 3.32
The simple head of a screw

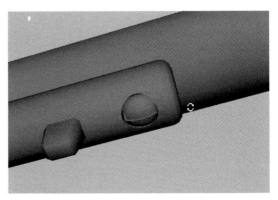

Figure 3.33
The screw inserted into the ejector rod

Now that you have all of the additional details created, you can finally do what you've been waiting to do all this time and carve out the hole in the frame to keep the revolver cylinder from intersecting all that geometry!

Figure 3.34

The large cube that will help carve out the cylinder space

7. In the Front view, create a cube that is the right size to encompass the entire cylinder object. Scale it out so that it sticks out both sides of the gun and duplicate it in place, making two cubes (Figure 3.34).

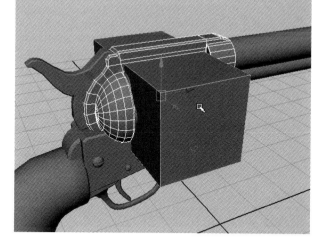

You need two cubes because when you perform a Boolean operation, it will remove the negative space object that you use. Since we have two pieces to the frame (the TriggerFrame and the CylinderFrame) we need a cube for each of them.

8. Deselect everything. Select the TriggerFrame, Shift-select one of the cubes, and select Mesh → Booleans → Difference.

9. Deselect everything again. Select the Cylinder-Frame, Shift-select the remaining cube, and do another Difference Boolean. The result of these two Boolean operations carves out a hole for the cylinder to sit in unimpeded.

Figure 3.35

The grip detail carved in

Now that you've carved out the frame, there's only one small detail left. You'll notice in the reference image that the top of the grip has a metal surface.

10. In the Front view, use the Cut Faces tool from the Edit Mesh menu to carve a horizontal edge loop through the grip geometry where the metal surface is in the reference image.

11. Select the faces that make up this carved section of the grip. Extrude them inward a small amount. Extrude them again back outward and scale them in slightly. You should get a result similar to Figure 3.35.

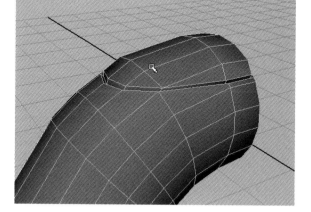

Creating the Low-Resolution Gun

Now that you have the high-resolution revolver, you can begin creating the low-resolution version. The low-resolution revolver will be the model that is used in your fictional game for this project. The high-resolution mesh was created simply to generate texture source details from it. These textures will be applied to the low-resolution mesh to create the illusion of detail, just as you did in Chapter 1 with the Brick Wall project. This is a typical procedure, not only in weapons but in game art in general.

However, don't feel like all that work is wasted on something you'll never use. You can extrapolate a large portion of your low-resolution geometry directly from the high-resolution geometry, making this mesh much faster to create in most cases.

1. First, select all of your high-resolution geometry and make certain it is all included in your HighRes layer by right-clicking the layer and choosing the Add Selected Objects option from the marking menu that opens.

2. Next, with all of your high-resolution geometry still selected, apply a new Lambert material by right-clicking; from the popup marking menu, going to Assign New Material → Lambert.

3. Make the Lambert's color dark, but not completely black. You still want to be able to make out the surface detail of your model.

4. You'll start with the grip. Select it and duplicate it. With the duplicate selected, right-click and select Assign Existing Material → Lambert1. This assigns the duplicate grip the default gray material.

5. With the duplicate grip still selected, enter Vertex component mode and select *all* the grip's vertices. Over in the Toolbox on the left, double-click the Move tool to bring up the Tool Settings dialog box. Under the Move Axis setting, change it to Normal.

   The Normal setting on the Move tool allows you to move a vertex along the surface direction of its individual position. The regular X, Y, and Z directions on your gizmo get replaced with U, V, and N, where N represents the Normal direction.

   With all the grip's vertices select and your Move tool set to use the Normal setting for its Move Axis, click and drag on the N-labeled handle on your gizmo. You'll notice that all of the vertices get *pushed* in or out along the surface direction. What you want to do with your duplicate grip's vertices is push them outward so that the mesh is slightly larger than the original grip mesh. The original grip will sit *inside* the duplicate grip.

   Having a dark material on the original and a lighter gray material on the duplicate helps you easily tell when the lighter gray color of your duplicate completely envelopes the dark color of the original. Then you can know that you've pushed the duplicate out far enough to stop.

6. After pushing the duplicate grip out to encompass the original, you can then modify its geometry to remove the detail, making it lower resolution. The main detail we want to remove is the horizontal cut that you inserted into the original grip earlier. Select those edges and delete them, removing them from the mesh with Edit Mesh →

Delete Edge/Vertex. Also, if there were any geometry completely hidden from view, that is, intersected within another piece of geometry and unseen, those faces can be deleted as well.

7. In the Layer Bar, create a new layer and name it `GameRes`. This will be the layer for all of your low-resolution geometry. Select the new grip, right-click the GameRes layer and Add Selected Objects.

REVIEW: CREATING THE LOW-RESOLUTION PARTS

The previous steps are essentially the same process you will use for each part of the revolver. Those steps for easy reference are as follows:

1. Duplicate the original high-resolution mesh.

2. Apply the Lambert1 material to the duplicate.

3. Select all the duplicate mesh's vertices.

4. Using the Normal setting on the Move tool's Move Axis, push the duplicate geometry out so that it completely encompasses the original geometry.

5. Remove small geometric details that can be handled by the normal map once you create them later. I'll go over some of these instances next.

6. Remove any geometry hidden from view.

7. Add the low-resolution object to the Game Res layer.

Keep in mind that even though some parts of the mesh may have a lot of geometry to create smoothness (such as the roundness of the barrel cylinder), don't remove that geometry just yet. Maintaining that roundness will assist in creating texture sources in a later section. Afterward, that density can be adjusted easily. Also, don't worry about creating a low-resolution version of the tiny screws and such as they will be details included in the normal map.

Creating the Low-Resolution Barrel

The barrel of the gun is essentially a hollow pipe. In the low-resolution version, that is a detail that you won't need because that kind of detail would be completely hidden from view—especially if the gun would be pointed away from the player most of the time when they are using it!

1. Once you have your duplicate geometry pushed outward along its vertices' normals, you can continue here. Select the face way down at the end of the interior of the barrel. Press the shortcut Shift+. to grow your selection. Keep growing your selection until you have the entire interior of the gun selected, along with the end of the barrel (but not the long cylinder that makes up the barrel's exterior). Delete them.

2. Select the edges bordering the open end of the barrel and select Mesh → Fill Hole to cap the end of the new barrel. Move the end of the barrel out until it covers up the end of the high-resolution barrel. You should end up with something like Figure 3.36.

In this image, I'm using Xray mode to demonstrate the two meshes on top of each other. The green highlighted mesh is the original high-resolution geometry and the white highlighted mesh is the new, low-resolution geometry surrounding it.

Figure 3.36

The low-resolution barrel surrounding the high-resolution barrel

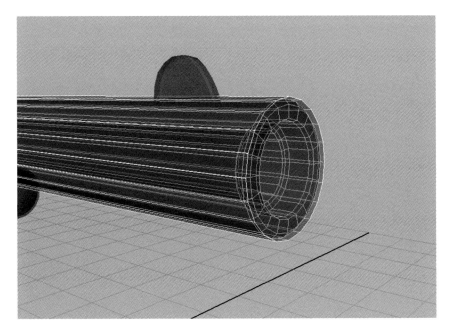

Creating the Low-Resolution Cylinder

The cylinder is a relatively complex object. It may even be easier to re-create it from scratch for the low-resolution version. However, I'll continue to use the method described here for this lesson to give you an alternative.

1. Once you have your duplicate geometry pushed outward along its vertices' normals, you can continue here. The first detail you can remove is the carved-in groove. That's a simple matter of selecting the edge loops and removing them with the Delete Edge/Vertex command from the Edit Mesh menu.

2. Next, select the faces that make up the six fluted indentations around the cylinder and delete them, leaving empty gaps where they were. You'll fill these in a bit later.

3. Before doing that, you can take care of the six square-shaped indentations that are also around the cylinder. Select the bottom face for each of them and press Shift+. to grow your selection until you have all the indentations' faces selected. Delete them.

4. Select the vertices for one of the holes left behind. Hold the V key to enable Snap To Point mode. Click and drag the vertices to the side to snap them along the edge that they intersect (Figure 3.37). Do this for all six holes.

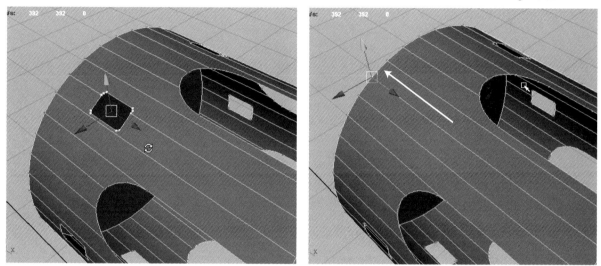

5. Use the Merge (Edit Mesh → Merge) command to merge the stacked vertices together, fusing them each into one point.

   Now that those holes are gone, you can focus on refilling the cylinder's fluted notches, this time, with a much lower resolution mesh. If you go into Vertex component mode, you'll see that there are a lot of vertices running along the edge of the holes that are left behind from when you deleted the faces that were there.

   An easy way to do this is simply to select all of the vertices that make up the curved area of the notches and press the Delete key on the keyboard. You'll notice that all of the hanging vertices (that is, vertices without edges) are deleted while the others are left alone. However this deletes too many, so undo that if you did it.

6. Select all the curved vertices again but this time deselect the vertices at the points where the notches begin to curve as well as the *second* vertex from there on each side of the curve. See Figure 3.38 for an example.

Figure 3.38

Deselecting the
circled vertices on
each notch

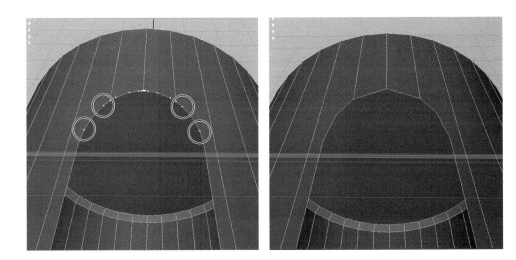

7. With those vertices deselected, you can delete the rest of them and end up with a low resolution result that you can work with. It won't be nearly as smooth, but the normal map later will help fake it.

8. On the other end of the notched gaps, you can do something similar, selecting every other vertex and pressing delete (Figure 3.39).

9. Select the edges on the back of each notch and extrude them toward the front, so they are aligned with the first row of vertices that make up the curve of the notches to begin filling in the holes.

10. Extrude the edges again and begin point-snapping the ends of them to the notch curve to fill in the gap. Once the gaps are filled, you can use the Merge command to fuse the stacked vertices together (Figure 3.40).

Figure 3.39

Deleting every
other vertex on the
other end of each
notch

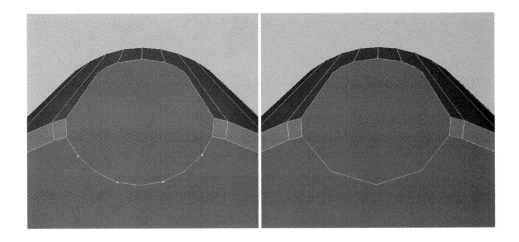

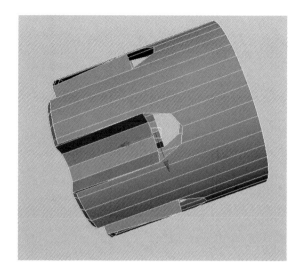

Figure 3.40

Filling in the notches

Finishing the Low-Resolution Details

The rest of the gun is pretty much a process of following the prior listed steps. If you get lost, feel free to refer to the video supplemental on the DVD. The videos in question are named `Pistol_Texturing`.

The main detail left to go over is the screws on the side of the TriggerFrame mesh. You don't necessarily need to devote an entire half sphere to each screw, even if they were low poly half spheres. Instead, you can use small pyramid shapes that are textured appropriately later with opacity and normal maps to effectively fake the details!

1. First, select Create → Polygon Primitives → Cone. Decrease the Subdivisions Axis down to 4, turning the cone into more of a pyramid shape.

2. Delete the bottom face (you won't need it), and squash the pyramid down so it isn't so tall.

3. Position the pyramid over one of the screws as in Figure 3.41. Do so for all three screws. (Not the one on the ejector rod. That one will be handled strictly by the normal map.)

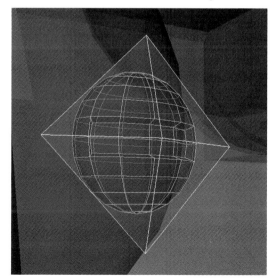

Figure 3.41

The pyramid shape covering the screw

That pretty much wraps up the work for creating the low-resolution revolver. When I finished, my high-resolution revolver was approximately 10,000 polygons while my low-resolution revolver was about 2,900 polygons, which is very doable in most next-generation action games. Figure 3.42 shows them side by side. If need be, the geometry density can be taken down even more without losing too much of the low-resolution gun's overall shape, but I'm going to leave mine here for now. You can continue to lower the geometry of yours as much as you want!

Figure 3.42

The high-resolution and low-resolution revolvers

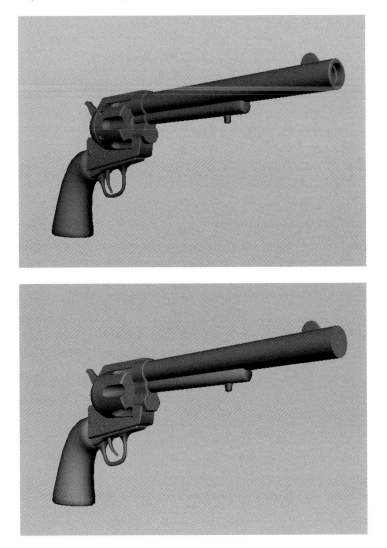

UV Mapping the Geometry

The next step is UV mapping the low-resolution geometry to get it ready for texturing. You'll start with the cylinder.

1. Select the cylinder mesh and press Alt+H to hide all the other geometry so you can focus your attention.

2. Select Window ➝ UV Texture Editor to open the UV Editor you'll be working in. I like to place the UV Editor window on the right and have my working camera view on the left.

3. You can see, with the cylinder selected, that the UVs are a mess in the editor. It's up to you to get them cleaned up. First, select the left cap face (facing the grip side of the gun) and select Create UVs ➝ Automatic Mapping. Because the face is round, it lays it out as a circle. Select the circle of UVs in the editor and move them to the side to get them out of the way.

4. Select the other cap face and repeat the Automatic Mapping, then move the result to the side.

5. With the two caps mapped, you can now map the cylinder itself. Select the remaining faces and select Create UVs ➝ Cylindrical Mapping. Take a look at the result in the UV editor.

    If your results are anything like mine, it probably doesn't look right. The cylindrical mapping manipulator is not aligned with the cylinder, creating a warped result.

6. Click the small red crosshair located at the bottom left of the cylindrical mapping manipulator. Clicking it brings up the transform gizmo, which allows you to rotate the manipulator 90 degrees, thereby aligning it with the cylinder and creating a much nicer result.

Continue to UV map pieces of the revolver using methods like this as well as what you learned in Chapter 2 when you UV mapped the trunk of the Savannah tree. If you get stuck or lost, you can refer to the video supplement found on the DVD. Eventually, you'll have everything UV mapped and strewn about the UV editor. You'll then need to lay the different UV shells out in the editor.

Figure 3.43

My example
UV layout

The idea behind laying out UVs is to make as efficient use of the UV space available as possible, as well as maintaining proportional UV density throughout the object. For instance, if the UV layout of the cylinder is much smaller in scale proportionately then the UV layout of the grip, it'll look too blurry or the grip will look too crisp—one or the other.

You can see my resulting UV layout in Figure 3.43. Notice

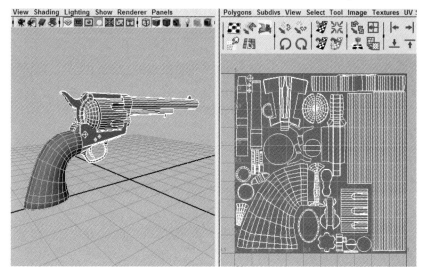

that I divided the UV shells of the grip and the cylinder and layered them on top of each other. This way, each half of the grip and cylinder can share UV space and share the texture.

Generating Texture Sources

After generating texture sources already for the previous two chapters, you are getting the hang of it, I think. You should be aware of just a couple of differences to pay attention to when generating texture sources for moving objects.

The AO maps that you generate for the moving parts should be generated separately from the rest of the model. Since the generated result is what you are using to bake in shadow information, you obviously can't have a shadow baked into, for example, the cylinder because you would notice it move unnaturally. So, when generating your source textures for Ambient Occlusion and Normals, generate the trigger, hammer, cylinder, and bullet caps separately.

Also, because in my example I'm stacking UV shells, you'll need to separate the stacked geometry and generate the texture sources for each half by itself. Then you can combine them back together afterward. So, in my example, I would need to separate half of the grip and cylinder before generating my texture sources. Eventually, I ended up with what you see in Figure 3.44, an AO source and a Normal source, both 1024×1024 targa files.

Figure 3.44

The AO and Normal source files

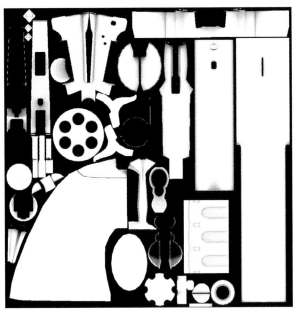 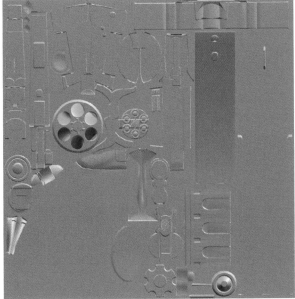

For this chapter, I won't be going over creating the final textures, but be sure to check out the DVD for supplemental files.

Animating the Weapon

Animation for a weapon, or any game prop for that matter, is just like animating anything else in games. The geometry is rigged with a skeleton and then animated by an animator on the team. Depending on how large a team you are working on, that animator could very well be you! So, it's important to understand at least some of the basics. With that in mind, you'll focus on creating a simple animation of the revolver firing.

1. Just so we're on the same page with this lesson, browse on the DVD to the Chapter 3 project directory and open the Maya file named Pistol3_AnimationStart.ma. This will be the starting point for animating the gun. It consists of the main revolver all joined together with its separated moving parts:

   - Revolver (main frame with grip and barrel)
   - Hammer
   - Cylinder
   - Trigger

2. Before beginning the actual rigging and animation, you'll need to do some minor animation setting adjustments. Open the Preferences window by going to Window → Settings/Preferences → Preferences or by clicking the Animation Preferences button near the bottom left of the screen, next to the AutoKey button.

   In the Preferences dialog box, open the Time Slider section under the Settings heading in the list on the left side. Check and see what the Playback Speed setting is set to. You want it to read Real-Time 30 fps (frames per second). If it says 24 fps instead, you'll need to make an adjustment.

3. Open the Settings header in the list on the left and change the Time setting to NTSC (30 fps). The majority of games are animated to this speed. If your particular project in the field requires something else, make sure your art lead informs you.

   Once you have the speed set, you can click Save and return to the project.

4. Press F2 to switch to the Animation menu sets. Select the Front view and press the 4 key to enter Wireframe mode.

5. Select Skeleton → Joint Tool to start creating skeleton joints. Place a joint near the center of the grip and press Enter to finalize its placement.

6. Select the joint and duplicate it. Place the duplicate near the base of the trigger where it meets the frame of the weapon. Duplicate the joint again.

7. Place this duplicate near the base of the hammer where it meets the frame of the weapon.

8. Duplicate the joint once more and place it at the center of the cylinder.

9. Rename the joints `Root`, `Trigger`, `Hammer`, and `Cylinder`, respectively.

10. Once you have them placed the way you want, select all of the joints *except* the Root joint. Shift-select the Root joint and press the P key on the keyboard. This will parent the other joints to the Root (Figure 3.45).

11. Select the cylinder and rotate it 30 degrees. After all, when the gun is loaded, the bullet needs to be lined up with the barrel!

Figure 3.45

The weapon's skeleton in place

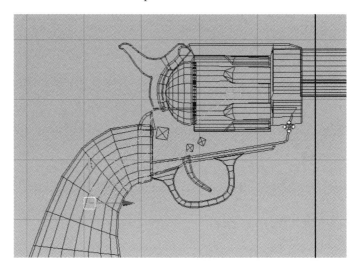

Binding to the Skeleton

Many games handle skeleton binding differently. Some simply parent geometry to joints if it's not going to deform. Other games require a Smooth Bind, whether it will deform or not. For this project, assume the latter and use Smooth Binding.

1. Select the revolver geometry (all of the non-moving parts) and Shift-select the Root joint. Select Skin → Bind Skin → Smooth Bind → Options. Change the Bind To option to Selected Joints and the Max Influences to 1.

   Smooth Binding is generally used for deforming geometry. However, for rigid meshes like props, you don't need anything to bend or deform. To ensure that doesn't happen, the above settings in step 1 will force the geometry to be bound 100 percent to the selected joint with no chance of being influenced by another.

2. Click Bind Skin. You can test this by selecting the Root joint and rotating it. The revolver geometry should follow suit.

3. Repeat these steps with the Hammer, Trigger, and Cylinder, binding them to their respective joints.

Setting Keyframes

Now it's time to start the animation! For the firing sequence, you'll need the following to happen in order:

1. The hammer pulls back, rotating the cylinder into place.

2. The trigger is pulled.

3. The hammer releases, and the gun recoils.

4. The trigger returns to the original position.

Easy, right?

1. Select Frame 1 in the Time Slider. Select the Hammer joint and set keys for its Rotation channels by selecting them in the Channel Box, right-clicking, and choosing Key Selected from the menu that opens.

2. You can probably time it out in your head, but for this lesson, you can assume it takes approximately a third of a second to pull the hammer back. Since we set it to 30 frames per second, select Frame 10 and rotate the Hammer joint about 40 degrees in the Z direction, pulling back into a cocked position.

   When the hammer is pulled back, what is actually happening is the cylinder is being locked into place with a fresh bullet. So, with that in mind, we want the cylinder to rotate *as* the hammer is being pulled.

3. Select Frame 3 and set keys for the Cylinder joint's rotation channels.

4. Then, select Frame 11 and rotate it 60 degrees. You'll recall that 60 degrees is the distance between bullets on our cylinder, so this will effectively portray the cylinder being primed for firing (Figure 3.46).

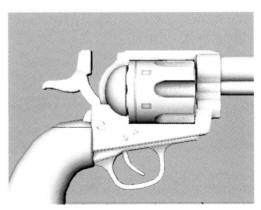

Figure 3.46

The gun is ready to fire.

5. With the gun now "loaded," go to Frame 30. Select the Trigger joint and set keys for its Rotation channels.

6. You can perhaps picture that it takes only a third of a second to pull the trigger, so go to Frame 40 and rotate the Trigger back about 30 degrees to a good position for firing.

7. The hammer shouldn't fire immediately. That would mean the trigger was a "hair" trigger with no give in it. Wait until Frame 35 and set another keyframe for the Hammer's rotation channels. This is halfway through the trigger's pull-back animation.

8. The hammer would clap down extremely quickly, so go to Frame 35 and rotate the Hammer back to 0 (its original location) and set another keyframe here.

9. This is about when the gun should recoil from the energy output of the gunpowder igniting! Go to Frame 37, about halfway through the Hammer's release animation. Set a keyframe for the Root joint's Rotation channels.

10. Go to Frame 40. Rotate the Root back about 20 degrees, as if it were kicking backward from the shot.

11. Go to Frame 50 and rotate the Root back the other way approximately -20 degrees, as if the person holding it overcompensated when trying to *push* the gun back into an aimed position.

12. Go to Frame 60 and return the gun to its original position and set a new keyframe.

13. Lastly, select the Trigger joint and set a keyframe at its last position for Frame 45. Then move forward to Frame 55 and rotate the Trigger back to its original position and set a new key.

If you rewind the animation and press Play, you should see an effective firing animation! All it needs now is a blast of particle effects bursting out of the barrel and a good sound effect to really sell it. But that's a different department. You can check out the `Pistol5_AnimationFinal.ma` file on the DVD to see my final animation as an example.

Moving Right Along

Hopefully by now, some of the patterns of creating game art are becoming apparent to you. While many steps may be repeated, they are never necessarily exactly the same. There are definitely differences that can be found on a per-project basis. Following along with these different projects should introduce you to many of those variables. Creating weapons can be one of the more fun props to create for an environment artist; second only to vehicles, perhaps!

CHAPTER 4

Vehicles

Vehicles can play a pivotal role in games. Racing games obviously make heavy use of them, such as the popular *Gran Turismo* series, which provides hundreds of cars to choose from! Other games may use vehicles as the player's primary mode of transportation within the game's world, such as in the aptly named *Grand Theft Auto* series. In general, even if it's not a racing game but features some form of civilization, you can bet vehicles will need to be made.

Understanding Vehicles

A game doesn't have to focus on driving to need vehicles. Even a game like Activision's *GUN*, set in the 1880s in America's Old West, had carriages and wagons populating the world. If a game features a city environment, even if the player never actually gets behind the wheel, you can bet there will be cars, trucks, and vans driving around or parked on the city streets. Even a one-on-one fighting game like Capcom's *Street Fighter 4* has vehicles populating the backgrounds of a few of its stages.

When it comes to creating a vehicle, the overall techniques involved are essentially the same as those used when creating any other prop. But you'll want to ask yourself several questions before you start creating any vehicles.

First, can the player see inside the vehicle? Adding interiors to the dozens, if not hundreds, of cars and trucks populating your game world will increase the polycounts and texture usages considerably. Many games opt to tint all the vehicles' windows or simply make them all highly reflective to hide or obscure whatever may or may not be inside them. Knowing whether the interiors are necessary for your game is obviously very important. After all, if no one is going to see the insides, there's no need to make them!

Next, will the vehicle get damaged? In action games that feature vehicle-based combat especially, such as THQ's *Saint's Row*, it's very likely that when the bullets, grenades, and missiles start flying, the vehicles will get caught in the crossfire. If they show damage effects like crumpled bumpers, caved-in canopies, busted taillights, and so on, these kinds of damage models will need to be created based on the game's implementation of such effects.

Finally, will the player be able to modify or upgrade the vehicle in any way during the game? Racing games especially can feature intense car customization features. These can range from adding decals to your car's hood to replacing your engine and fine-tuning your suspension. Adding decals to certain parts may require certain specifications in the UV layout of the car model, and all of those different customizable parts will need some sort of art-related presentation, showing under-the-hood as well as under-the-frame views in many cases.

Project: Building a Dune Buggy

For the project in this chapter, you'll tackle a vehicle that's mildly complex; specifically, you'll create an extreme sports–style dune buggy! These durable vehicles can range greatly in style and shape, so search the Internet to find some image references for inspiration.

> Before starting, make sure you set your project to your project directory by going to File ➜ Project ➜ Set.

The first step is to create the basic roll cage that will make up the overall shape of the buggy's cockpit. You'll do this with a number of basic pipes arranged to create the shape and merged or fitted together where they meet.

1. Select Create ➜ CV Curve Tool ➜ Options. In the Tool Settings dialog box that opens, change the Curve Degree setting to 1 (Linear). This will cause the curve you lay out with the tool to be rigid rather than smooth. This will help you lay out the roll cage more precisely.

2. In the Side view, draw the shape of the cockpit roll cage however you desire, using reference or your own idea. You can use extra points on the corners to create a rounded shape. Mine looks like Figure 4.1.

Figure 4.1

Initial roll cage curve in the Side View

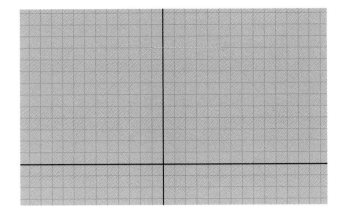

3. Switch to the Perspective view, and move the curve to the left or right of the origin, approximately 5 units or so, depending on how large you drew it.

4. In the Top view, draw out a new curve, using four or five points, that fits around the cockpit roll cage curve and extends forward to the front end where the hood of the buggy will eventually be (Figure 4.2).

5. Select both curves and duplicate them (Ctrl+D). With the duplicate curves selected, group them (Ctrl+G). With the group selected, change the ScaleX attribute in the Channel Box to -1 to mirror the curves to the other side of the origin. Select Edit → Ungroup to remove them from the group.

   Removing the curves from the group will keep your scene clear of miscellaneous group nodes, which can build up quickly if you do this method of mirroring often, as I sometimes do.

6. With the curves now mirrored, you can more clearly see what your overall shape is starting to look like and begin making adjustments with a fuller picture in mind. For example, I noticed that I had made the hood of the buggy much too narrow and therefore widened the curves accordingly.

   Reshape the curves as you like, but be sure to grab the top of the roll cage (that makes up the roof of the cockpit) and move them in as in Figure 4.3.

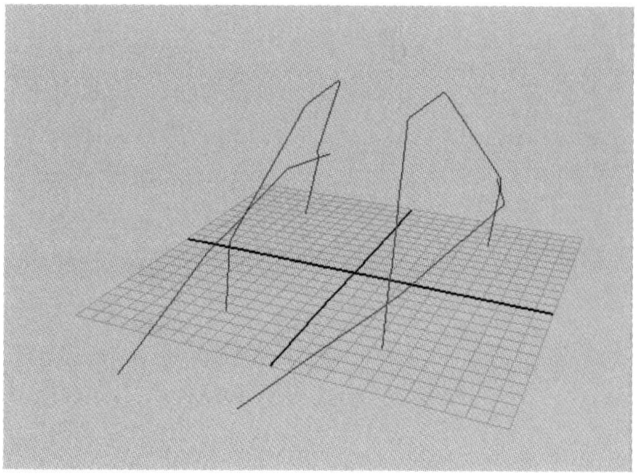

7. In the Top view, draw out a straight curve using three points that joins the front corners of the cockpit roof. Repeat for the back corners. Switch to the Perspective view to position them at the top corners of the cockpit. Create two more lines for the base of the cockpit in the front and back. These will act as the roll cage's support bars.

8. Back in the Top view, hold the C key to toggle Snap To Curve mode. While still holding the button, left-click on the frame's left profile curve and drag to its front end. Release the left mouse button, and let go of the C key. Continue to draw out a curve, merging the left frame profile curve with the right. For the last point, hold the C key again to snap the last point to the front end of the right profile curve. You can see my result in Figure 4.4. If you like, you can use a few extra points to round the corners.

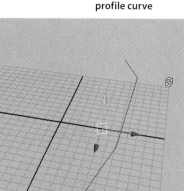

Figure 4.2

The buggy profile curve

Figure 4.3

The cockpit profile is beginning to come together.

Figure 4.4

Merging the front
profile curves
together

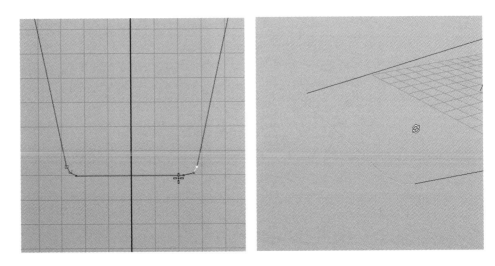

9. Return to the Perspective view, and make sure the curve is aligned with the frame's curves. Select the left frame curve, and Shift-select the front curve you just made. Change your menu set to Surfaces, and select Edit Curves → Attach Curves → Options. In the Options dialog box that opens, make sure the Keep Originals check box is unchecked and the Attach Method is set to Blend. Click the Attach button. This will merge your two selected curves together.

10. With your newly merged curve selected, Shift-select the other frame curve and attach them again. Delete the curve's history (Edit → Delete By Type → History).

11. Repeat steps 8–10 with the back end of the frame, creating a curve between the two ends of the back frame curve and merging the curves together. Since you'll be creating a closed (or periodic) curve with the second attachment, you'll instead need to use the Open/Close Curves command (found under the Edit Curves menu) to merge the last corner of the curve.

12. Adjust the curve's shape how you like. Duplicate it and lower it down to form the lower bar of the buggy's frame (Figure 4.5).

Figure 4.5

The buggy's frame
curves in place

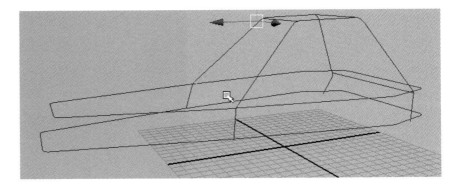

13. Switch to the Side view. Draw out a curve forming the top of the hood, curving it at the front to act as the lip of the hood.

14. Back in the Perspective view, reposition the hood curve so that its base is at the corner of the cockpit and the hood curve ends at the front corner of the buggy frame, as in Figure 4.6. Mirror the hood curve for the other side.

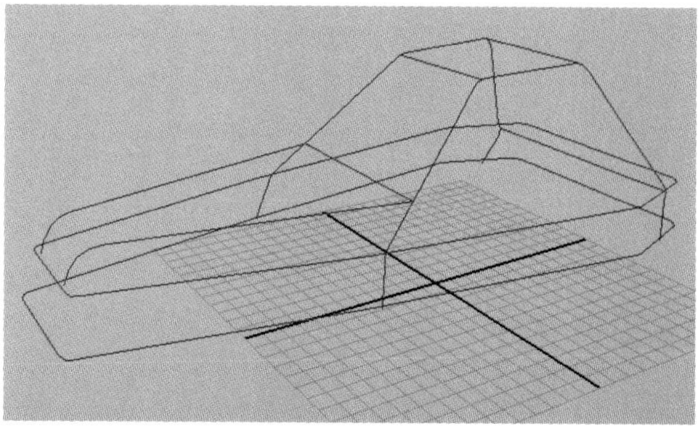

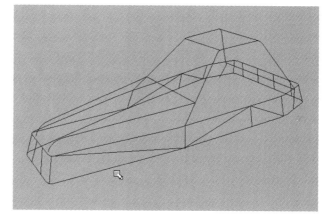

Figure 4.6

The hood curves in place

15. Position several small, straight curves around the frame, connecting the top and bottom frame curves together with what will become support bars. You can see in my example (Figure 4.7) that I put several in the front and back and added diagonal bars to the sides.

Figure 4.7

Frame support curves in place

16. Now, you can start creating the actual pipe geometry. Select Create → NURBS Primitives → Circle and drag out a circle in your scene. This circle will represent the diameter of your pipes, so scale it accordingly to a thickness you like.

17. Select the circle and Shift-select one of your many curves. With them both selected, select Surfaces → Extrude.

> For your Surfaces → Extrude commands, make sure you go into the options and set the output geometry to Polygons. I'm using a General tessellation method with the Per Span # of Iso Params set to U—1 and V—2.

Take note of how thick the pipe is that resulted from your Extrude. If you want to change it, you can do so by simply scaling the circle. Since history is still active, your pipe will update in real time. Once you have a thickness you like, you can continue.

18. Next, begin extruding the rest of the curves by repeating step 17. Make certain that for each one, you first select the circle and *then* select the path curve for each pipe in

turn. Don't forget that you can use the G shortcut key to redo the last command. You should eventually have something like Figure 4.8. Feel free to add more pipes to the frame to make whatever kind of support frame you want for your buggy!

Figure 4.8
The buggy is
taking shape!

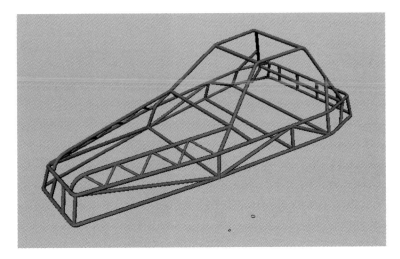

At this point, you can continue to create more pipes to shape the buggy's frame however you like. You also can change the shape and add more support structures to your liking. Once you have the frame the way you want, you can continue to the next section.

Creating the Wheels

With the basic frame and shape of the buggy worked out, you can begin placing the wheels. For this project, I've chosen a more "off-road" style of dune buggy, with large, gripping rear wheels and smaller front wheels. This will require the roll cage to tilt downward from back to front. Before you know how much tilt it needs, however, you must first create the wheels with the following steps:

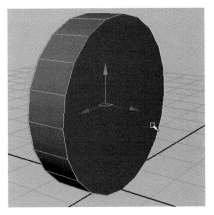

Figure 4.9
The wheel's humble beginnings

1. Hide your roll cage. You'll then start with a cylinder placed on its side. If you're following along with me, the cylinder should be scaled up about 1.5 units in the X and Z directions and .4 units in the Y, which creates a wheel shape, as in Figure 4.9.

2. Select both round cap faces of the cylinder and bevel them to begin rounding the wheel.

The next series of moves will be dependent on what you want the hubcap of the wheel to look like. After a series of beveling and extruding processes, my result ended up like Figure 4.10. (See the "Using Object History" sidebar for more information regarding using history.)

3. To achieve the opposite side of the wheel, you'll cut the wheel in half and duplicate the front of the wheel to the back. Using Edit Mesh → Insert Edge Loop tool, insert an edge loop down the middle of the wheel. You can grid-snap the resulting loop to make certain it is centered. Then delete the backside faces of the wheel.

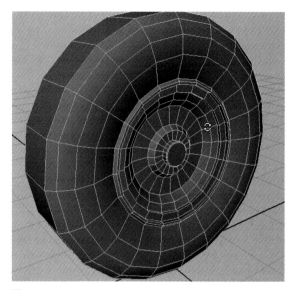

Figure 4.10

Using Extrudes and Bevels to create the hubcap detail

USING OBJECT HISTORY

From the blank cylinder face to the hubcap detail you see in Figure 4.10, I used about a dozen or so Bevels and Extrudes. You may believe that exhaustive planning and knowing exactly what you are going to do is required before beginning, but that really isn't the case. It may seem daunting, but it really is quite easy to achieve such a result. First, I recommend having a good reference for the kind of hubcap detail you want to achieve. But otherwise, the trick is to make good use of your history.

Each time you use a Bevel or an Extrude (or almost any other command), it gets added to the object's history in the long list you see on the right side of the screen in the Channel Box. In this example, for instance, the list contains several Extrude commands and a couple of Bevels thrown in for good measure:

This list exists for more than simply telling you what you've already done. This list is a *time machine*! It allows you to go back in time to something you did several steps ago and make a change. That change then propagates *forward* in time to the present, changing every step you did in between to match the new change.

By simply clicking nearly any editable input in the Channel Box, you get access to the options of that input. You can also use the Show Manipulator tool (the Y shortcut key) to manipulate the past in your scene.

What does this mean for the buggy wheel? Well, if you've made several Extrudes and Bevels and then realize that six steps ago you really should have pushed that extrude a little further inward, you can! Remembering that you can access your history will help you with not only this project but hundreds more to come.

4. Duplicate the remaining half, scale it -1 in the mirroring direction (the x-axis in my case), and select Edit Mesh → Combine to combine the wheel halves together. Use the Edit Mesh → Merge command to weld the bordering vertices together.

5. Unhide the roll cage mesh, and reposition and rescale your wheel in relation to the size and position of your buggy's frame. Mine looks like Figure 4.11.

6. The hubcap detail that looks great for the front of the wheel is a bit too complex for the back of it. Select the faces that make up the middle detail of the hubcap and delete them. Then select Mesh → Fill Hole to cap it like in Figure 4.12.

7. Duplicate the front wheel, and move it to the back of the buggy. Resize the wheel as you see fit. In my case, I made the rear wheel about 50 percent larger overall and made the rubber part of the wheel thicker and wider.

8. You can create a different hubcap detail for the rear wheel if you want. I made the rear wheel hubcap a bit less complex, for instance.

Figure 4.11

The front wheel positioned

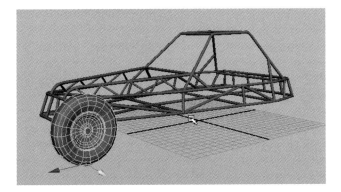

Figure 4.12

The back of the front wheel

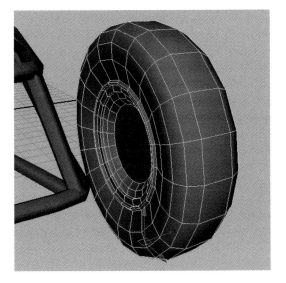

9. After you've resized the rear wheel like you want, position it on the buggy. If yours is like mine, you'll need to angle the buggy's frame to match the elevations of the two wheels. Select all roll cage pipes and group them together (Ctrl+G). With the new group selected, reposition the roll cage to match the new wheel positions.

   This can be made easier by repositioning the group's pivot point at the front or back wheel position. Then you simply rotate the group to adjust the elevation.

   The next step is to create the tread detail. For this project, the rear wheel will have the heavy-duty tread detail, while the front wheel has less extreme tread detail.

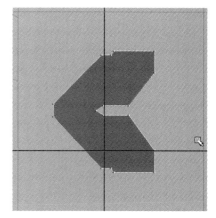

Figure 4.13
Starting the tread detail

10. Working around the axis will make the next steps easier, because it will require a lot of precise rotations. However, you don't want to lose your wheel position, especially if you have it dialed in perfectly and don't want to fight to find it again. You'll get around that by creating a surrogate. Duplicate the rear wheel, center the pivot (Edit → Center Pivot), and grid-snap it to the origin. You can hide the rest of the buggy.

11. In the Top view, select Mesh → Create Polygon Tool, and create a shape that will form a pattern on your tire's tread. I used a pattern similar to one I found in reference photos online, which looks like Figure 4.13.

12. Move the tread detail to the top of the wheel's rubber surface and extrude it upward, giving it thickness. Delete the two faces on the ends where the pattern would meet.

   The next step will require a bit of experimentation on your part, because the exact values involved depend on how big your tread detail and wheel diameter are.

Figure 4.14
The duplicated tread detail

13. With your tread detail selected, press the Insert key on the keyboard to enter Edit Pivot mode. Point-snap the pivot point to the center of the wheel. Press Insert again to exit Edit Pivot mode.

14. Duplicate the tread piece. Now, in my case, rotating the tread 10 degrees in the x-axis rotated the duplicate tread enough to butt up next to the original. Pressing Shift+D at this point will invoke the Duplicate With Transform command, creating additional duplicates that each rotate an additional 10 degrees around the wheel, meeting on the other end (Figure 4.14).

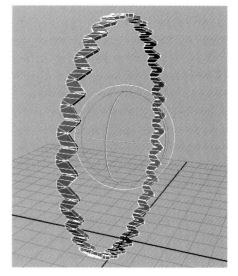

   If your geometry doesn't meet up perfectly at the end of the circle, undo the duplicates, and try again with a different rotation value until you get it just right.

15. This part can be pretty tedious. Select all of your tread pieces, and combine (Mesh → Combine) them together. Next, go through and merge the pieces' vertices together using the command found under Edit Mesh → Merge. Eventually, you'll have them all merged together and ready to go!

16. Repeat the process with a new tread pattern that complements the first. I went with a shape that you see in Figure 4.15.

17. For this detail to go on the rounded edge of the tire, you'll need to cut in some bendable geometry that you can then adjust to follow the surface direction of the tire (Figure 4.16). You can do this by hand or by using a Bend deformer that can be found in the Animation menu set under Create Deformers → Nonlinear → Bend.

18. Once the tread detail is curved, you can then duplicate it around the wheel in the same way you did before, merging the resulting segments together to form one piece. For this curving edge piece, duplicate it and mirror it to the other side of the wheel to curve along the opposite edge.

19. Once you have all the tread detail you want, position it on the wheel the way you like it. I placed my first tread along the middle of the wheel with the edge tread on either side, positioned so that the pointed ends fit into the concave ends of the adjacent pieces (as shown in Figure 4.17).

    You can continue creating all the tread detail you want. Once you're done, you'll then need to transplant this tread detail onto your original rear wheel and delete the surrogate.

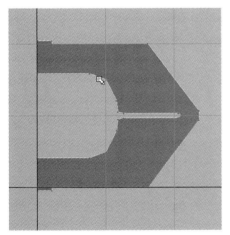

Figure 4.15
A new tread pattern

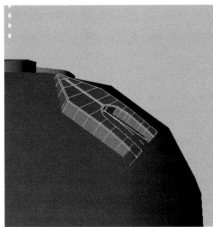

Figure 4.16
Curving the tread detail to fit the wheel

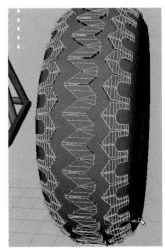

Figure 4.17
The tread in place

20. Select all the tread detail and group or combine it together. Center the pivot and unhide your hidden buggy parts. Delete the surrogate rear wheel. Point-snap align your new tread detail onto the real rear wheel.

> The Align tool can assist you in aligning objects together. First, select the object that will move and then Shift-select the object you'll be aligning to. Then select Modify → Align Tool and select the corresponding indicator on the gizmo that represents the point on the object you wish to align to.

21. For the front wheel, you can create whatever kind of tread detail you like. For my own, I used the Extrude tool and a couple of Bevels to create a few raised ridges along the circumference of the wheel—a large, thick ridge in the center and two small, thin ridges on either rounded edge (Figure 4.18).

Figure 4.18

The front wheel's tread detail

22. Create a small cylinder. This will be a bolt for the front wheel's hubcap. Depending on the hubcap design you've chosen, position however many duplicate bolts on the hubcap to add detail to the wheel. In my case, I placed them around the outer rim of the hubcap as well as around the inner area, around the center of the hubcap.

23. If you are following along with me, you can also add some details to the hubcap, such as some support struts. In the Side view, drag out a tall cube, with its Subdivisions Width set to 5, which gives it several divisions along its vertical length. Bevel the forward-facing edges and position it on the wheel. You can adjust the vertices to make the shape of the strut curve outward from the center of the wheel and duplicate them around the hubcap's center as in Figure 4.19.

Figure 4.19

Adding detail to the front wheel's hubcap

24. As with the front wheel back in step 2, you can do the same with the rear wheel in creating hubcap detail. Using a series of Extrudes and Bevels, manipulating the history to manipulate the shape, I got something like Figure 4.20. You can detail your own in any way you like!

Figure 4.20

The rear wheel hubcap before (left) and after (right) adding details

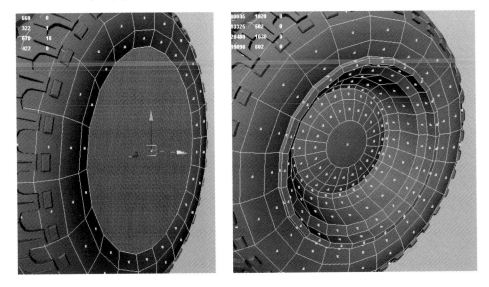

25. As with the front wheel, you can also place bolts on the hubcap to add detail in any way you see fit.

26. Now that you have the two wheels created, you can begin attaching them to the frame. In the Top view, use the CV Curve tool to draw a curve from the front corner of the roll cage to the wheel. When the curve meets the wheel, draw a point above (from your vantage point in the Top view) the last, making the curve angle abruptly toward the rear of the wheel. Be sure to position the curve on the wheel with its base touching the frame and its curved end placed flush against the upper part of the wheel's inner hubcap. You may need to adjust its control vertices to make the curve fit correctly (Figure 4.21).

Figure 4.21

A curved connector from frame to wheel

Figure 4.22

The wheels con-
nected to the frame

27. Once you have the curve positioned, duplicate it and lower it to the lower side of the wheel with its base connected to the lower corner of the roll cage framework. Rotate the curve upward slightly if needed and adjust the control vertices to fit the new position.

28. Using the Surfaces → Extrude command from the Surfaces menu set, create two new frame pipes with these two curves. Because the ends of these two pipes are exposed (and not buried into another pipe like most of the others), you can cap them with the Mesh → Fill Hole command and add a slight bevel if desired.

29. You can then add two straight support pipes joining the two together. Once you're done with that, you can select all the wheel parts as well as the connector frame that you just made, duplicate them, group them, and mirror them over to the other side (Figure 4.22).

30. Repeat this process for the rear wheels, connecting them to the frame as well.

Adding the Shock Absorbers

Most of these heavy-duty dune buggies have some equally heavy-duty shock absorber coils connected to the wheels. Some have them on both the front and rear wheels, but for this project they'll just be on the front. However, if you'd like to add them to the rear of your buggy as well, you're more than welcome to do so!

1. Create a tall thin cylinder, and decrease its Subdivisions Axis to 12. Select the face on the top and then the bottom of the cylinder, and use a series of extrusions and Bevels to get a result similar to Figure 4.23. This will be the shock absorber frame that will attach the roll cage and wheel together.

Figure 4.23

The shock absorber frame made from a cylinder

2. For the coiled spring of the shock absorber, you will create a helix primitive object. It can be found under Create → Polygonal Primitives → Helix. The settings for this coil will depend a lot on just how large your shock absorber frame is; in my case I used these options:

Coils:	13
Height:	3.35
Width:	0.7
Radius:	0.05
Subdivisions Axis:	8
Subdivisions Coil:	12
Subdivisions Caps:	0

Position the spring to be centered on the shock absorber frame. You can adjust the coil to match your own frame if my settings didn't work for you.

3. Select the coil and the frame and group them together. Reposition them to join the frame and wheel together at an angle like you see in Figure 4.24. Duplicate and mirror the shock absorber to the other side.

Figure 4.24

Positioning the shock absorber on the buggy

Creating the Hood

The next step will focus on the hood of the buggy. Not all dune buggies have coverings, but for this project, the idea is to create a racing buggy, with decals and such.

1. Create a U-shaped curve and place it over the front of the car, near the cockpit. Duplicate it and position it near the front end of the buggy between the front wheels.

Select Surfaces → Loft (from the Surfaces menu set) to create a surface between the two curves as in Figure 4.25. Don't worry about clipping through the shock absorbers or anything at this point. You'll make space for them in a later step.

Figure 4.25

The beginning of the hood

2. You can bevel the sides to soften them and curve them more around the hood.

3. Insert an edge loop down the center of the hood and delete the left side. You will later duplicate the completed half of the hood for the other side. Select the edges along the bottom side, behind the front wheels, and extrude them downward to cover the exposed roll cage framework.

4. Insert an edge near the cockpit, and lift up on the border edges to create a lip like in Figure 4.26.

5. With the Split Polygon tool (from the Edit Mesh menu), cut a shape out of the hood mesh that you'd like your hood to be, and delete the excess faces. I made a cut along the side of the hood that curved upward toward the front of the buggy. Then, I cut out a divot in the hood that the shock absorber could stick through. You can see my results in Figure 4.27, but you can shape yours however you like.

Figure 4.26

Adding a lip near the cockpit

6. Select the two edges on the forward end, and lower them down to follow the downward curvature of the roll cage frame beneath it. Extrude the edge a few times, each time repositioning the extruded edge to follow the hood's curvature until you get about even with the wheel's connecting frame.

Figure 4.27

The shaped hood
(before and after
cutting excess faces)

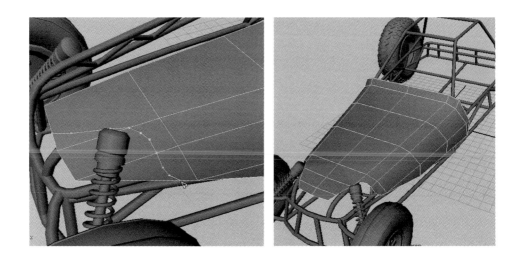

7. Select the edges on the outer edge of the newest faces and extrude them a couple of times outward to the sides, pulling them in to follow the curvature of the hood. Examine Figure 4.28 to see what I mean.

Figure 4.28

Extending the hood,
following the curva-
ture of the frame

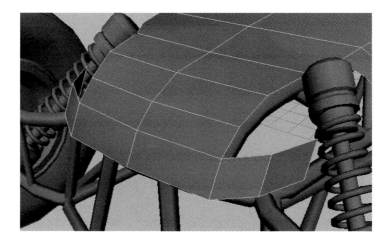

8. Next, use the Append To Polygon tool from the Edit Mesh menu to fill in the gap between the hood and these two extension pieces. Again, don't worry about clipping through the shocks.

9. You can use the Split Polygon tool again to cut the necessary hole for the shock absorbers into the hood.

Continue to modify the shape however you like, adjusting the curvature and the profile of the hood. When you're done, you can duplicate and mirror it to the other side.

10. Extrude the entire hood by a very small amount. I used an amount of about 0.02 units.

11. You can continue creating any additional hood details you want. I added a molded form to the hood by selecting the faces on top of the hood, extruding them up a few inches, and scaling them inward. I then beveled the center and border edges to round it out like in Figure 4.29.

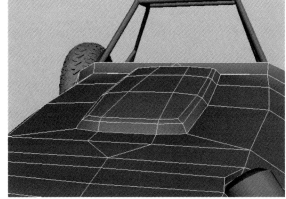

Figure 4.29

Adding some details to the hood

Creating the Axle and Steering Wheel

The rear wheels will not be pivoting to the left and right for steering, so for the next few steps, you'll create the rear wheel axle that would connect to a drive shaft that causes the wheels to spin, pushing the buggy along. You don't have to be too detailed for this particular project. The important thing you need is the axle because it will be the main part of the rear wheel drive that will be visible.

1. Create a cylinder and position it between the two rear wheels, aligned to the wheels' center point and centered on the buggy.

2. Select both end cap faces and extrude them outward a couple of times, with perhaps a Bevel or two thrown in for good measure, to create something like Figure 4.30.

3. If you like, you can thicken the center of the axle to give it some heft.

   The next step is the steering wheel. As you may expect, it starts with a ring— a torus, to be exact.

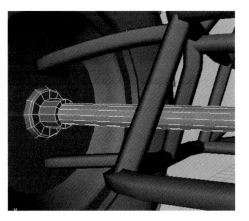

Figure 4.30

Creating the end caps of the axle

4. Select Create → Polygon Primitives → Torus. Depending on your scene, your adjustments may vary from mine, which are as follows:

Radius:	1.5
Section Radius:	0.2
Subdivisions Axis:	40
Subdivisions Height:	8

5. Next, you'll add the support struts to the steering wheel. Create a thin cube with a Subdivisions Height value of 2, splitting it in two sections. Lower the center edges down to cut the cube by a third and scale the opposite end inward, thereby tapering the width.

6. Move the tapered end toward the front, creating a leaning L shape. Bevel the long edges to smooth them a bit.

7. Position the shape on the steering wheel so that the tapered end meets the top of the wheel. You should get something like Figure 4.31.

8. If it's not already aligned, move the strut's pivot point to align with the center point of the steering wheel torus. Duplicate and rotate a new strut 120 degrees in the z-axis. Do it again for a third one. You should have three steering wheel struts placed equidistantly.

9. You'll probably notice that they all intersect at their base. Go ahead and create a small beveled cube to hide their intersection at their base. Once you have all the details you like, group them all together (Ctrl+G), reposition, and rescale the group to fit the buggy (Figure 4.32).

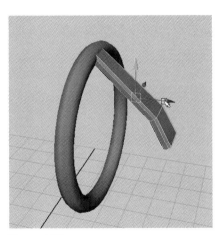

Figure 4.31
A steering wheel support strut

Figure 4.32
The steering wheel in place

Creating the Side Panel

You have a hood covering the front of the buggy's frame, but the sides are still exposed. The next stage will focus on creating a side panel to cover the exposed framework on the sides of the buggy.

1. In the Top view, use the CV Curve tool to draw a path along the side of the buggy. Select the Perspective view, and reposition the curve to fit the side of the buggy side frame at its base.

2. Duplicate the curve and move it up to the top of the buggy's side frame. Loft (Surfaces → Loft) the two curves, creating a surface in between (Figure 4.33). Don't worry if it's clipping through the frame; you're about to fix that.

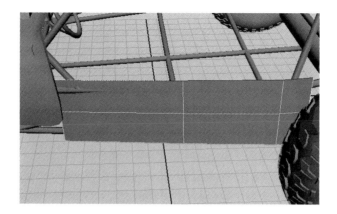

Figure 4.33

The start of the side paneling

3. If the Loft command didn't result in having an edge cutting through the middle of the panel horizontally (as in the prior Figure 4.33), use the Cut Faces tool from the Edit Mesh menu to make one.

4. Raise this center line up and outward, creating a slightly curved lip at the top of the paneling.

5. Select the entire panel and extrude it approximately 0.1 units to give the paneling some thickness. If it's still visibly clipping through the frame, you can reposition it.

6. The idea is to make the panel look as if it is below the hood. Grab the side faces that are facing the hood and extrude them forward. Reposition them to be beneath the hood and flush with the buggy's frame.

7. Grab the bottom forward-facing edge and bevel it. You should have something similar to Figure 4.34.

8. Continue to adjust the side panel however you like, adding any details you wish to see. For example, I beveled the outer edges slightly, giving the entire panel a more rounded appearance.

Figure 4.34

The side panel

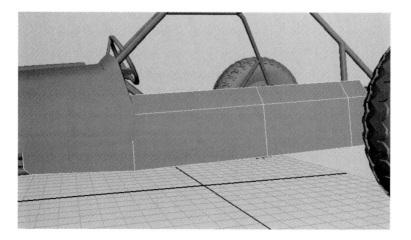

Creating the Base Undercarriage

This would be a good time to create a new layer for your buggy so you can easily hide all the geometry you've created so far when your scene starts getting complex. Create a layer called **HiRes**, and add the current geometry to it. You'll notice that there's an obvious lack of floor to the buggy. Before you get started on it, ask yourself—how will the underside of the buggy be seen? Some games will allow you to focus on the underside quite closely. If that is the case, many details may need to be made. If it's not going to be seen at all, you don't need to spend as much time creating detail.

1. In the Top view, use the Create Polygon tool under the Mesh menu to draw an outline of the underside of the buggy.

2. Return to the Perspective view and reposition the mesh to align with the base of the frame.

   This is about all you need to do for now. You'll return to the undercarriage later. However, if you'd like to add more details to the undercarriage, you can.

Creating the Chairs

In this section, you'll create the all-important chair that the player could potentially sit in. You can do this in any number of ways and with different methods, but you'll try something a little different here: You'll try using curves, rather than starting with a cube or something (which is also a viable method). Using curves to build a profile of the chair allows you a better chance at previewing the profile of the mesh and getting that part right before filling it in with the rest of the details that follow.

1. First, you'll add to the roll cage by attaching a bar that will serve as a chair brace. In the Front view, draw an upside-down U-shaped curve from the left side to the right that will sit behind the chairs.

2. As with the prior roll cage pipes, use the Surfaces → Extrude command along with the profile circle created previously to extend a pipe along the curve's path. Set the pipe in place as if it were behind the (soon-to-be-made) chairs, like in Figure 4.35.

Figure 4.35
The seat brace positioned

3. Back in the Front view, draw another upside-down U-shaped curve that will act as the profile of the back of the chair.

4. Duplicate the curve and rotate it 90 degrees to form the shape of the chair's seat, making sure both curves' end points are touching.

5. Modify the curve's vertices to curve the chair's form to fit the shape of a normal chair, like in Figure 4.36.

6. Select both curves and, under the Surfaces menu set, select Edit Curves → Attach Curves to connect the two curves together. However, this will attach the two only on *one* end.

7. To connect the other end as well, select Edit Curves → Open/Close Curve.

Using the Open/Close Curve command could noticeably modify your curve's overall shape. If this happens, you can just edit the curve back to where you want it.

8. Once you have this curve shaped the way you want, select it and select Edit Curves → Offset → Offset Curve. Adjust the Distance value to be about -0.25.

9. In the Side view, adjust the control vertices of the new curve to make the distance between curves about equal all along the curve's path (Figure 4.37).

The plan is to loft a surface between these two curves; however, if your curves are anything like mine, doing so will result in a surface similar to this:

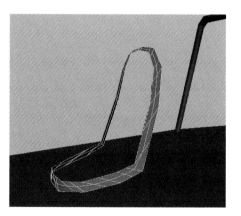

The geometry twisting that you see here is definitely not ideal. To fix this, you'll need to use the Rebuild Curve command.

10. Select one of the curves and press Ctrl+A to bring up the Attribute Editor. Make note of what the spans number is. In my case, the spans count was 16. Whatever span count you have is the number you'll want to use in the next step.

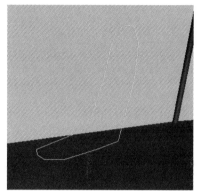

Figure 4.36
The start of the buggy chair using curves

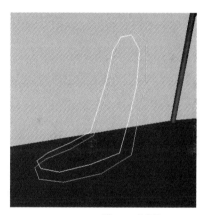

Figure 4.37
The two offset curves

11. Select *both* curves, and select Edit Curves → Rebuild Curves → Options. In the options, make the following changes:

Parameter Range:	0 to #Spans
Number of Spans:	Your number (mine is 16)
Degree:	1 Linear

    Click Apply. This makes the two curves match in their makeup and provides a much cleaner result when you apply the Loft in the next step.

12. With both curves still selected, select Surfaces → Loft. As you can see, this time, the surface is much cleaner (Figure 4.38).

13. Select the central edge loop using the Select Edge Loop tool (from the Select menu) and press Ctrl+F9. This shortcut command will convert your selection from edges to vertices. Double-click the Move tool to open the Tool Settings dialog box and change your Move Axis to Normal mode. Drag the N labeled directional handle on your move gizmo and pull out the row of vertices to add a slight curve to the shape of the lofted surface.

14. Use the Append To Polygon tool to fill in the front-facing center gap of the chair.

15. Select the gap faces and apply an Extrude, scaling the extrusion inward to create a curved indention to form the bucket seat of the chair, like in Figure 4.39.

16. Use the Append To Polygon tool to fill in the gap in the back of the chair. Reposition the chair to fit the buggy's cockpit and scale and tweak the geometry to your liking, if it isn't already. If you'd like to add a fluted appearance, you can use Booleans to cut out holes or add divots.

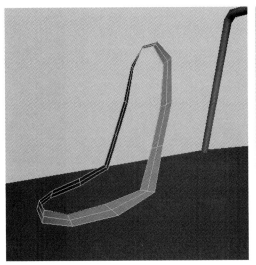

Figure 4.38
A much cleaner Loft

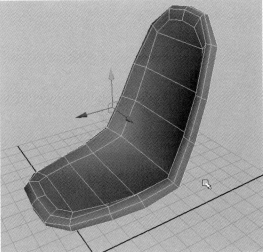

Figure 4.39
Filling in the chair

Creating the Headlights

For this project, you'll create some globe-style headlights attached to the hood of the buggy. The idea is that the headlights were tacked on after the initial construction as a way of customization.

1. Create a sphere and decrease the Subdivisions Height to 12. Rotate it 90 degrees so that the poles are facing left to right and delete the back half's faces.

2. Scale in the remaining half to flatten the protrusion and make it not quite so extended outward. Use Mesh → Fill Hole to cap the backside.

3. Select the back face and use the Grow Selection Region command from the Select menu to grow the selection to include the next ring of faces. Extrude these outward to give the headlight a thicker frame border.

Figure 4.40

The headlight model

4. Again, select the back face and apply an extrude command. Scale it in about a quarter of the thickness of the back face. Apply a second Extrude and pull it out to give it some thickness. You should have something similar to Figure 4.40 when you're done.

5. Position the headlight on the front end of the hood on either the left or right side. In the Front view, draw a rounded, upside-down, V-shaped curve to serve as a support anchor for the headlight. After extruding a pipe along it, you should have something like Figure 4.41.

6. Duplicate and mirror the headlight and anchor frame to the other side.

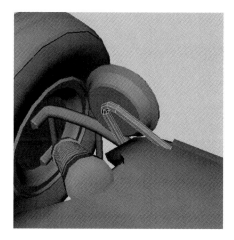

Figure 4.41

The headlight anchor frame

Adding a Rear Spoiler

As an optional part, you can add a rear spoiler onto the buggy. A spoiler is usually added for the purposes of aerodynamics and improving handling at high speeds. It also just looks cool!

1. First you'll create an addition to the buggy frame to put the spoiler on. In the Side view, create a rounded, V-shaped curve that extends from the top rear of the cockpit,

out beyond the rear wheel, and then curves downward back to the top of the base frame.

2. As with the rest of the frame pieces, extrude a pipe through the path you made, and adjust the shape as you see fit.

3. Position the pipe to be on one side of the buggy, duplicate it, and mirror it over to the other side. You should have something like Figure 4.42.

4. Create a long, thin cube and position it on the end of this new frame extension. Increase the width of the cube to be about even with the rear wheels.

5. Taper the end of the cube facing the front and widen the rear end, beveling the corners to round them. Make sure the cube is set on the frame properly.

6. Duplicate it and raise it up to create a second tier to the spoiler. Grab the front end vertices and push them back, shortening the second tier of the spoiler and angling it down to create an angle of approximately 30 degrees, like in Figure 4.43.

Figure 4.42

Adding the spoiler frame to the rear of the buggy

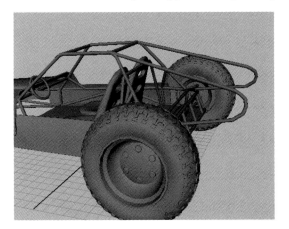

Figure 4.43

The spoiler's two-tiered blades in place

7. In the Side view, use the Create Polygon tool from the Mesh menu to create a shape that would act as a frame to hold the two spoiler blades. You can create any kind of shape, as long as it holds both spoiler blades. The one I made looks kind of like the state of Delaware or something, but that's OK, I guess!

8. Extrude the polygonal shape you create about two inches or so to give it some thickness and place it on the far end of the spoiler blades. Duplicate it and move it over to the opposite side. You should get something similar to Figure 4.44.

9. Next, you can create additional frame support by adding more pipes to the frame to reinforce the spoiler if it looks like it needs it.

Figure 4.44

The spoiler end caps in place

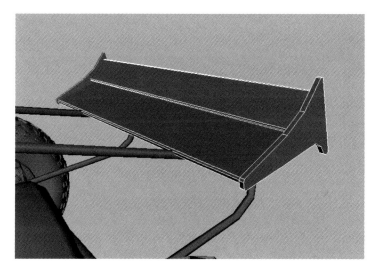

Keen-eyed readers will notice that the dune buggy's support strut was featured in Figure 4.43 but not in Figure 4.44. This is just a result of how I captured the images for this book and not me removing it. It's still there, just not shown, in Figure 4.44.

Creating the Engine

The engine for most dune buggies is located in the back of the buggy, so it depends on what kind of game you're working on to determine how detailed your engine should really be. You can truly be as detailed as you want for this project. For the purposes of this lesson, I'll demonstrate the creation of an engine of medium-level detail. I'll allow you to fill in any additional details you'd like on your own. Or if you prefer, you can simply follow along with me.

1. First, you'll need to create a platform for the engine to rest on. The way you can do this is by adding onto the base undercarriage mesh you made earlier. Select the edges

around the back of the buggy, and extrude them up to fill in the area of the frame that surrounds the axle.

2. Extrude again and pull the edges forward to fill in the gap behind the chairs, then again to close off the gap, similar to what's shown in Figure 4.45.

3. Create a cube and place it on the platform. This will act as an engine cover that the engine will be placed inside. Taper the top of the cube and scale it to fit. Add a bevel to the front to create a lip to the engine cover shell.

4. Create another cube, insert it into the engine cover, and use a Difference Boolean to carve out (Mesh → Booleans → Difference) an opening in the cover in which to place the engine (Figure 4.46).

Figure 4.45

Creating a platform for the engine

Figure 4.46

The engine cover in progress

5. Create a cylinder and rotate it to face the back of the buggy. Position it in the front area of the engine cover's opening. You can extrude it a few times to give it some additional details and grooves if you like.

6. Duplicate it and scale it in the three axes so that it has a smaller diameter, but a similar thickness as the first. Mine was scaled 0.6 in the x- and z-axes and 0.3 in the y-axis, and it worked well. Place this smaller cylinder above and to the right of the original.

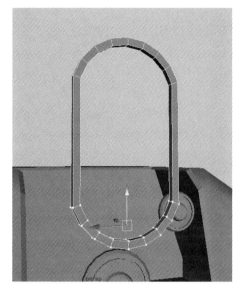

Figure 4.47

The gear belt made from a torus

7. Create a torus and rotate it so that it faces the back of the buggy. This will act as a gear belt for the two gear cylinders you just made. Lower the Subdivisions Height to 4, and increase the Twist to 45.

8. Select the edge loops on the left middle and right middle of the torus and use the Edit Mesh → Delete command to remove them. This will change the torus from a circular shape to more of a pill shape.

9. Grab the lower half of the vertices and lower them down, stretching the shape like in Figure 4.47.

10. In the Front view, reposition the belt geometry to wrap around the two gear cylinders like in Figure 4.48.

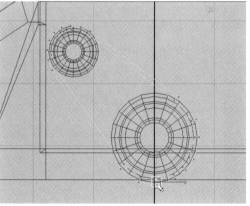

Figure 4.48

Wrapping the gear belt around the gears

11. Create a cube and place it within the engine cover, setting it on the base of the opening behind the gears. Bevel the topside edges to taper the shape. This will serve as the engine block.

Keep in mind that the engine of the buggy in this lesson will not be focused on very closely during play, so the details are rather minimal. If you'd like to go nuts and model a highly accurate engine block, please do!

12. Continue to model the engine to the level of detail that you prefer. I added a few more basic engine parts simply to identify the engine as an *engine*. You can see how mine turned out in Figure 4.49. These engine parts were all created using simple

cylinders and Extrudes and Bevels. If you need some more step-by-step instruction for this part, feel free to check out the video supplement on the DVD.

13. Next, you'll add some detail to the engine cover. Some simple Extrudes and Bevels can easily give you a metal paneling look. Create a small cylinder and place it on the cover to look like a bolt. Duplicate it however many times you feel necessary and place the bolts along the panel borders (Figure 4.50).

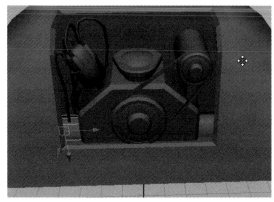

Figure 4.49
A simple engine model

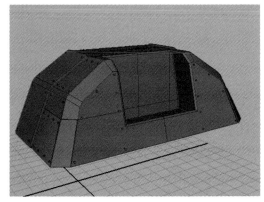

Figure 4.50
Bolts and panels added to the engine cover

Filling in the Final Details

At this point, the high-resolution model is nearly complete. Continue to fill in any additional details that you want to add to this project to make it your own. The last bit that I added was a front grill to fill the gap in the frame.

1. Select the front edges of the undercarriage mesh that runs along the front and sides of the hood.

2. Extrude them upward, filling in the gap.

3. Adjust the vertices to line up with the shape of the frame, like in Figure 4.51.

Figure 4.51

Adding a front grill mesh to the undercarriage

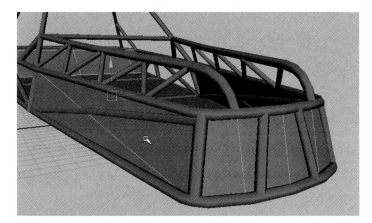

Creating the Low-Resolution Buggy

Just as you did in Chapter 3, you'll now create the low-resolution mesh for the buggy that you'll burn your normal and AO maps to. The process for doing so is the same as with the revolver in the previous chapter. I'll reiterate the steps that you'll want to follow:

1. Assign all the current buggy meshes to the HiRes layer.

2. Create a new layer called `GameRes`.

3. Assign a new Lambert material to the high-resolution mesh and lower the color value to make it darker.

4. Duplicate the original high-resolution mesh.

5. Apply the Lambert1 material to the duplicate.

6. Select all of the duplicate mesh's vertices.

7. Using the Normal setting on the Move tool's Move Axis, push the duplicate geometry out so that it completely encompasses the original buggy's geometry.

8. Remove small geometric details that can be handled by the normal map once you create them later. I'll go over some of these instances next.

9. Remove any geometry that is obscured by other geometry and hidden from view.

10. Add the low-resolution object to the GameRes layer.

11. Return to step 4 and repeat for each mesh.

Figure 4.52

The low- and high-resolution meshes

You can watch a step-by-step video of each low-resolution mesh being created on the DVD that is included with this book.

In Figure 4.52, you can see the difference between the high-resolution and low-resolution dune buggies.

UV Mapping the Low-Resolution Mesh

UV mapping the buggy will be just like UV mapping the revolver from the prior chapter. Take each piece and focus on it individually. Be patient, as all of those pipes in the roll cage *will* take a while, but the end result will be worth it.

One thing you'll do differently with the buggy is UV map it with the intention of creating two textures—one for the frame and one for the rest. The reason for this is twofold. First of all, the pipe-based frame has so many pieces that it will take a significant amount of UV space to accommodate them all. Therefore, giving them their own texture allows you to give the rest of the buggy the amount of space its pieces require.

The other reason is that having a separate frame texture allows you to create multiple dune buggy variations using the same frame. Since the frame has its own texture, you can completely re-do the rest of the accompaniments to redesign a new buggy and not have to duplicate the texture for the frame itself.

1. Start first with the hood. Select the low-resolution hood mesh and apply an Automatic Mapping command from the Create UVs menu. You should get a result similar to Figure 4.53.

   Obviously, this result is not satisfactory, so it will require some editing. The goal is to end up with two UV shells—one for the top of the hood and one for the bottom.

2. Focus first on the top of the hood, as that's the main part that people will naturally see. Select the largest UV shells (most likely the middle of the top and bottom of the hood) and move them to the side. For the remaining small parts, enter Edge component mode and select all the edges. Press the Cut UV Edges button (on the UV Editor toolbar or under Polygons → Cut UV Edges) to separate each selected face.

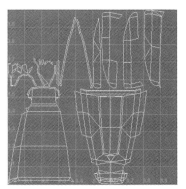

Figure 4.53
The result after auto-mapping the hood

3. Select the left and right edges of the large UV Shell of the top of the hood and use the Move And Sew UV Edges command to attach the side faces to the side of the shell.

4. Because each face was separated from the small UV shells before, each face that you just connected is separate from each other face. The easiest way to attach them together is to select *all* the edges of the hood UV shell and then *deselect* all the highlighted edges that are separate from the UV shell. This will result in only the wanted edges being selected. Use the Sew UV Edges command to merge them together.

5. Continue to sew edges together, attaching UV shells to either the top or bottom UV section until you have both the top and bottom UV shells complete. If you accidentally attach a bottom section to the top UV shell, you can simply select the edges that attach them, cut them, and sew them where they belong. You should eventually get a result similar to Figure 4.54.

The reason the bottom of the hood is so much smaller than the top in this example is because the scale of the UV shells needs to be relative to each piece as well as dependent on their visibility. While the bottom of the hood is obviously the same size as the top, because it isn't really seen, the shell can be scaled much, much smaller.

Continue to UV map the rest of the buggy in the same way, skipping the frame for now. When you're done, it'll be time to arrange each UV shell into a workable texture sheet. In Figure 4.55, you can see how I arranged mine.

Notice that the pieces are, for the most part, correctly scaled in relation to each other. The hood, wheels, and chairs are the largest portions of the UV shell because they are the largest portions of the buggy. The major exception is the undercarriage, but since the undercarriage shouldn't be seen all that often, the scale doesn't have to be one-to-one with the rest of the vehicle.

For the frame's UVs, you'll be following the same steps and arranging the UVs for their own frame texture. Be sure to lay out the UVs so that the longest pipes are the longest UV shells and so on. You can see how mine turned out in Figure 4.56.

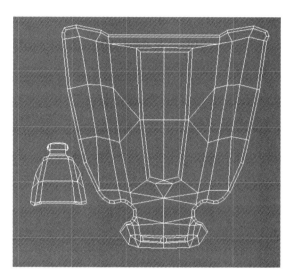

Figure 4.54

The finished hood UV shells

Figure 4.55

The final UV layout for the buggy (sans frame)

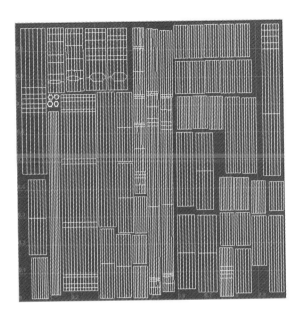

Once the UVs have been completed, you are able to bake normal and AO source textures for both the frame and the buggy. As you did in the prior chapters, you'll bake 1024×1024 resolution textures for the maps.

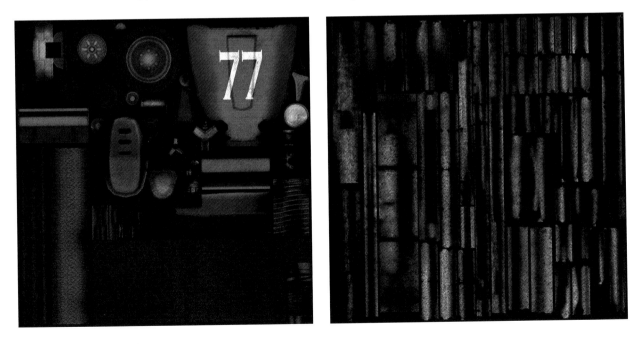

Check out the DVD for the video supplement to this chapter to watch the texturing process.

Where to Go from Here?

Aside from character work, a vehicle is arguably one of the more complex kinds of props you can create. Sometimes vehicles are simply props for the background. Other times, they *are* the focus of the entire game. In the next chapter, you'll tackle the challenge of creating the most common type of prop for an environment artist—a building!

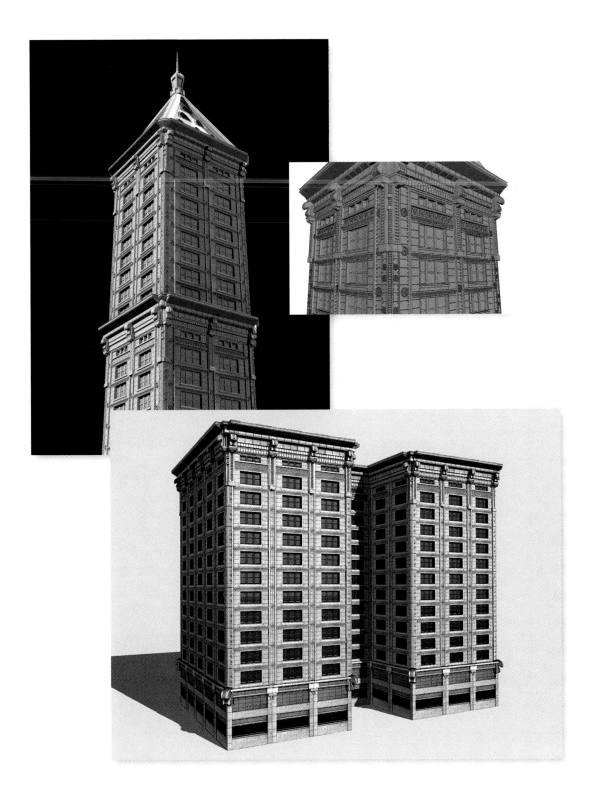

CHAPTER 5

Buildings

As an environment artist, you can bet that buildings will be a big part of what you do on the job. In fact, most environment artists get their start doing miscellaneous background structures. As you get more experienced and more responsibility, more of the foreground elements will be assigned to you. But even the most experienced environment artists get called upon to do buildings and structures from time to time. The trick is to enjoy it, no matter what level of experience you have!

Understanding Buildings

Just saying the word *building* can bring up hundreds and thousands of different images in your mind. Or in a Google image search! There are limitless combinations of shapes, styles, and uses for any structure. To create that same sense of limitlessness in a video game is impractical, not to mention entirely impossible. If you look at the buildings in any of the popular games that are set in a large city, such as *inFamous* or *Grand Theft Auto IV*, you'll inevitably run across the same building being used in multiple locations.

The main reason for this is simply resources. Sure, it is possible to create hundreds or thousands of completely unique buildings to populate a city, but what about the memory requirements of such a task? Even considering the dense amount of information that modern consoles and computers can handle, there's just not enough space on the disk for that much information. But let's say that space on the disk is no issue. How long do you think it would take to make that many structures with the average development team? Years? And at what cost?

No, it's much more practical to reuse buildings in different parts of the city as much as possible, but in ways that aren't obvious and that don't take away from the player's experience of the game or the setting. One method that is used to help speed up the process of city building is building *modularly.*

The process of building modularly is creating a series of parts (or *modules*) that can be put together in different ways to create several variations. For instance, if you create a block of windows, a door, and a roof, you can pretty much arrange them in any number of ways to create differently shaped, generic buildings. Do this on a large scale, and your city can become unique looking.

Project: Building a Skyscraper

For this lesson, you'll create a skyscraper using the process of modular building. You'll create 10 modules and use them to put together the structure. At the end, I'll demonstrate a few different examples of this.

Creating Module 1: A Block of Windows

Even if you're building modularly, having a reference to use as a guide is always useful. I chose to use the Smith Tower in Seattle, Washington, as the model for this project. I took the liberty of snapping a few photos to use here as reference in Figure 5.1. You can also use the Internet as a valuable reference resource.

Figure 5.1

The Smith Tower

You aren't necessarily going to copy the images precisely. The idea is to use the image as an idea resource. Some details you can expand on yourself; others you can gloss over completely because they are unnecessary. Take a look at Figure 5.2. In this image, I've highlighted the key parts (or modules) that your modularly built skyscraper could be composed of, using this reference image.

If you look at what is highlighted in the figure, you may be able to tell that you wouldn't be able to duplicate the building 100 percent perfectly using just those individual pieces, but you would be able to create a pretty good representation of it in a game. That is the ultimate goal. Not only that, you could create several more variations of the building using the same pieces. So, with the work you do for this one building, you'll end up with the pieces to create a dozen more structures if you want.

> Before starting, make sure you set your project to your project directory by going to File → Project → Set.

To get started, you will create a generic block of windows that can be used to make up the majority of the building's surface detail.

1. Start a new scene and set your project to a new project directory.

2. In the Front view, create a plane that is 35 units wide and 15 units high. Position it so that the left side is even with the origin and the rest of the plane extends to the right.

3. In the Perspective view, choose Create → Polygon Primitives → Pipe. Draw out a quick pipe and then change the settings under the Inputs in the Channel Box to be as follows:

Radius:	1.75
Height:	1.15
Thickness:	0.5
Subdivisions Axis:	40

Center the pivot and point-snap it to the upper-left (or upper-right, depending on the orientation of your scene—my example is to the left) corner of the plane.

4. Select the forward-facing edge loops of the pipe and apply a Bevel command to round them.

5. Duplicate the pipe and point-snap the duplicate to the lower-left corner of the plane.

6. Back in the Front view, create a tall, thin cube next to the two pipes that extends beyond the top and bottom of the plane. Just as with the pipe meshes, bevel the two forward-facing edges.

7. Duplicate both pipes and the cube and mirror them to the other side of the plane. You should have something like you see in Figure 5.3.

8. Select the plane and apply an Extrude command. Without pulling the extrusion out any, scale it inward. Then apply a second extrude

Figure 5.2

The highlighted modules for the skyscraper

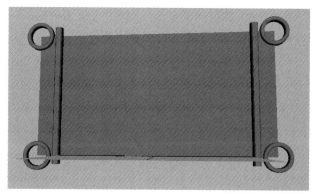

Figure 5.3

The window block beginning to form

and push it inward, creating the frame that will house the windows. You'll have to delete the extra face that is left behind when extruding from a plane. Also, don't worry too much about the exact shape of the window cavity. You'll get back to that in a later step.

9. Next, create a cube that is about 6 units long, 3 units tall, and 3 units thick. This will be a brick that will cover the majority of the surface between all the windows and columns on the skyscraper.

10. Bevel the front face of the brick. Then bevel the four corner edges to round them out as well.

11. Place the brick on the lower-left corner of the plane, so that its right side is flush with the tall cube. Also, make certain the bottom face is even with the grid. Duplicate the brick and move the duplicate up until it sets on top of the first brick. Do so again until you have 5 bricks set on top of one another on the left side of the plane. If you need to adjust the bricks to fit within the 15-unit-tall area that the plane marks out, you can.

12. Duplicate the column of bricks and mirror it to the other side. Duplicate them again and move them on the other side of the cube divider, so that their left side is flush with the side of the tall cube. Duplicate and mirror this brick stack to the other side as well.

13. You'll more than likely need to adjust the size of your window cavity to fit within this brick border on either side. You may also need to bring the four circular pipe shapes and the two tall cubes outward some to stick out from the bricks. At this point, you should have something like Figure 5.4.

14. Next, in the Front view once again, create a long horizontal cube that stretches across the top of the wall from the left cube divider to the right. Pull it out to extend beyond the bricks and is even with the two bordering cubes.

Figure 5.4

Adding the brick border

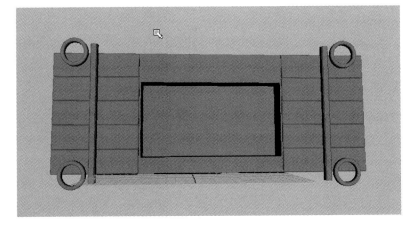

15. Select the bottom edge of the front-facing side of this new cube and pull it up, creating a wedge shape. Bevel the two front-facing edges. This cube will serve as a frieze, which is a structural band that runs along the tops of doors or windows. You should have something like Figure 5.5.

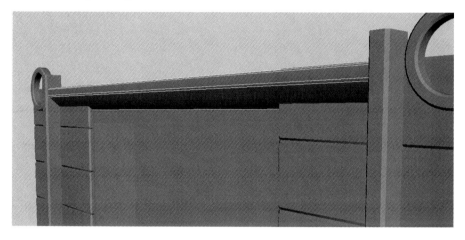

Figure 5.5

The frieze along the top of the windows

16. Duplicate one of the top bricks and place it above the windows, flush with either the left or right brick columns. Grab the vertices on the opposite side of the brick and pull them to the other side of the window, creating one long brick above the window opening.

17. Duplicate it and place it below the window as well, filling in the rest of the blank space.

18. In the Side view, use the Create Polygon tool (under the Mesh menu) to create an upside-down, L-shaped polygon similar to Figure 5.6. This will become one of many in a series of dentil molding that forms a decorative band along the top of the window blocks below the frieze.

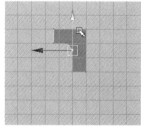

Figure 5.6

Creating the L-shaped polygon for the dentil molding detail

19. Return to the Perspective view. Extrude the polygon out about 1 unit to give it some thickness. Bevel the sharp corners to round them a bit. Place the polygon below the frieze and above the window, leaving a little space between it and the left-side dividing cube. If you need to adjust the shape to make it fit, do so now.

20. Duplicate the dentil block and move it to the right, leaving a space between the two that is about the same width as the dentil block. Press Shift+D several times to use the Duplicate With Transform command, until you have the entire row filled with the molding blocks like in Figure 5.7.

Figure 5.7

The band of dentil molding above the window

Figure 5.7

The band of dentil molding above the window

21. Duplicate the frieze and position it below the window. Shorten it so that it extends just a small amount beyond the left and right sides of the window and raise up the bottom edge, removing the wedge shape. Push it inward slightly so that it isn't extending beyond the bricks quite so much. This will simply be a window sill.

22. Next, you'll add the windows. In the Front view, choose Create → Polygon Primitives → Cube. Draw out a cube that fills in the hole that you made for the windows.

23. In the Inputs section of the Channel Box, increase the Subdivisions Width setting to 3, thereby dividing the cube into three sections.

24. Select the two dividing edge loops and bevel them, adjusting the offset to be about 0.2. This gives you two thin strips of geometry placed equidistantly apart.

25. Select all the faces except the two strips and extrude them, pushing them inward to cause the two strips of geometry to protrude outward from the cube. Position the cube into the window cavity.

26. Bevel the forward-facing edges of the two strips of geometry. This will give you the shape of three windows divided by a frame (Figure 5.8).

27. Create another pipe. Change its Thickness to 0.4 and its Subdivisions Axis to 4 to create a square shape. This will be the main frame of the window.

Figure 5.8

The windows within the frame

28. Rotate the frame 45 degrees to straighten it and select Modify → Freeze Transformations. This command will bake the object into place, removing all transform changes and keeping it at its current position and shape. Rotate the frame 90 degrees forward to stand it up.

29. Go into the Front view and reshape the frame to fit the window cavity. The easiest way is to grab the top vertices, and move them into position, then grab the left side's vertices and move them, and so on. Work your way around the shape in this manner until it's completely in position.

30. Bevel the forward-facing edges as well as the four corner edge loops (Figure 5.9)

Figure 5.9

The window frame beveled and in position

31. Create a long cube and place it in the middle of the windows horizontally, forming a horizontal bar for the frame to separate the panes of glass. Bevel the forward-facing edges.

Figure 5.10

A simple design for the corners of the window block

32. Add a decorative shape (or combination of shapes) in the center of the four corner circles. This can be whatever you want. I created a few beveled cubes and arranged them in a flowery pattern as in Figure 5.10. Duplicate this pattern to all four corner circles.

This block of windows will form the majority of the building. It will be duplicated and snapped end to end and top to bottom to form a large wall of windows. Next, you'll create a corner column to go on the corners of the building.

Creating Module 2: A Corner Column

At the edge of a building's walls, where two walls at 90 degrees form a corner, there is usually a column. The corner column forms a supporting as well as a framing structure. This structure will add a framing shape at the corners, which will help relieve a building's sharp edges and make it look much more structurally believable.

1. Create a cube that is 5 units wide, 5 units deep, and 15 units high. This will act as the base of your column. For the purposes of this lesson, the front-right edge will be the corner that will face the exterior of the building.

2. Select that front-right edge and bevel it, making the Bevel Offset about 0.25 if you are following along with my measurements.

3. Increase the bevel's Segments value to 2, creating a new edge through the middle of the beveled surface.

4. Select the connector edge that forms on the top and bottom caps of the column and delete them.

5. Select the center edge and move it inward, forming a square-shaped cavity that runs along the entire column like in Figure 5.11.

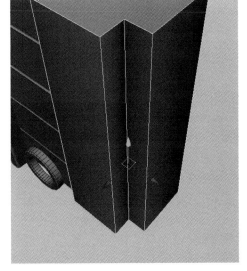

Figure 5.11
Forming the column's forward-facing corner

6. Select all the vertical edges of the column (none of the ones bordering the top and bottom) and bevel them slightly, rounding the hard-edged corners.

7. Delete the top and bottom faces of the column for now. You won't need them in later steps.

8. Go to the Front view. Select the front face and with the Cut Faces tool (under the Edit Mesh menu) hold Shift and cut a straight, vertical edge through the center of the selected face.

   If you didn't quite cut it in the center and need to adjust the cut's position, you can by clicking the polyCut1 Input item in the Channel Box on the right side of the screen and change the Cut Plane Center X value to 0. This will move the cut to the center of the face.

9. Select the newly cut edge and bevel it, giving it an Offset value of about 0.7 to create two thin, vertical faces running along the sides of the forward-facing side.

10. Select the center face and extrude it inward, creating a cut path through the center of the column's forward face (Figure 5.12).

11. Go to the Top view. Create a cylinder and using Maya's interactive creation, draw it out to fit within the corner alcove of the column, as in Figure 5.13.

12. Back in the Perspective view, adjust the cylinder's Subdivisions Caps to 0. Select the top vertices and lower them down to make the cylinder about 1 unit tall.

13. Select the top and bottom faces of the cylinder and bevel them slightly to round the hard edge.

14. Duplicate the cylinder and place the duplicate directly above the original. Continue duplicating the cylinders (you can use the Duplicate With Transform command with the Shift+D shortcut keys to make this easier) and placing them above the previous one until the cylinders form a small column all the way up the height of the main column shape.

    If you find that the topmost cylinder extends beyond the top of the column's base shape, you can select all the small cylinders, group them together, and scale the group down until they fit perfectly. Then make certain you Ungroup (Edit → Ungroup) them afterward (Figure 5.14).

15. At this point, you can start adding whatever details you want. If you want to skip to the next module now, you can. If you'd like to follow along with me, create a small cube.

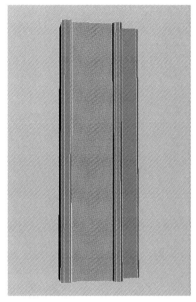

Figure 5.12

Creating surface detail on the column

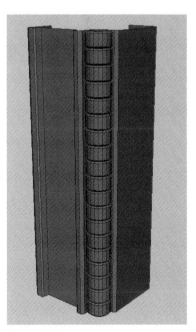

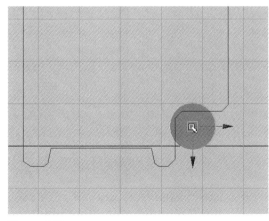

Figure 5.13

Placing a cylinder within the column's corner edge

Figure 5.14

The small column within the larger column

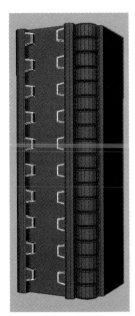

Figure 5.15

Smaller details added to the column

16. Bevel the cube and make one end shorter than the other. Place it within the forward-facing ridge. Duplicate it and place it every two units or so down the height of the column. Duplicate the cubes for the other side of the ridge, and you should get something like Figure 5.15.

    You can place these teeth-like details along the left and right edges of the first module and the window block as well, if you want. You may come up with a detail later in the project that might look good on an earlier piece. Don't hesitate to go back and add it to improve the earlier work!

17. Select the circular corner details of the earlier module and duplicate them to use with the column module. Scale it down to fit and place two of them in the center of the large forward-facing side like in Figure 5.16.

18. Another detail you can trade between modules is the bricks. Duplicate a brick from the window block module and resize it and reposition it to fit with the column. Duplicate it and stack the bricks to fill the height of the column behind the teeth detail.

19. Once you've added all the details you want, you can duplicate and mirror one side of the column for the other and you'll have your completed column module (Figure 5.17).

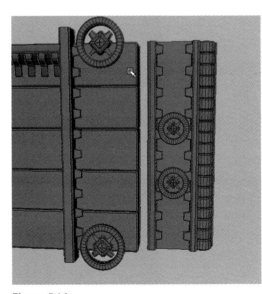

Figure 5.16

Duplicating details from the window module to the column module and vice versa

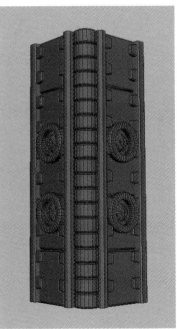

Figure 5.17

The completed column module

Creating Module 3: A Smaller Window Block

It's good to have some variation. Allow yourself to have some details look different and, thus, more visually interesting. Of the 10 modules you'll be making for your building, two of them will involve windows. If you want, you could continue to make more variations on the window blocks. The more variation, the better—to a point. In a real project, you'll always want to make sure you are keeping within your rendering budget. The more variation you have, the more textures you'll be required to make, which will making the rendering of it all much more computationally expensive.

This second block of windows you'll be making in this section will share many of the elements of the first window block. This will keep their design consistent and allow them to be used together.

1. Create another plane. This one should be the same width as the first window block's plane (35 units wide to be exact), but this time, make it 10 units tall instead of 15. The windows in this module will be a bit shorter, so the plane will be shorter as well.

   Place this plane directly above your first module. This will make it easier to duplicate consistent details between the two and keep them lined up correctly.

2. Grab the bricks from your first module, duplicate them, and move them upward to line up with the new module's plane. Do the same with the left and right dividing cubes. This will give you a result like you see in Figure 5.18.

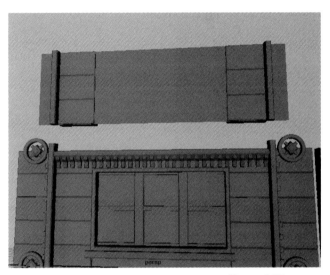

Figure 5.18

The small window block with shared details from the large window block

3. Select the bottom brick on both sides and delete them. Grab one of the duplicated dividing cubes and rotate it 90 degrees to make it lie horizontally. Scale it so that it reaches across the module from the left dividing cube to the right and place it below the remaining bricks.

   This will create an area for more decorative details that will act as a border.

4. Duplicate the horizontal cube you just placed and move the duplicate up to the top of the module to serve as a border.

5. Select the plane backing and apply an Extrude. Scale the extruded face to fit within the space that remains between the bricks. Extrude again and push back to create an opening for windows to be placed later. You'll probably need to delete the extra face that is usually left behind to reveal the window cavity (Figure 5.19).

Figure 5.19

The window cavity in place for the small window module

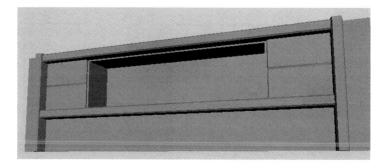

6. In the Front view, using the Create Polygon tool, use 6 points to draw out an L-shaped polygon. Extrude it outward to give it some thickness and bevel it, rounding the hard-edged corners.

7. Duplicate it, rotate it 180 degrees vertically and position the duplicate so that the two L shapes fit together like a puzzle, leaving a small gap between them (Figure 5.20). Scale them so that they fit within the gap below the window area.

Figure 5.20

Two interlocking L-shaped surfaces

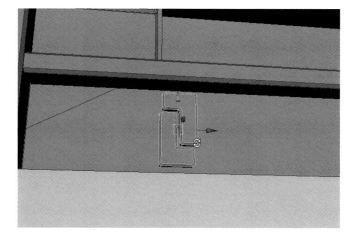

8. Move the two pieces to the left side of the area beneath the windows. Duplicate them both and group the new duplicates together (Ctrl+G to group them). Scale the group -1 in the x-axis to flip them so that the shape faces the opposite direction.

9. Ungroup the two shapes and select all four L-shaped objects. Group all four together and duplicate them a few times. Move each duplicate to the right so that the shapes fill up the space. If you have any space left over, you can create a few vertical, beveled blocks to go in between, like in Figure 5.21.

10. You can grab the window details from the first window block module to use in the second. Simply resize them to fit the window cavity and you're done (Figure 5.22)!

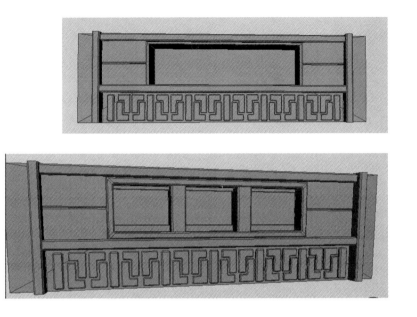

Figure 5.21

Filling in the detail space

Figure 5.22

The finished small window module

Creating Module 4: A Roof Ledge

The roof ledge module will act as the top border of your structure. Rather than having the windows simply stop when they reach the top of the building, you can add this ledge to the top of the building to make it look more complete and rooted in reality.

Before beginning, think about how your game project handles the rooftops of buildings. In many games, the player will never be able to get to the roofs, so they don't necessarily need to be created. However, if your characters can jump over buildings in a single bound or pilot a helicopter and fly high above the cityscape, you may need to make sure that there actually *is* a roof. For this project, I'll be assuming that, like in a typical game, the player will not be able to see the tops of the buildings.

1. Create another plane to act as the base that you'll build from. Make it 35 units wide and 8 units high. You can place it above the other modules you've made to help you with placement and to make sure things line up.

2. In the Front view, create a tall cube that is 8 units high that will act as a section of dentil molding to form a band at the base of the ledge where it meets the windows below it.

3. Bevel the forward-facing edges of the cube to round its edges.

4. Place the cube at the far left of the plane. Duplicate it and move it to the right so that the duplicate cube is flush with the original. Use the Duplicate With Transform command (Shift+D) to continue to duplicate the cube across the surface, like in Figure 5.23.

Figure 5.23

A band of dentil
molding to serve as
the ledge's base

5. Duplicate one of the molding cubes and rotate it 90 degrees so that it lies horizontally. Then flip it 180 degrees so that the beveled side is facing the structure. Grab one end of the cube's vertices and stretch it across the band of dentil molding, inserting it partially into the band.

6. Select all the original dentil molding cubes and combine them together (Edit Mesh → Combine). Delete the new combined object's history (Edit → Delete By Type → History).

7. Select the combined dentil molding mesh if it isn't selected already and Shift-select the horizontal cube that runs across them. Perform a Difference Boolean (Mesh → Booleans → Difference), cutting an indention across the surface of the dentil molding like that shown in Figure 5.24.

8. For the purposes of adding interest, you can select the top side of the indention and pull the vertices out, making the upper half of the dentil molding jut farther forward than the lower half.

9. Create a rectangular cube above the dentil molding that is 35 units wide and about 4 units tall. Reshape the cube into a wedge shape that angles upward and extends out beyond the dentil molding that is below. Bevel the forward edges to round out their hard lines.

10. Select the topmost face of the wedge and extrude it upward about 4 units. Pull the forward-facing top edge outward, making it extend even farther forward.

Figure 5.24

An indention
carved through
the center of the
dentil molding

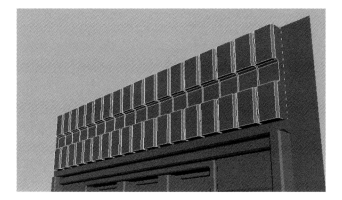

11. Select the topmost face again and extrude it up about 2 or 3 units. You should have something similar to Figure 5.25, a ledge that demarks the boundaries of the roof.

12. Bevel the forward corners to round them off and soften their lines.

13. Duplicate the ledge. Select the vertices on the right side and move them over to the left until the duplicate ledge is only about 3 units wide.

14. Select all the thin duplicate ledge's vertices. Hold the W key and left-click and hold. This combination of key and mouse click is a shortcut to access the Move tool's options.

Figure 5.25

The ledge extended above the dentil molding

While still holding the left mouse button, drag the cursor to the left to hover over the word *Axis*. This will open a new marking menu. Move the cursor to hover over the word *Normal* and release. This changes your Move tool from its regular mode to Normal Axis movement.

Now that you are within Normal Axis movement, click and drag on the handle labeled N (demarking the surface normal direction) and pull all the vertices outward slightly.

Using the Normal Axis movement like this makes every vertex move outward relative from its own position rather than all of them moving in a singular direction as a group. It's very similar to the Push command in Autodesk's 3D Studio Max, if you are familiar with that application.

15. Return to World Axis movement by accessing the Move tool's options again (either the way you did above or by double-clicking the Move tool in the Toolbox and setting the Move Axis back to World). Move the small duplicate ledge (we'll call it a ledge block from now on) to the far left of the main ledge shape, making it flush with the left side.

16. Bevel the edges of the ledge block.

17. Duplicate the ledge block and move it to the right, positioning it flush with the original. Continue to Duplicate With Transform (Shift+D) across the ledge. If the ledge blocks extend too far off the right side, you can select them all, group them, and scale them as a group until they fit snugly (Figure 5.26).

18. Select one of the horizontal cubes from a previous module, such as one of the ones above and below the windows in the

Figure 5.26

The ledge with ledge blocks arrayed across its surface

small window block (from Module 3). Duplicate it and move it up to the topmost forward-facing surface of the ledge. Scale it to stretch across the entire front face of the ledge and position it at the top of the ledge on the corner. Duplicate it and position it on the lower corner of the ledge's top face as well. It should look something like Figure 5.27.

Figure 5.27

Two horizontal bars along the top of the ledge

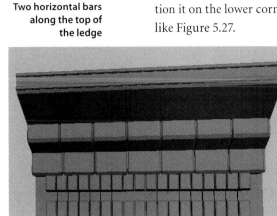

The ledge module is pretty much complete at this point. Feel free to continue to add all the details you want. At this point, with these four modules (large window block, small window block, corner column, and roof ledge) you can make a pretty convincing surface. By duplicating and stacking modules and placing them side by side, you could create a wall of detail similar to Figure 5.28. That's made just with *four* of our final 10 modules. Let's keep going!

Figure 5.28

An example of what the current modules are capable of creating when used together

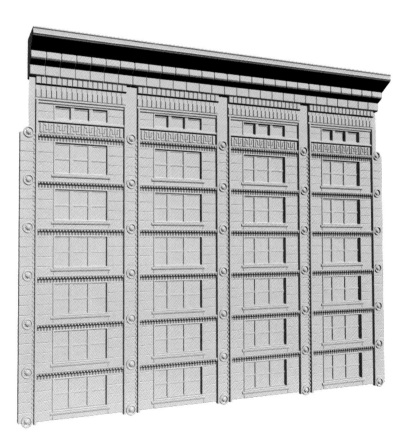

Creating Module 5: Large Corner Column

Back in Figure 5.2, you can see that toward the top of the building, near the ledge, there's a different type of column being used on the corners. It is a bit larger and acts as a platform for the corner ledge. It also helps add more variety, which is always a good thing, especially when building modularly.

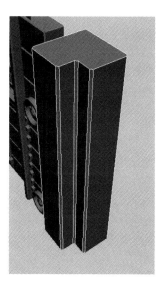

Figure 5.29

The creation of the large column begins just like the smaller one.

1. Create a cube that is 6 units wide, 6 units long, and 25 units high. Just as with the previous column (back in the Module 2 section), select the forward, right edge and bevel it, adding a second Segment and repositioning the center segment edge to carve an L-shaped wedge into the corner of the cube as in Figure 5.29. Don't forget to use Snap Align to help keep things square. Bevel all the vertical edges to round them a bit.

> Snap Align is simply the action of snapping in one dimension to align one (or more) points to another point in that same dimension. For example, to snap align two vertices in the y-axis, hold the V key (for Snap To Point) and left-click and drag the green y-axis handle from one point to another. The original point will snap to the second point's y-axis position, but remain unchanged in the other two dimensions.

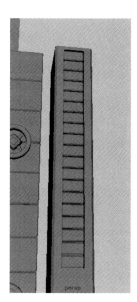

Figure 5.30

Creating a column of beveled bricks

2. Select the forward face and apply an Extrude from the Edit Mesh menu. Scale it inward. Select the bottom edge of the extruded face and lift it up, adding some space between the bottom of the column and the bottom of the extrusion.

3. Select the extruded face and apply a second Extrude. This time, move the extrusion in, pushing a cavity into the column's surface.

4. Create a small rectangular cube. Bevel all the cubes edges and place it within the column's cavity at the top. Duplicate the cube and move the duplicate down so that it is flush with the original. Continue to Duplicate With Transform (Shift+D) to create a column of small bricks stacked on top of one another within the cavity of the column, like in Figure 5.30.

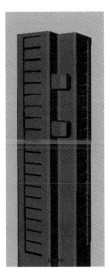

Figure 5.31

Adding two bricks
to the corner wedge
of the column

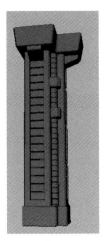

Figure 5.32

Adding a base and
cap to the column

5. Delete the other side of the column and mirror the details that you have so far to create an L-shaped column with both sides containing the brick column.

6. In the Top view, create another small cube and place it within the corner wedge of the column. Bevel its forward-facing edge to round the corner. Bevel the top and bottom faces of the cube as well to remove their hard edges.

7. Return to the Perspective view. Position this new cube about a quarter of the distance from the top of the column. Duplicate this new cube and move the copy down until it's a little above halfway down the side of the column. It should look something like Figure 5.31.

8. Select the column of cylinders from the small column (that you created in Module 2's step 14) and duplicate all of them. Place the duplicate cylinders in the larger column's corner wedge. Duplicate more cylinders to fill the space on the large column to run up the entire height.

9. To create a base and cap to the column, create another cube and add a wedged gap to its forward, right-side corner just as you did to create the column in step 1. Make this cube about 3 units tall and place it at the base of the column.

10. Duplicate the base and place it on top of the column as well. Modify the vertices of the cap to make it larger and extend farther out from the column so that it will effectively act as a support for whatever will be placed above it in a future step.

11. Create two wedge-shaped cubes to be placed beneath these flanges of the cap to act as further support.

12. You can continue to add details as you see fit, but in the end, you should end up with something like Figure 5.32.

Creating Module 6: Corner Roof Ledge

The next module on your list is to create a corner piece for the roof ledge. With the roof ledge piece you have now (Module 4) you can create straight and diagonal roof ledges, but when it comes to the corner, you'd need a new corner piece to fill in the gap that can been easily seen in Figure 5.33.

1. In the Side View, use the Create Polygon tool (from the Mesh menu) and draw out a profile shape for a decorative stone support. Mine is *sort of* seahorse shaped. You can, of course, make whatever kind of shape you'd like.

2. Extrude the drawn out profile polygon to give it thickness. Position it to sit on top of the larger column you made (Module 5 if you recall) so that it is centered on top of one of the platforms that make up the column's cap, like in Figure 5.34.

Figure 5.33

The corner gap that needs a new module to fill it in

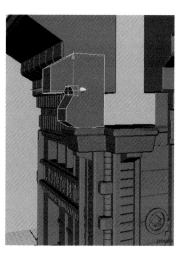

Figure 5.34

The decorative support set on top of the column

3. Select the ledge structure from Module 4 and duplicate it. Select the rightmost vertices and move them to the left to shorten the ledge piece to fit within the gap. It should be flush with the ledge that is to the left of the corner gap and extend to the edge of the large column, which in my case, is about 7 units wide.

4. Duplicate this small ledge piece and flip it 90 degrees to fit on the right side of the corner gap as well.

5. For this corner module, you'll create a stepped style corner. In a future module, you can create a more rounded corner module. First, create a cube and place it between the two ledge pieces to fill in the gap. You can make it the same height as the topmost section of the ledge, like in Figure 5.35.

6. For a moment, return to the decorative supports. You can continue to modify them to be as decorative as you'd like. I took my base shape and added a few details (Figure 5.36). They don't need to be too fancy as they will never be seen up close in the game. These little supports will be near the tops of the buildings most of the time.

Figure 5.35

Beginning to fill in the corner with a stepped style of architecture

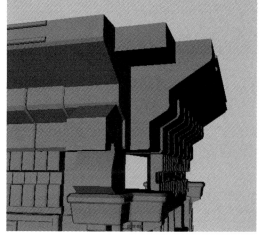

7. Duplicate the support object and place it on the other side of the column so that it is centered on its cap ledge as well.

8. Now return to the corner ledge details. Select the two horizontal bars that run along the top of the original ledge you made, duplicate them, shorten them, and place them on the ledge corner section you have. Duplicate them and position them to follow the shape of the stepped corner.

9. You can also duplicate the other details of the ledge module onto this corner ledge module, such as the bricks and the dentil molding and whatever else you may have created that is different from my examples.

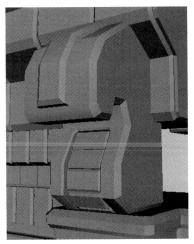

Figure 5.36
The finished support structure

10. Remember the cube that sits within the gap from step 5? It's time to finish that bit. Select the bottom face of the cube and extrude it down to be even with the next section of the ledge. Scale this new extrusion inward to match the angle of the ledge. Once that is done, bevel the edges to round off the corners. You should have something like what you see in Figure 5.37.

11. Duplicate this corner cube and position it below the first so that it fills the gap below. Move the top of the cube's vertices upward to intersect into the cube above it.

12. Continue to modify this corner ledge module however you'd like. You can see my final results in Figure 5.38.

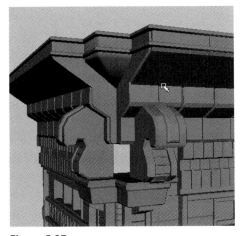

Figure 5.37
The corner ledge module is coming along nicely.

Figure 5.38
The finished corner ledge module

Creating Module 7: The Roof

The roof module isn't so much a puzzle piece that can be plugged in like the rest, but more of a cap piece to any tall building you may make with this set of pieces. Not all buildings necessarily have to have a cap piece, but having it on top of a building instantly changes the building from a typical square building to a centerpiece structure with an intrinsic visual value that is different from the more typical buildings.

1. You can create a rooftop piece that looks however you like, but if you'd like to follow along with me, select Create → Polygon Primitives → Pyramid.

2. Using the interactive creation, drag out a tall pyramid that can be placed on top of a building, similar to the reference image in Figure 5.2. Rotate it 45 degrees to align its square base to be parallel with the rest of the modules.

3. Select the pyramid's apex vertex and select Edit Mesh → Chamfer Vertex. This will create a new square face on top of the pyramid, which will flatten its tip. Under the polyChamfer1 Inputs in the Channel Box, you can adjust the Width value down to something around 0.13 units to make the new face not quite so large.

4. Select the top face and bevel it to round the corners some. Select the edges running up the four sides of the pyramid and bevel them as well, increasing their Segments value to 2 and shrinking their Offset value down to something like 0.2 to give the edges a rounded profile.

5. Select one of the pyramid's four large faces. It doesn't matter which. Extrude it and scale the extrusion inward, giving the face a thick border. Scale this new Extrude again and push it inward, carving into the surface.

6. Select the large inner face of this new cavity and extrude it again, once again scaling it inward to create a border. And then once again extrude and push inward. This gives your border two distinct tiers.

7. Select the forward-facing edge loops that run around both tiers and bevel them to round the hard edges. You should have something similar to Figure 5.39.

8. In the Front view, use the Create Polygon tool to draw out the shape of an alcove. It can be whatever shape you want, but

Figure 5.39

The two-tiered border on the pyramid-shaped roof

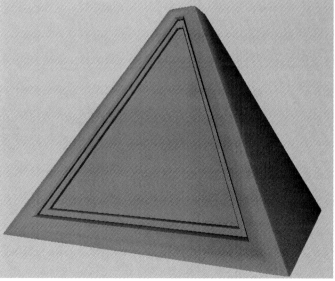

I followed the reference image from the start of the chapter and made it an arch shape.

9. Extrude this shape out to give it some thickness.

10. Duplicate it. Hold down the Control key and scale the forward directional handle on the scale gizmo (in my case, this was the Z direction).

Holding the Control key like this will lock the selected scale axis, causing the shape to scale only in the other two directions. This will make it keep the same depth as the original alcove, but expand it outward in the width and height.

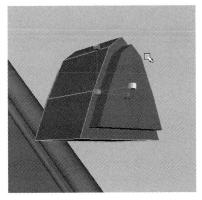

11. Once you've expanded the duplicate arch, you can then let go of Control and scale the duplicate inward in the depth direction to make it not quite as deep as the original alcove. You should have a shape similar in style, as in Figure 5.40.

Figure 5.40

Creating an alcove

12. Place these alcove arches together at the top center of the large center face of the pyramid. Duplicate them and place two in the middle of the face and then place three more near the bottom of the face so that they are set almost like pool balls in a rack (Figure 5.41).

13. Now, using Difference Booleans (from the Mesh → Booleans menu), cut the alcove shapes out of the pyramid.

Figure 5.41

Setting up the alcoves on the roof

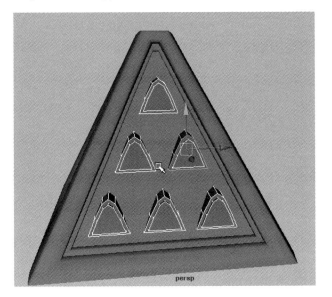

14. You can now detail the rest of the roof however you see fit. I took the rows of teeth-style cubes that were used on the window modules and ran them along the inner tier of the roof's border. I also beveled the edges of the alcoves to smooth them.

    I would normally say you could now duplicate this side of the pyramid for the rest of the sides, but you don't actually need to do that (even though I did on the DVD video supplement material). Later on, you'll only be using one side of the pyramid to bake texture information, so for now, you need only make one side.

15. For the top of the pyramid, you can create a spire. Or make a steeple or a weather vane or a radio antenna—whatever you want. I created a simple steeple shape using a cylinder for a base and a cube that I extruded upward for the steeple itself. You can see it in Figure 5.42.

Figure 5.42

A simple steeple on top

> Don't forget that if you expect your player to be able to get up to the roof and view it close-up, you should spend the time to detail it as much as you would any other part of the building. If it's going to be seen only from way down below, at street level, however, a little detail can go a long way toward the illusion.

Creating Module 8: Support Strut

As we get closer to the end of our 10 modules, you'll start to see that some of the modules you make are based on or even simply just parts of other modules. For example, the sea-horse-shaped support structures from the corner roof ledge module (Module 6) will actually be duplicated and broken off to form their own support strut module. These support structures will run along the top of the ledges, to give the roof more structural support as well as to serve as a decorative way to break up all the straight lines that are up near the top of the building.

And, you don't necessarily need to be doing this right now because you will use the *low-resolution* version in the actual game. Since you will have the low-resolution version of the support structure completed for the corner roof ledge, you can simply use *that* support strut in the game as your eighth module. Creating it right now actually doesn't serve any purpose, but I'm going over it so you understand that when I said there would be 10 modules, I was telling the truth!

Creating Module 9: Round Roof Ledge

Module 9 is another module that takes parts from a previous module. The round roof ledge module is simply a variation on the corner roof ledge module. Instead of a cornered ledge shape to form a 90 degree angle, this one will be rounded, forming a smooth shape between each side.

1. Duplicate the corner roof ledge module and move it to the side. Delete the cube in the middle of the two ledge extensions.

2. Create a cylinder that is the same height as the top horizontal face of the ledge. Bevel the bottom.

3. Place it in the center of the corner. Scale it to fit, if it doesn't already.

4. Select the bottom face and extrude it downward. Scale the extrusion inward to fit the angle of the ledge's downward slope like in Figure 5.43.

Figure 5.43

The rounded corner coming together

5. Use the Insert Edge Loop tool (from the Edit Mesh menu) to insert an edge loop around the top ring of faces to be level with the top border geometry of the ledge extensions on either side.

6. With the new edge loop selected, bevel it. Adjust the Offset value to make the width of the new ring of faces match the width of the top border geometry.

7. Select the ring of faces now, and use the Duplicate Faces command from the Edit Mesh menu to duplicate them as their own mesh.

UNGROUPING

Don't forget that after duplicating faces from a mesh, Maya will automatically put both the original and duplicate meshes within a new group node. You can easily remove these unwanted nodes (assuming they *are* unwanted on your project) by following these steps:

1. Select one of the two meshes, either the original or the duplicate.

2. Press the up arrow key on the keyboard to move up the hierarchy to the group node.

3. Select Edit → Ungroup to remove the two objects from the group and delete the group node.

4. You may also want to delete the two objects' history, as they will retain their "memory" of this event in their history list in the Channel Box (selecting Edit → Delete By Type → History *or* by pressing Alt+D).

Also, be aware that if the original mesh had been assigned to a layer or was within another group already, it has most likely been removed from the group or the layer after ungrouping. The original mesh will need to be reassigned or regrouped.

The reason for this is the way Maya handles nodes. Before the meshes were duplicated, they were a node that Maya had named, such as pCube476 or something similar. After duplicating faces from the original, Maya groups the two together and names the *group* pCube476. The original and duplicate meshes now get new names. So when you ungroup them, you are essentially deleting the original mesh according to Maya. You are left with two brand-new meshes with new names. Therefore, their original layer assignments and group affiliations are no longer retained.

Keep this sort of thing in mind when extracting or duplicating faces of a mesh to avoid unwanted group nodes or confusion about why an object is no longer within a group or a layer that it had been in before.

8. Extrude this new ring of faces to give them thickness that matches the thickness of the border geometry to its left and right.

9. Bevel the forward-facing edge loops to match the beveling of the border geometry.

10. Duplicate the piece and move it down to match the elevation of the bottom border geometry. When they both match, you should have a flowing border such as the one seen in Figure 5.44.

Figure 5.44

Border geometry flowing along the entire surface

Creating Module 10: The Base

The last module is a base wall support. This will be what goes around the base of the building so that it's not just windows at the bottom street level. Keep in mind that if the building is one that the player will actually enter, a door piece would also need to be made.

It can be difficult to find good reference of the base of buildings on the Internet. However, thanks to the magic of Google Maps' Street View technology, you can probably find what you are looking for with a quick address search. Luckily, I live near the Smith Tower, so I was able to take a photo to use here (Figure 5.45). You won't be duplicating this exactly, but it serves as a good reference.

Figure 5.45

The Smith Tower reference from the street

1. Create a tall cube that is 6 units wide and deep, and 45 units tall. Center it on the origin. You can place Module 1 up above it as a size reference.

2. Bevel the four vertical edges to round the corners.

3. Duplicate the cube and select the top row of vertices. Move them down to shrink the duplicate so that it is about 5 units tall. Scale it up slightly so that it is slightly thicker than the original.

4. Select the top and bottom faces of the smaller cube and bevel them. This will serve as a large stone brick.

5. Duplicate the brick and move the duplicate up so that it is flush with the top of the original. Continue duplicating bricks up the height of the column until you have covered it.

6. Duplicate the entire column and group it together (Ctrl+G). Move the new column 35 units over. This gives you the two sides of the base module (Figure 5.46).

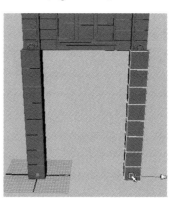

Figure 5.46

The left and right sides of the base module

Now to fill in the details between the two columns. These details can be whatever you like. Bricked walls, window paneling, or decorative molding designs. The sky's the limit. For a real project, you'd actually want a couple of different variations for this module so that the base isn't exactly the same all the way around.

7. Select one of the columns (not one of the bricks) and rotate it 90 degrees to lie horizontally. Select the front vertices and push them back, making the column half the depth. Place the horizontal column a little lower than halfway down the vertical columns and between the two.

This will be a horizontal border block between the windows and the bricks that you will add in later steps.

8. Select the top bricks of both columns and scale them up about 125 percent. This will give the two bricks more heft to act as support for the weight above them.

Figure 5.47

A ledge on top of the base module

9. Create a few long, flat cubes along the top to create the beginning of a ledge. Have the top cube stick farther out than the ones below it for a tiered look.

10. Grab a brick and select the bottom vertices. Move them upward to flatten the brick and place a few along the top within the ledge pattern.

This ledge is for decorative purposes. You can adjust it to be whatever looks good to you. If you're following along with me, you should have something similar to Figure 5.47.

11. Just like the windows you created for the two window block modules (Modules 1 and 3), you can create another set of windows here. Think of these as storefront windows, so make them taller than the office/apartment windows you made previously.

    Alternatively, you can create a different kind of wall here as well, as an addition if you want to give yourself more variation, which is, within reason, not a bad thing (Figure 5.48).

Figure 5.48

A storefront window added to the base module

12. To fill in the space above the center dividing block, you can literally do whatever you'd like. I simply filled it with a brick pattern that will eventually be textured slightly differently than the rest of the area to give it some color variation.

13. At the top of the columns, below the large support blocks, add in some sort of decorative detail. I used the reference image and created a row of dentil molding with an upside-down omega shaped below it. Simple shapes can go a long way in architecture (Figure 5.49).

    With that finished, you have created all 10 modules in this lesson. Please don't hesitate to create more if you like, to give yourself more variations. Keep in mind, however, that each additional module you make will add to the number of textures that will be needed for the final set of building modules. Also, in a real game project, you'll probably be creating a dozen different sets of modules, where each set can create another dozen different buildings. So, don't necessarily try to pack every idea you have into a single

Figure 5.49

Adding some decorative details to the top of the columns

set. Save some for other building designs. Using this modular system, you'll be surprised just how quickly a city can come together.

But don't get me wrong, you're not done yet. These meshes were the high-resolution meshes! Now comes the low-resolution mesh building. But don't worry. These low-resolution meshes are pretty simple compared to what you just did. Speaking of what you just did, Figure 5.50 is an example of what can be created with the 10 modules you've made.

Figure 5.50

The 10 modules (left) and an example of what they can do when they work together (right)

Creating the Low-Resolution Modules

Given how detailed that last image looked, you'd be surprised at just how low the poly-count of the low-resolution modules will be. Only if you're expecting your game to be like the game *Champions Online* and allow your players to literally climb tall buildings with Spider-Man style powers should your low-resolution meshes be very detailed.

1. Before beginning, create layers for each of your high-resolution modules. You can name them specific names for easy identification, such as `Window_Block_Hi` and `Roof_Corner_Hi`. The "Hi" designates them as the high-resolution versions of the modules. Assign each module's pieces to its respective layer.

2. Hide all the modules except Module 1, the main window block.

    As with the previous chapters, I find it easier to see what is going on by assigning a darker-colored material to the high-resolution mesh. The low-resolution mesh will have the original gray material so it stands out against the dark color for easy visibility.

3. Create a plane that is 35 units wide and 15 units tall. Pull it out so that it is in front of the main window details. The upper ledge and side border shapes will still push through (Figure 5.51).

4. The goal is to add as few details as possible to cover the surface of the high-resolution mesh. For instance, for this window block, you can simply extrude in the window and cut in a few faces for the border and ledge and you are all ready to go (Figure 5.52).

Figure 5.51

The plane positioned on the window block

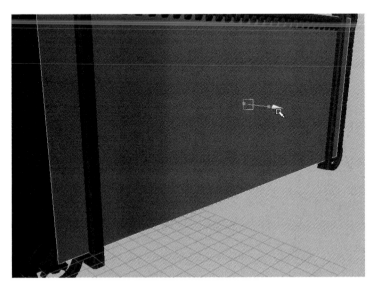

Figure 5.52

The low-resolution window block

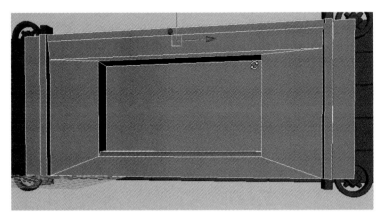

Notice that the four corners of the low-resolution version of the window block go directly to the center of the round corner designs at each corner of the high-resolution mesh. When you duplicate and stack window blocks on top of each other and to their left and right, these details should tile together very nicely.

5. Repeat this process with each module, encompassing each high-resolution module with a lower resolution shell. You'll be surprised at just how easy this process can be for many of these modules, especially the columns. If you need a little extra help, though, you can consult the DVD video supplement, where I recorded each step. Eventually, you'll have something like Figure 5.53.

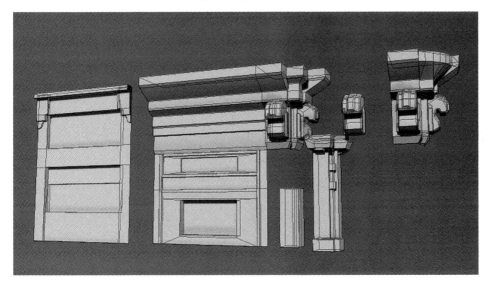

Figure 5.53

The low-resolution building modules (roof not pictured)

UV Mapping the Low-Resolution Meshes

The next step is to UV map each module. Because each module is mostly rectangular, this process is much easier than some of your previous projects in this book.

1. Open the UV Texture Editor from under the Window menu. Select the low-resolution window block module and use the Automatic Mapping command found under the Create UVs menu. The result should be something similar to Figure 5.54.

   You'll notice that it has the front of the module mostly put together, with a few of the other elements laid out to the side. With these kinds of shapes, it can be very easy to put the UV shells back together again. I'll show you how in these next steps.

Figure 5.54

The result of auto-mapping the low-poly window block module

2. In the UV Texture Editor (found under the Window menu), right-click and choose UV from the component selection marking menu that opens. This will turn on UV component mode and allow you to select UVs.

3. Select a UV from the main part of the mesh, the part containing the window opening. If your Automatic Mapping resulted in anything like mine did, you'll probably need to rotate it 90 degrees to make it right side up. In the UV Texture Editor's menus, choose Select → Select Shell. This will modify your selection to include all the UVs of the current shell you have selected. You can then use the Rotate Clockwise or Rotate Counterclockwise commands on the upper toolbar.

4. Once the UV shell is rotated uprightly (if it needed to be), you can right-click within the UV Texture Editor and choose Edge as your component selection. Select the top edge of the main UV shell and use the Move And Sew UV Edges command (found on the toolbar or under the editor's Polygons menu).

5. Do the same for the bottom edge of the shell. This will attach the UV shells on top and at the bottom of the main UV shell, merging them together properly.

6. Continue to do this for the top and bottom edges until every top and bottom UV shell is attached. You can then do the same for the left- and right-side UV shells.

7. Then you can select the edges that make up the window opening and use Move And Sew to join their respective UV shells together as well. Once you're done, you may need to manually move some UVs around to straighten them up if they came in at a strange angle. But you should eventually get something similar to Figure 5.55.

With so many pieces, it can be a big resource saver to have multiple objects share the same texture. So for this project, the two window block modules can share a texture, as can the ledge and corner ledge modules. The base and columns can share as well. Or they can be put together in some other combination. The goal is to make them fit together as well as possible with as little wasted, empty space as possible and with as little deformation as possible. To avoid deforming UV shells, you may have to break some shells up into separate pieces. In Figure 5.56, you can see that the 10 modules in this lesson can be laid out to share only four textures.

Figure 5.55

The window block UVs in place and ready for texturing (image's contrast modified for easier viewing)

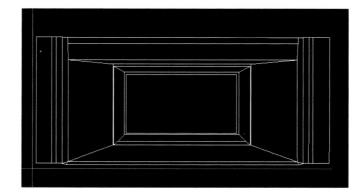

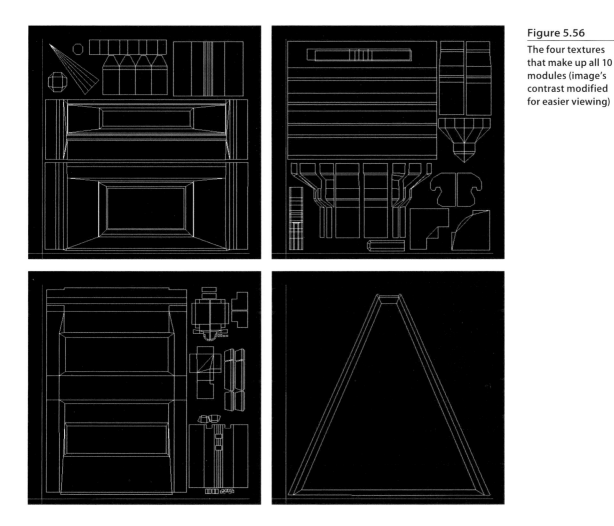

Figure 5.56
The four textures that make up all 10 modules (image's contrast modified for easier viewing)

Texturing the Building

The textures can be handled many different ways, depending on what the player will be seeing. I hope that since I mention it so often, you can see how important it is to make certain that no time or energy is wasted, especially in a project as big as the construction of a city. So if the player will only see a building from the street level, the only vantage point that needs to look good is the player's vantage point.

MAKE YOUR WORK SEEN

The idea that you should not work as hard on unseen aspects of a game's art sometimes offends some artists' creative sensibilities. I know that it offended mine at first! As an artist, you naturally want to do the best job you can. And that's great, you should! But when it comes to a commercial product like a game, you need to do the best work you can on work that will actually *get seen*. For example, you could spend hours constructing the most detailed, most awesome-looking birds' nest ever. And then you could meticulously place it at the base of the spire on top of the tallest skyscraper in the game's city. You could then model little baby chicks and animate them breaking out of their shells. And it looks great! You imagine the glee that a player will have when they discover this little secret you placed in the game's world. But, will the player actually see it? If you're making a game in which the player is unable to get to the roofs of buildings, the answer is no. And where did all that effort go?

Another example from my own experience—I know of a particular artist who spent a month constructing the best-looking teeth you have ever seen in a character's mouth. He did an amazing job getting every detail right. He individually modeled every tooth and wrapped the teeth in a pristine gum line that a dentist would cherish. Yet these teeth could have been a simple alpha plane, as far as the viewer could tell. All that work was completely unnoticed and unseen. This is the same reason the undersides of most shoes in a game are not all that detailed. They are rarely ever seen.

The point is to do the best you can on the work that will be seen and make an impact on the player. Do *not* do subpar work and use the excuse, "Well, the player won't really see this *all that often*." That's not acceptable. You have no idea what the hundreds and thousands of players will do after the game leaves your studio and enters the general public's hands. *All* of your work that makes it into a game should be as excellent as you can make it because it *can and will* be seen. If it won't be seen, then why do it at all?

The textures you make can be as detailed as you like. For mine, I'm going to make them simple, yet easy to read and understand the shapes. Feel free to follow along:

1. Just as you have in the previous chapters, you can use the Transfer Maps command to bake an Ambient Occlusion (AO) and normal map base texture for each of the four textures you UV mapped in the previous section (Figure 5.57).

2. If you are following along with me, you will begin with texturing the window blocks. Open Photoshop and open the baked window block AO texture (either your own or the one included on the DVD).

3. From the DVD texture sources, open the concrete-looking texture called con004 (or use your own texture source that you like). Drag it into your Photoshop file and move its layer below the AO layer.

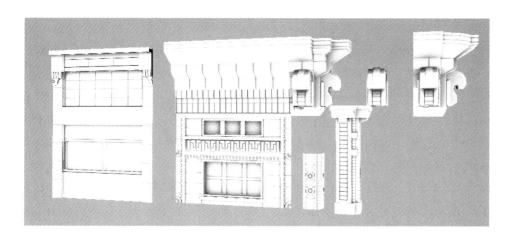

Figure 5.57
The AO textures baked for the low-resolution meshes

4. Change the AO layer's blending mode to Multiply. This will make the dark values of the AO render on top of whatever is below it.

5. Use the Free Transform tool (Ctrl+T) to resize the concrete image to fit on the window block module's portion of the texture space. You can rename the layer **Base**, indicating that it is the base texture layer that other layers will build on.

6. With the Base concrete layer selected, create a new Hue/Saturation adjustment layer above it. Change the color to a tan hue. If you are following along with me, I used a Hue value of -16 and a Saturation value of 68.

7. Next, create a Brightness/Contrast adjustment layer and increase both the brightness and contrast to give the surface a slightly more whitewashed look, as if it had been in the sun for years and years. I used a Brightness value of 15 and a Contrast value of 41. You'll have something similar to Figure 5.58.

8. Now you'll start adjusting the highs and lows of the surface and adding in some color variation. Create a new Hue/Saturation adjustment layer and increase the Lightness to 18.

Figure 5.58
A base wall texture

This brightens the entire image, which you don't want. Select the adjustment layer's mask (the white box on the layer next to the image thumbnail) and invert it using the Ctrl+I keyboard shortcut.

This makes the layer mask black and thus hides the effect of the adjustment layer. You only want this layer's brightness to affect the raised portions of the window block.

9. Make white your selected brush color (press D to change your colors to the default white and black, if they aren't already). Select the brush tool (or the B shortcut key) and with the layer mask still selected, paint strokes along the raised sections of the window block, such as along the vertical divider blocks on the left and right as well as the ledges and supports, and anything else you may have in your image that represents a surface that is higher than the rest of the surface around it.

10. Create another Brightness/Contrast adjustment layer. Increase the contrast levels to add more readability to the image. I used a Brightness value of -5 and a Contrast value of 23.

11. Once again, invert the layer mask so that it is fully black. Then paint white strokes on the raised-up areas of the image.

Those two adjustment layers take care of the highs. Now you'll add the lows using shadow and lowlights.

12. Create a new Hue/Saturation adjustment layer and decrease the Lightness value to something like -30, darkening the image substantially. Once again, invert the mask to make it black and use a white brush to paint along the lower areas of the image. You can also paint a thin stroke along the brick borders to make them pop more. With the highs and lows painted on, you can see something like Figure 5.59 beginning to emerge.

13. Now the texture may look a little too whitewashed. It did in my case, so I went back and added one more adjustment layer. To do the same, create a Levels adjustment layer. Increase the lower range of the Input Levels to something like 80, leaving the mid and high input level values alone.

Figure 5.59

Adding highlights and lowlights to the texture

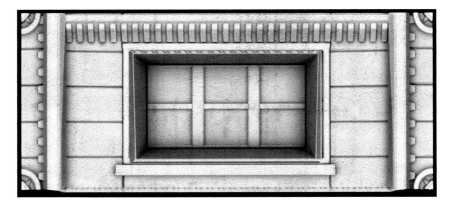

14. This time you won't invert the layer mask. Hold down the Control key and left-click the mask of one of the highlight adjustment layers from before. It doesn't matter which one. This will load the mask as a selection.

15. Select the layer mask for the new Levels adjustment layer. Choose black as your brush color and use the Fill command from under the Edit menu (or use the Alt+Delete shortcut key). This fills the selection with black and masks out the new Levels adjustment where the highlights are, making the Levels adjustment only affect the lower surface.

Texturing the Windows

The windows of the building can be done lots of different ways. You could even let them be their own textures so that you could have many different varieties of windows to choose from. For this project, you'll keep it relatively simple and give all the windows just dark tinted glass. Of course, feel free to adjust this to your own liking.

1. First, select the area that makes up the window frame. Open up a relatively simple metal texture, such as the Aluminum2 image from the DVD's source files.

2. With the metal image active, select all (Ctrl+A), copy (Ctrl+C), switch to your building texture with the window frame selection still active, and Paste Into (Shift+Ctrl+V).

   The Paste Into command will paste the copied image into the active selection as its own layer, making the selection an automatic layer mask.

3. Press Ctrl+U to open the Hue/Saturation adjustment command and lower the Lightness value down to something like -70, making the window frame a dark metal like in Figure 5.60.

4. Select the window area again, but deselect the window frame. This leaves only the glass window panes left in your selection. Create a new layer and place it below the window frame layer. Fill the selection with black.

Figure 5.60

The window frames now are in.

5. Ctrl+click the black windows to load them as a selection. Press Shift+Ctrl+V to use Paste Into once again, pasting the Aluminum texture into the glass window panes as their own layer. Change this new layer's Blending Mode to Linear Dodge, which creates a slight noise pattern.

6. Tune down the noise to be more subtle by lowering the layer's Opacity. This can be done to your preference. I lowered mine down to about 20 percent.

For the rest of the modules, you will literally do the same steps. You want all the modules to look consistent, so copy the adjustment layers you use for the first texture to use on the rest. The main difference you may want to make is adding some color variation for a few things, such as the decorative detail on the lower half of the small window block or the brick detail on the higher half of the base module. Once you're done you could have something similar to Figure 5.61.

Figure 5.61

The consistently textured modules

With the modules completed, you can then go about creating your buildings. It's simply a matter of putting the modules together like a big jigsaw puzzle (Figure 5.62).

Don't forget to break off the support strut to form Module 8!

Let's Light It Up

With modular modeling, you can create a system of modules (also called tinker toys by certain aspects of the industry) to create practically any environmental structure. You could create a modular system of dungeons for a game with a medieval theme, a modular street system to go along with the city, or modular spans to create bridges of any length. There are many possibilities that modular building can afford an environment artist.

Next, let's cast some light on the situation. In the next chapter, you'll learn about illumination and objects that cast light. Campfires, spot lights, street lights, flashlights, lanterns—all sorts of objects may need to illuminate in some way. Turn the page to learn more!

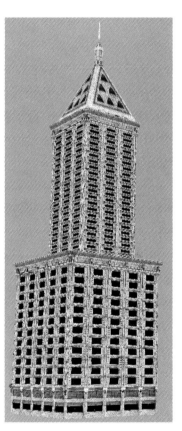

Figure 5.62

An example building constructed with all 10 modules

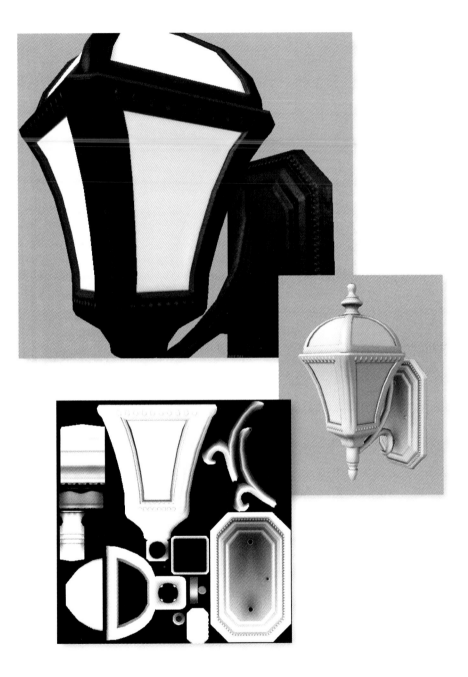

CHAPTER 6

Illuminators

There is no exact term, per se, for objects that cast light in a game. So, I'll just refer to such objects as illuminators. Sounds cool, don't you think? Illuminators are created the same way as other objects in that they are modeled, UV mapped, textured, and so on. The main difference is that illuminators are utilized as light sources and should have some sort of illuminating ability, whether it is a light bulb or magical innate glow of subterranean mushrooms. In this chapter, you'll create a simple illuminator and learn about the differences between illuminators and other, non-illuminating objects.

Understanding Illuminators

In most game engines, a light source is *not* a piece of game art. That is, when you see a glowing light bulb model in a video game, the light being cast from that model is not coming from the model at all but from an invisible object that is created and placed within the game engine (usually by a level designer but possibly by a skilled lighting artist). I'll refer to this invisible object as a *light source*. The light source and the illuminator are two separate things. The illuminator is the object that is meant to *represent* the light source, and that is what this chapter focuses on.

> There are a few game engines (such as the more current versions of the Unreal Engine) out there that are able to recognize the glow from an illuminator object and dynamically create a light source from it. But for most game engines, that isn't the case.

This is much the same as it is in Maya. You could model a light bulb with all the necessary components for illumination—the filament, the wires, the insulation, and so on—yet it still cannot turn on. It isn't real, after all. So, you must create a light source from the assortment of lights that Maya provides. Point lights, directional lights, area lights—all created from the ether to provide illumination. *These* are the sources of the light. The light bulb model is simply the illuminating object—the illuminator.

For this chapter, you'll create a light sconce. The sconce is modeled, UV'd, and textured much the same way as you have done for the other projects in this book; however, this time, you'll add one additional texture type—the emissive map or "glow" map.

The emissive map can either be grayscale or have color. If the map is grayscale, the color of the glow can sometimes be tinted with controls found in the game engine being used. Otherwise, the glow will be white. If the emissive map is colored, the glow will be of the same hue. Before you get too far into the ins and outs of the emissive map, first you need to create the model.

MAYA LIGHTS

Maya offers several different types of lights that you can use. Although not all have counterparts in most game editors, many do, so it's important to know the difference between a spot light and a point light when dealing with game levels. The relevant light types are as follows.

Directional lights Directional lights shine light in one specific direction on an infinite plane. For example, you could have a directional light at the origin of your scene and it will cast its light on every object in your scene from its designated direction, regardless of how close the object may be to the light.

Spot lights Spot lights light the environment within a cone of influence, just like a spot light in the real world. They have a point of origin, so they don't illuminate along an infinite plane like the directional light does. They also have settings for "barn doors" just as real life spot lights do. Adjusting a spot light's barn doors allows you to square off its sides, in case you don't want a circular lighted area, or to prevent the spot light from lighting certain objects on the edges of its cone of influence.

Point lights Point lights are lights that shine from a single point outward within a spherical area of influence. Point lights are probably one of the more widely used light types in game engines, as they are very versatile and are one of the cheaper light sources to render, in terms of the processing power required.

Ambient lights Ambient lights illuminate the entire area within its influence evenly. So there is no real "hot spot" to speak of. With a spot light, the closer an object is to the light source, the brighter it is lit. With an ambient light, every object is lit evenly with no regard for an object's relative position to the light source. By default, ambient lights do not cast shadows either, so they will illuminate an object on all sides. Ambient lights are generally used as fill lights, which illuminate an entire scene with a subtle amount of lighting while other light types handle the key lighting roles.

Lighting is extremely important in video game environments. A weak environment can be made extraordinary with excellent lighting. Conversely, an excellent environment can fall flat if its lighting doesn't hold up to the same level of excellence. Having knowledge of lighting and lighting techniques can make you invaluable to an environment team.

Project: Creating a Wall Sconce

Just as in the previous projects, you'll begin with creating a model of the wall sconce. This sconce will be a flared square shell design. Modeling the light bulb itself may not be necessary if the sconce is always on and glowing: The bright glow from the light can hide the interior of the lamp and therefore hide the bulb. If the sconce can be turned off, however, the interior may be visible and the bulb displayed. For such cases, the bulb would need to be created.

1. First, create a cube that is 3 units wide, 5 units tall, and about 0.25 units deep. This will be the wall bracket.

2. Line the cube up so that the back is even with the origin. The origin line will act as the "wall" that the sconce is attached to.

3. Select the four corner edges and bevel them. If you are following along with my scale, the default Offset value should work fine.

4. Select the beveled edges (all eight of them) and bevel them again. This time, decrease the Offset down to 0.1.

5. Select the front face and bevel it, decreasing the Offset to about 0.2.

6. Use the Extrude and Bevel commands to create three tiers to the wall bracket, as in Figure 6.1.

7. In the side view, create a tall cube that is 3 units tall, and 1.5 units wide and deep. Increase the Subdivisions value to be 5 along the height of the cube. These subdivisions will allow the cube to be flared in the following steps.

8. Change the menu set to Animation, which gives you access to the animation class of menus. Select the new cube, if it isn't selected already, and select Create Deformers → Nonlinear → Flare. This will apply a Flare deformer to the cube.

9. Increase the End Flare X and Z values to 2 to flare out the top of the cube. Modify the Curve value until you have the curvature that you want for the sconce (Figure 6.2).

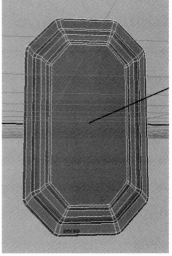

Figure 6.1

The three-tiered wall bracket for the wall sconce

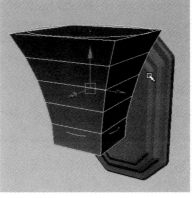

Figure 6.2

The start of the sconce shape using the Flare deformer

10. When you have a shape you are happy with, delete the sconce's history. This will remove the Flare deformer and finalize the shape change.

11. Bevel the vertical edges of the sconce, adjusting the Offset to about 0.3.

12. Select the top and bottom faces of the sconce and bevel them as well, using an Offset of approximately 0.15.

    At this point, you may want to rescale the sconce in relation to the wall bracket. I scaled mine slightly shorter and a tad wider.

13. Select the bottom face and extrude it down about 0.25 units and scale it inward a bit to curve the edges toward the center. Select the bottom face again and extrude down about 0.5 units. Scale it inward to about half the original width.

14. In the Channel Box, scroll down to the bottom of the most recent Extrude's options to the Divisions value. Increase the Divisions to 3, adding some horizontal cuts to the extruded shape. Select

Figure 6.3

The tapered base of the sconce

the middle row of edges (or faces) and, locking the y-axis, scale your selection inward to curve the shape as in Figure 6.3. You can slightly bevel the bottom face.

15. Select the eight vertical edge loops on the corners of the sconce and bevel them slightly to soften their sharpness.

16. Using the Insert Edge Loop tool (from the Edit Mesh menu in the Polygons menu set), insert four edges that form the boundary for the selection of faces you can see in Figure 6.4. This is for the opening that the light will shine through.

17. When you have the window faces created, select them and extrude them inward slightly. Scale the extrusion in to create a beveled edge to form the lip of the window. Then, extrude again, this time extruding deeper into the sconce.

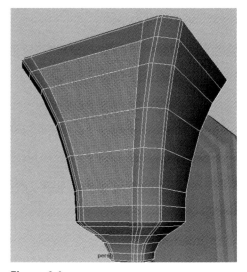

Figure 6.4

The selected area that is created using four inserted edge loops

Instead of doing this extrusion process four times, to keep all four sides identical, you can delete the other four sides' faces and duplicate the edited side. Delete the other three sides, being sure to leave the top and bottom faces. Don't duplicate the fourth, remaining side just yet. You're not quite done with it.

At this point, rather than having flat corners, you can add any decorative details that you like. I'm going to add a rounded ridge up the center of the corner faces.

18. Using the Insert Edge Loop tool, insert three vertical edge loops up the center, left, and right sides of one of the corner surfaces.

19. Select the edges in the center, next to the window cavity, and move them outward. To soften the edge here, you can bevel your selection (Figure 6.5).

20. Create three duplicates of the remaining side of the sconce and rotate them around for the missing sides. Delete any faces you don't need and combine them together, merging the edges where they meet.

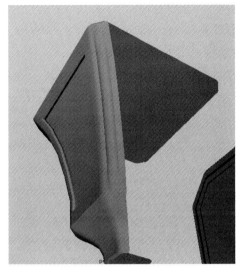

Figure 6.5

Adding a rounded ridge up the middle of the corner's surface

Creating a Domed Cap

To cap the sconce, you'll add a domed shape that the light can escape through. It'll follow the main shape's design in that it will have a square base. To start, you'll use curves to create a quarter of the shape and then duplicate it for the remainder.

1. In the Top view, create a circular curve by selecting Create → NURBS Primitives → Circle. Scale it up to encompass the entire sconce but have it cross over the tops of the sconce's corners.

2. Rotate it 90 degrees along the x-axis to stand vertical, and 45 degrees in the y-axis to point it diagonally from corner to corner. Position it so that it is halfway inserted into the sconce. If you need to, scale the circle up so that it extends across the sconce at the corners.

3. Scale the circle down in the y-axis slightly to squash it a bit. You can see what I mean in Figure 6.6.

4. Select the circle and look for the Sweep Input value found in the Channel Box under the makeNurbCircle1 node. Decrease the Sweep value to 90. This makes the curve only extend 90 degrees rather than the full 360 degrees.

Figure 6.6

The circle positioned on the sconce

5. Duplicate it and rotate the duplicate 90 degrees to form a wedge shape with the two curves.

6. Next, you'll create a third curve that connects the two wedge curves at their base. Select the CV Curve tool from the Create menu. Hold down the C key to toggle Snap To Curve mode and middle-click and drag on one of the curves. A point will appear on the curve, following your cursor. Move the point down to the bottom of the curve and release the middle-mouse button.

7. With the C key still being held down, middle-mouse click and drag on the other curve, dragging a point down to the base of it. Release the C key and the middle mouse button and press Enter to finish the curve.

8. This is the perfect opportunity to use a new tool, the Birail tool. Switch your menu sets to Surfaces. From here, select Surfaces → Birail → Birail 1 Tool → Options. In the options, change the following settings:

Output geometry	Polygons
Type	Quads
Tessellation method	General
U type and V type	Per span # of iso params
Number U and V	1

9. With the Birail 1 tool active, simply follow the onscreen prompts found down in the Help Line at the bottom left of the screen. I'll also walk you through it here:

   a. First, select the Profile curve. That would be the line that connects the two rounded "Rail" curves at their base.

   b. Next, select the two Rail curves.

   c. Watch in amazement as the surface appears!

   You should have a shape similar to Figure 6.7 appear.

Figure 6.7

The Birail surface formed for the domed cap

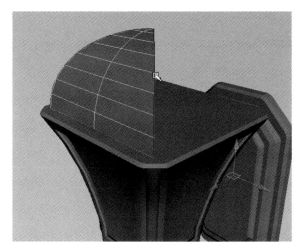

10. In the Channel Box, under the nurbs Tessellate1 Input item, increase the V Number value to about 12. This will add a lot of geometry to the surface, but it will give you the ability to create another window cavity for the light that will eventually shine through.

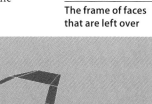

11. First, delete the tip of the geometry wedge where all of the faces come to a point. Then, select all the faces in the center of the wedge of geometry, leaving the outer row of faces unselected. Delete the selected faces. You should have a frame of faces remaining, as you see in Figure 6.8. You can delete the edges that are left over along the top and bottom faces (using the Delete Edge/Vertex command from the Edit Mesh menu).

12. Duplicate the frame around to make the other three sides of the shape. Combine and merge them together.

13. Use the Select Edge Loop tool from the Select menu and double-click an edge from each of the four corners to select the vertical edge loops on each corner. Apply a Bevel to them to round off the hard edges. Feel free to increase the Segments value to 2 if they don't seem rounded enough for your tastes.

14. Select the entire frame and extrude it about 0.1 units, giving the entire object some thickness.

15. In the Front view, use the CV Curve tool to draw the profile shape for a decorative top for the dome. It can be whatever shape you like. Make sure your first and last points are on the origin line (toggle grid snap by holding the X key if you need to). Mine is sort of chess-piece-shaped, like you see in Figure 6.9.

> You only need the profile curve to form one half of the shape you want, not the entire thing.

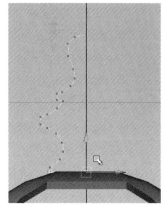

Figure 6.9

The profile curve for the top piece of the dome

16. Once you have the profile shape you like, switch your menu set to Surfaces and select Surfaces → Revolve → Options. In the options, make certain that you are using the polygon output settings that you set back in step 8. When your settings are correct, click the Revolve button.

If you want to adjust your shape after revolving, you can simply adjust the control vertices of the profile curve and the history that is still present on the mesh will update its shape in real time. Once you are happy with the revolved results, you can delete the history on the revolved shape and delete the profile curve.

17. You can use the same process to create another decorative piece at the base of the sconce as well, or you can create a cylinder and use a series of Extrudes and Bevels to get the results you want. With whichever process you decide to use, make sure to create it with the same style as the one on top of the sconce so that they match stylistically. You can see how mine looks in Figure 6.10.

18. Next, you can fill in the space on the dome by creating the glass that will be illuminated in a later step. This can easily be done by using the Snap To Point command while creating the polygon using the Create Polygon tool.

    Hold the V key to toggle Snap To Point and use the points along the inner edge loop of the dome frame to create the glass surface. Duplicate it to fill in the dome on the other three sides. (Figure 6.11)

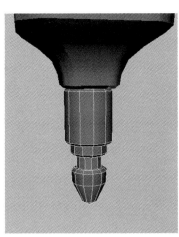

Figure 6.10

The bottom decoration for the sconce

Figure 6.11

The filled-in glass dome on top of the sconce

Attaching the Sconce to the Bracket

The sconce shape is pretty much in place, so now you can work on creating the attachment to the wall bracket. This can, of course, be done any number of ways with whatever style you choose. I'll be using a decorative vine-like design.

1. In the Side view, use the CV Curve tool to draw out an arcing curve from the base of the sconce to the top of the forward-facing surface of the wall bracket.

2. Draw another curve starting from the lower middle half of the first curve and curve it into a loop that flows near the lower part of the wall bracket.

    You can edit these curves to shape them however you'd like. Mine look like Figure 6.12.

3. Once you have the path curves shaped the way you like, you can create a profile curve. It could be just a simple circle, but for the sake of visual interest, you could create a more interesting shape. If you'd like to follow along with me, first create a NURBS circle from the Create → NURBS Primitives menu.

Double the circle's Sections value to 16. With the increased points on the circle, you have more control to edit the shape. I manipulated mine to look sort of mushroom-shaped, like in Figure 6.13.

4. Select the profile curve and Shift-select one of the path curves. Within the Surfaces menu set, choose Surfaces → Extrude. Do it a second time with the other path curve.

At this time, you can modify the path curve points to continue to adjust the vine-like shapes to your liking. You'll want them to be at equal distances from the bracket, with about an inch or two of space between them.

Figure 6.12

The initial curves for the wall bracket connection

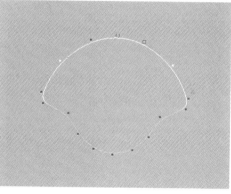

Figure 6.13

The profile curve shape

You should have already set the polygonal output settings for the Extrude from a previous step, but in case you haven't, make certain you use the settings found in step 8 of the prior section in the Extrude options.

5. Select the edges that border the end of one of the vine-like objects and use the Mesh → Fill Hole command to fill it in with a polygon.

6. Select the new face and use the Extrude command to extend and taper the end of the shape. You can also scale the existing edge loops to smoothly taper the end of the surface. Do the same for the other (Figure 6.14).

7. Once you are happy with the shape of the connector shapes, you can create a simple cylinder with a beveled lip to serve as the connection between them and the bracket, like you see in Figure 6.15.

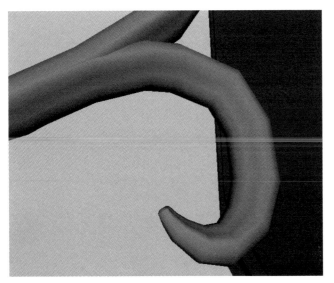

Figure 6.14

Tapering the end of the connecting shapes

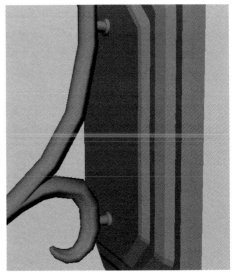

Figure 6.15

Attaching the sconce to the bracket

Adding Decorative Details

The sconce is essentially complete, but you don't necessarily have to be finished. You can continue to add details to the sconce and the bracket to decorate and detail it to your heart's desire. I took a bunch of spheres and arrayed them around the bracket as well as the sconce itself. These will catch the light in an interesting way and add visual interest (Figure 6.16).

Figure 6.16

The final details on the sconce

Creating the Low-Resolution Mesh

With the high-resolution mesh complete, the low-resolution geometry can now be created. Just as with other projects in this book, the low-resolution mesh will receive the details from the high-resolution mesh through baking normal map details. You can create the low-resolution geometry in many ways. I find it easiest to simply duplicate the high-resolution geometry and remove the unnecessary polygons to get the low-resolution geometry that I want, but this method isn't always possible if the geometry is too complex.

1. First, select your entire high-resolution wall sconce and apply a new material by right-clicking and choosing Assign New Material → Lambert from the marking menu that opens.

2. The attributes of the new material should open. Lower the Color slider, making the mesh a dark hue.

3. Create a new layer in the Layer Bar. Double-click to open its properties and rename the layer **Hi**. With your wall sconce meshes selected, right-click the layer and choose Assign Selected.

4. Create another new layer and name it **Lo**. This will be the layer your low-resolution mesh will be assigned to.

5. Select the wall bracket (not any of the decorative details). Press Ctrl+D to duplicate it.

6. With the duplicate selected, right-click the Lo layer and assign the new mesh to it. With the mesh still selected, right-click in empty space and from the marking menu, choose Assign Existing Material → Lambert1. This will assign the existing default material to the duplicate wall bracket.

7. Next, select all of the duplicate bracket's vertices. Hold the W key and click to bring up the Move tool options. Hover your cursor over the Axis option. From the new options that appear, hover your cursor over Normal and release the left-mouse button.

    This switches your Move tool to Normal Axis movement, which allows you to perform the next step.

8. With all the vertices selected and with the Move tool set to Normal Axis movement mode, click and drag on the move handle labeled N to slightly expand the mesh to encompass the original wall bracket geometry.

9. Now that the duplicate mesh encloses the original, you can begin to remove unnecessary geometry to lower the density of its polycount. The goal is to remove geometry that will not affect the duplicate's ability to continue to encase the original high-resolution mesh.

    In Figure 6.17, you can see that my low-resolution wall bracket, although very low in polygonal density, is still able to encompass the entire high-resolution mesh. (This is hinted at by the bits barely poking through in the upper-right side. Don't worry, that won't affect the quality of the normal map that you'll eventually bake.)

10. The next piece of geometry you can simplify is the bottom decorative element below the sconce's light. Select it, duplicate and expand it just as you did with the wall bracket in the previous steps, and remove edge loops that are unnecessary for the shape.

11. For the looping, vine-like pieces that connect the sconce to the bracket, you'll follow the same process. Duplicate and expand both pieces. Remove edge loops that aren't necessary to keep the mesh surrounding the high-resolution geometry.

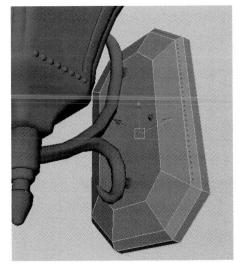

Figure 6.17
The low-resolution wall bracket encasing the high-resolution geometry

12. Once you have the two shapes, select them both and select Mesh → Booleans → Union. This will combine the two meshes together while deleting the geometry that intersected them. This will leave behind some ugly geometry (Figure 6.18).

13. Clean the geometry here so that it flows better between the two shapes and still encapsulates the original high-resolution meshes. Using Snap To Point and Merge, you can merge the extraneous points together to form the cleaner lines necessary for the part.

Figure 6.18

Ugly geometry left over from the Union Boolean operation

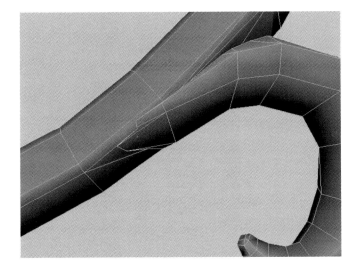

You can continue this process with the rest of the geometry, creating a low-resolution version of the sconce. Once you have the low-resolution mesh completed (Figure 6.19), you can start the UV process.

UV Mapping the Sconce

For UV mapping the sconce, you'll find it easier to stack UV shells of identical parts of the sconce. For instance, you can stack each of the four sides of the sconce on top of each other so that each side uses the same texture space. This will save space on your texture and allow for more detail. You can do this for the four sides of the dome on top of the sconce as well. It's best to choose a forward-facing side so as to limit the amount of influence the other surfaces of the object will have on the resulting texture bakes.

As always, keep in mind the size of the item in relation to the scale of its UV shell in the UV Texture Editor (found under the Window menu). If the object is tiny, its UV shell should be equally small in relation to the rest of the UV shells in the texture. There are exceptions, however. The main detail of an object—that is, the main part of the object that people will focus their attention on—could have a slightly larger scale attributed to its UVs. This is the same sort of method used in character texturing, where the character's face and eyes are given a larger amount of UV space, since that is where most people will focus their attention.

Just as focused parts have larger UV space, parts that are completely out of focus, such as the bottom of shoes, the interior of a character's mouth, or (in this case) the back of a wall bracket, should have smaller UV space given.

Figure 6.19

The low-resolution wall sconce

1. Select the faces that make up three of the four sides of your low-resolution sconce. Delete them. With the remaining geometry (the side, top, and bottom), UV map them normally.

2. Once your UVs are laid out for the remainder of the sconce, duplicate the faces on the side of the geometry (you may want to extract the top and bottom faces first using the Mesh → Extract command) and rotate them around the sconce to fill in the empty space.

   The four sides of the sconce will now share the same UV space. If you need to reposition the UV shells for the sconce, make certain you select the UV shells for all four sides, as it is easy to accidently move one side and not the others.

   You won't combine the four sides together just yet. You will do so after the textures are baked in the next section. You can UV the squared dome shape on top of the sconce in the same manner, sharing UV space for all four sides. For the rest of the object, however, you can UV map them normally (Figure 6.20).

Figure 6.20

The final UVs
of the sconce

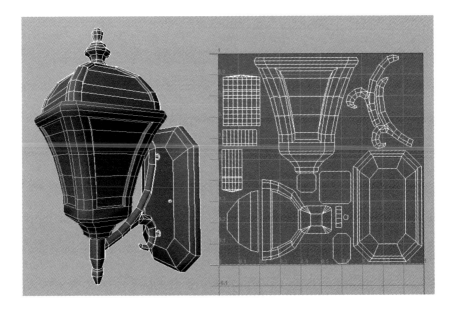

Baking Texture Sources

As with all game assets, the next stage is to bake the high-resolution details to the low-resolution mesh to create the ambient occlusion (AO) and normal map source files.

1. Select your low-resolution geometry, excluding the duplicated sides of the sconce that share UV space. You only want *one* side of the low-resolution sconce and dome meshes to be selected. (The same is true with any other meshes that share UV space.)

2. Switch to the Rendering menu set and choose Lighting/Shading → Transfer Maps. Since your low-resolution meshes were selected, they'll automatically be loaded in the Target Meshes section of the Transfer Maps dialog box.

3. Select all of your high-resolution meshes and click the Add Selected button under the Source Meshes section of the Transfer Maps dialog box. If you have a lot of high-resolution meshes, it may take a minute or so for them all to load.

4. Next, indicate which maps you want to bake. You'll want an ambient occlusion map and a normal map. Click the appropriate buttons under the Output Maps section to make them appear below.

5. In each map's given section, indicate a location to save the image as well as the file format. As always, you'll choose Targa (tga).

Targa is probably the most common image format used in games, but occasionally, other file formats are used, such as DDS and BMP formats. Consult your supervisor for details regarding the map types used for your project.

Below, in the Common Output sections, you can specify a file resolution. For the previous projects in this book, you've generally used a relatively large resolution, such as 1024×1024. This is fine for larger objects (like the dune buggy or building), but for small items, you generally want a smaller resolution.

6. For this project, choose 512×512 for both the Maya Common Output and Mental Ray Common Output settings.

Once your settings are ready, click the Bake button and wait for Maya to finish generating the texture sources. You can see how mine turned out in Figure 6.21.

At this point, you can combine and merge the separate sides of the sconce to make one single mesh. You can also continue to lower the geometry resolution of the low-resolution mesh even further, if you want; however, be careful not to affect the UV shell boundary geometry, or you may see your texture stretch badly.

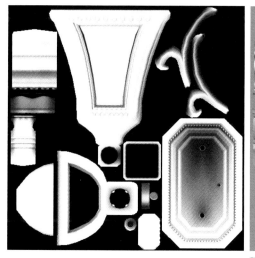
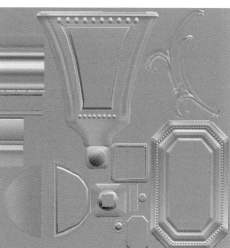

Figure 6.21

The generated AO and normal maps applied to the sconce

Creating the Final Textures

Using your generated texture sources, you can create the final textures in Photoshop. For this project, you'll be making the usual diffuse, normal, and specular maps. In addition, you'll also create an emissive map (or "glow" map) to control the sconce's glow effect.

1. First, start Photoshop and open your baked AO texture. Double-click it and click OK on the dialog box that opens to change the image from a locked *background* to an editable layer. You can rename this layer AO.

2. Click the New Layer button (at the bottom of the Layer palette). Drag the new layer below the AO layer. Click the Foreground swatch on the left side of the interface and choose a dark color. Fill the empty layer with this color (Alt+Delete) and rename it BaseColor.

3. Select the AO layer and change its Blending Mode from Normal to Multiply. You should get something like Figure 6.22.

Figure 6.22

The sconce with a base color

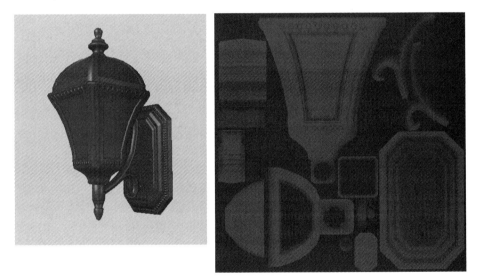

To help in the texture creation process, you can create a UV snapshot. The UV snapshot will produce an image of your UV layout that you can bring into Photoshop to use as a guide.

4. Back in Maya, select all of your low-resolution sconce meshes. Open the UV Texture Editor window and choose Polygons → UV Snapshot.

   In the UV Snapshot dialog box, choose the 512 for Size X and Y, Targa for the Image Format, and choose a save location and name (such as UV.tga) for the File Name setting.

5. Return to Photoshop, and open the UV.tga file you just created. Drag and drop it into your texture's Photoshop file and drag its layer to the top of the layer palette's stack.

Set its Blending Mode to Screen and lower its Opacity down to something like 20 percent. Rename this layer UV.

You can toggle this layer on and off to get a guide for your mesh's UV layout that is helpful for knowing where exactly a texture detail will show up on the final mesh.

> Make certain to hide the UV layer when saving your textures. Otherwise, your model will have wireframe lines all over it!

Figure 6.23

The area on the texture that will eventually illuminate

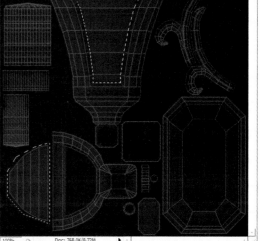

6. Create a new layer above the BaseColor layer. Name it Glow. Use the Polygonal Lasso selection tool to select the area that will be glowing on your sconce. Remember to have the UV layer visible to help you make your selection accurately (Figure 6.23).

7. Choose a yellow-orange color and, with the Glow layer active, fill in the selection.

8. Open a suitable, low-contrast metal source texture. On the DVD, you can find and use the aluminum.jpg file that I have provided if you don't have something you like better. Drag the source into your Photoshop file above the ColorBase layer but *below* the Glow layer.

9. If you're using my provided texture, position it on the image so that it covers all of it and change its Blending Mode to Color Dodge. This causes the metal detail to soften enough to look like it has had relatively mild weathering. Rename this layer Metal.

10. Above the Glow layer, create a Hue/Saturation adjustment layer (by clicking the Create New Fill or Adjustment Layer button at the bottom of the Layer palette). Increase its Lightness setting slightly—to about 8. Then click OK.

11. Select the masking swatch next to the adjustment layer's thumbnail icon and fill it with black (or simply invert the white color with the Ctrl+I shortcut command).

12. With a white brush and with the adjustment layer's mask still selected, paint over the raised portions of the sconce, increasing their brightness slightly (Figure 6.24).

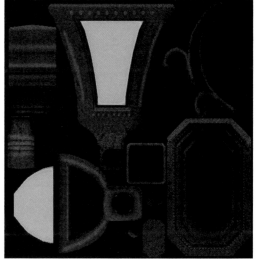

Figure 6.24

Highlights added to the sconce texture

13. Create another Hue/Saturation adjustment layer, this time decreasing the Lightness setting to about -35. Fill its mask with black and with a white brush, paint in the low areas of the texture with shadow.

This will be your diffuse texture! Save it as `Sconce_Diffuse.tga`, and save the Photoshop file as well.

Creating the Specular Texture

With the diffuse texture completed, now start the specular texture. We want the specular texture to be subtle, but not so subtle as to make no difference.

1. First, why don't you get a little organized? Select all of your current layers (except the UV layer) and select Layer → New → New Group From Layers. Name the new group `Diffuse` and click OK. Your diffuse texture layers will all go into their own group folder.

2. Select the Metal layer and duplicate it by dragging it to the New Layer button. Drag the duplicated layer out of the Diffuse folder and below the UV layer.

3. Ctrl+left-click the Glow layer to load it as a selection. With the duplicate Metal layer still selected, fill the selection with black. Change the

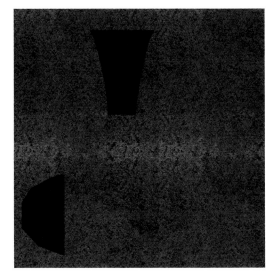

Figure 6.25
The specular texture

duplicate Metal layer's Blending Mode to Normal and rename it `Metal_Spec`. If you like, you can make a new group folder for this layer called Specular. Save this as your specular texture and call it `Sconce_Specular.tga` (Figure 6.25).

The reason you filled in the glowing area with black is so that there won't be a specular highlight visible within where the light should just be glowing brightly.

Creating the Emissive Texture

The normal map that you generated is actually suitable just as it is. So, all that's left is the new emissive texture! The emissive texture will indicate where on the model it should glow and with what color.

1. Select the Glow layer and duplicate it by dragging it to the New Layer button. Drag this new layer out of the Diffuse folder and place it above the Specular folder (not in it!). Rename it `Glow_Em`.

2. Create a new layer and place it below the Glow_Em layer. Fill it with black.

   This is actually all you really need to create an emissive texture. However, you can add a lot of interest to the emissive texture by paying attention to how the glow of the light should actually work.

3. Create a new layer and place it above the Glow_Em layer. Hide the black layer that is below it and hide the Specular folder. You should be able to see the diffuse texture beneath the visible emissive layers. Rename your new layer Glow_Falloff.

4. With the same yellow-orange color as the glow, start painting around the sconce where the light of the glow should hit it. You would see it on each of the decorative spheres surrounding the sconce and wall bracket, as well as on the arm of the support frame.

5. Also pay attention to where the light of the glow would *not* cast, such as the shadow the support arm would cast onto the wall bracket. Continue to think logically about where the light would cast and paint in those details.

6. Lower the Glow_Falloff layer's Opacity down to around 25%. It should look something like Figure 6.26.

7. Once you're happy with how the glow looks, unhide the black layer separating the emissive and diffuse layers and save the result as Sconce_Glow.tga.

   With the falloff details of the emissive texture included, you can create a lot more believability.

Figure 6.26
The glow falloff to be applied in the emissive texture

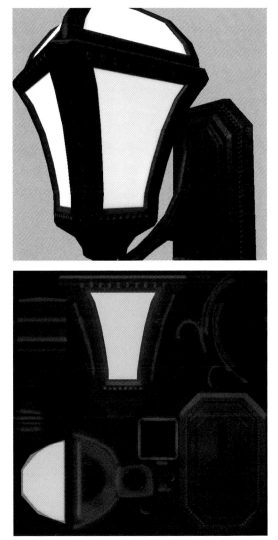

In the Home Stretch!

With this project I hope you were able to see that, even with a small, seemingly insignificant prop like a wall sconce, you can create a lot of detail and get a lot of added atmosphere for any environment. Another element that adds depth to an environment is movement. You'll explore this concept in the next chapter.

CHAPTER 7

Ambient Movement

There is no exact terminology used in the game industry for objects that *move*. It generally just comes down to the art lead asking an artist, "Hey, can you animate this?" So for the sake of this chapter, I'll just refer to such objects as *movers*. Movers are just like any other object and they are created using the same methods. The main difference is that movers are bound with a skeleton and, obviously, animated so that they move. In this chapter, you'll create a simple mover and go through the process of rigging and animating it.

Understanding Movers

Not too long ago, back when 3D was still relatively new in the game industry, animation was rather expensive. There were only so many moving parts that could be rendered per frame, and these were usually maximized by spending them on the characters and enemies rather than on the environment. The original *Resident Evil* is a good example of this. It used prerendered backgrounds to achieve its level of environment detail because real-time graphics just weren't up to snuff back then. The downside of prerendered graphics, however, is that they don't move. They're static. It's like a photograph with 3D characters running around on top of it.

Another example is the popular *Final Fantasy VII*, the first 3D game in the *Final Fantasy* series. At the time it was revolutionary, but if you were to look at it with today's standards in mind, you may notice that the characters are all made out of separate pieces, almost like action figures or Lego people.

Today, game engines are very robust and capable of doing things barely imaginable by the designers of the first generation of 3D games. And the benefit to the environment artist is that, finally, a game's locale can have just as much interesting movement as the characters that inhabit it. Switches can be flipped, doors can open and shut (without switching to a loading screen!), and miscellaneous background machines can actually look as if they are doing something suitably mechanical.

Project: Creating an Industrial Fan

For this chapter, you'll create an industrial fan. Industrial fans are a staple of the factory environment and easily add a lot of movement to a scene. Having some rusty contraption spinning slowly in the background with suitably grating sound effects can add a lot to making a scary scene that much creepier. Or in a more functional environment, it can make a scene seem as if it is actually working and that something is happening behind the walls, even if the player can't actually see it.

> Before starting, make sure you set your project to your project directory by going to File → Project → Set.

1. Start by going to the Side view and creating an elongated U-shaped curve about 10 units high in the y-axis, as shown in Figure 7.1.

2. Select it and, under the Surfaces menu set, select Surfaces → Revolve → Options. Make sure the output of the Revolve command is polygons, as it has been in other projects in this book, and choose Z as the Axis Preset. This will make the z-axis the axis used to revolve the curve. Press the Revolve button.

   You should then get a circular, spool-like shape. This will be the beginning of the fan's circular housing.

3. Increase the V Number value under the nurbsTessellate1 Input node (found in the Channel Box) to 3 or 4 to make the shape's roundness smoother.

4. Select the entire shape and return to the Polygons menu set. Apply an Extrude command from the Edit Mesh menu and extrude the shape outward slightly, about 0.17 units—just to give it a bit of a lip on the edge and some thickness.

   You can adjust the shape's edge loops to get a shape that's pleasing to you. Mine turned out like Figure 7.2.

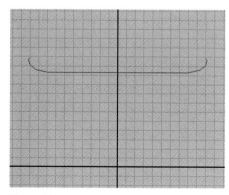

Figure 7.1
Beginning the fan shape with a simple curve

Figure 7.2
The fan housing

5. For the center of the fan, you'll use the Revolve function once again. Create a curve in the Side view that looks something like Figure 7.3. This will be the start of the fan's motor.

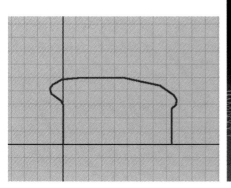

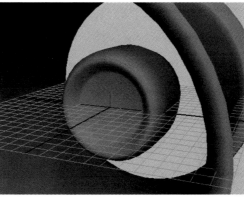

Figure 7.3

The profile curve for the fan motor and the result after revolving

6. Once revolved, place it in the center of the fan housing. Select the front face and, using a couple of simple Extrudes and Bevels, bring out a central detail to serve as an axis, such as my example shown in Figure 7.4. You can add more details, such as bolts or screws, to your own preference.

Figure 7.4

The motor's axis given more details

7. The next step is to create the fan blades. Create a cube that is about 1 unit wide, 7 units tall, and about 6.5 units deep. Increase the cube's Subdivisions Height to 5 and Subdivisions Depth to 2, giving it a single division in the middle of the wide side of the cube.

You want the blade to be shaped like the blade of an airplane propeller—curved with a slight twist to make the circulation of air pull in a certain direction.

8. Select the outer vertical edge loops and scale them inward slightly, tapering the ends like you see in Figure 7.5. Once they've been tapered, bevel them with a slight rounded edge.

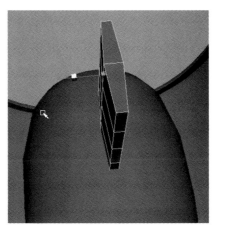

Figure 7.5

The fan blade tapered toward the outer edges

9. Now select the middle vertical edge loop and bevel it, which gives you two edge loops in the middle of the blade to work with. Scale them inward to your own preference, making the bulged center of the blade curve out a bit more gradually.

10. Once you have the blade shaped to your liking, you can add more details such as divots or screws and bolts. I used a few Difference Boolean operations to carve some divots into my blade.

It's time to do the twist! There are two major lines of thought when it comes to something like this—accuracy and dynamism. It'll be up to your individual project director to determine the project's preference for you. Some people want to ensure that everything is done to the utmost accuracy. Others just want the fan to look cool! Keep your own preference in mind when doing the twist in the next step. You can twist the fan blade to look accurate, or you can just make it look cool to you. Sometimes, accuracy *does* look cool, so don't rule accuracy out completely if cool is the look you are going for.

11. In either case, select the fan blade geometry, switch to the Animation menu set, and select Create Deformers → Nonlinear → Twist. A Twist deformer will be applied to your mesh.

In the twist1 Inputs (in the Channel Box) you have several settings for your Twist deformer. Adjust these to your liking and style. I ended up with a more realistic twist using a Start Angle value of 13.75 and an End Angle value of 24. You may also need to rotate your fan blade geometry if you're having trouble getting the exact look you want.

12. When you have the fan blade geometry completed, duplicate and rotate several fan blades around the motor like in Figure 7.6. If you need to, you can adjust the size of the fan housing to make the fan more proportional now that you have a better idea of the size of your fan.

13. Just as you did with the axis detail in the front of the motor, you can create an exhaust port in the back of the motor. For this detail, I went with a more "make it look cool" attitude instead of strict accuracy. It's more fun that way! By just using a series of simple Extrudes and Bevels, I came up with Figure 7.7. You are free to do whatever detail looks good to you.

14. You can continue to detail your industrial fan however you see fit. I added

Figure 7.6

The fan blades in place around the motor

some bolts along the outer rim of the fan housing as well as an array of indentions along the rim of the exhaust port to add a little bit of visual interest (using the Extrude command). You can see what I created in Figure 7.8.

Figure 7.7
Adding an exhaust port to the back of the fan motor

Figure 7.8
Continue adding details as you see fit

Creating a Base

Next, you can add a base to the fan to ground it to the floor, although sometimes these types of fans are suspended in the air or embedded into a wall system.

1. Create a thin, trapezoidal cube that intersects the base of the fan, as in Figure 7.9.

2. Duplicate it for the opposite side. Duplicate it a third time and scale it thicker to fill in the area between the two outer cubes. Shrink its width so that it's not as wide as the outer cubes of the frame.

Figure 7.9
The start of the industrial fan's base

3. Insert an edge loop in the middle of the center cube and scale it wider, matching the width of the cube's widest point. Lift it up slightly so that it's off the floor line. You should have something similar to Figure 7.10.

Figure 7.10

The base in place

4. In the Front view, create a large cylinder that matches the size of the industrial fan housing's opening. Scale it out so that it extends beyond the width of the base shapes. This will be the negative-space object that you use to carve out the unwanted sections of the base.

5. Duplicate the large cylinder twice, giving you a total of three. In turn, use the cylinders to carve out the unwanted space of each of the three meshes that make up the base using the Difference Boolean command. When you're done, it should look like Figure 7.11.

6. Bevel the outer edges of the base shapes to round their corners. You can also add two thin cubes below the two outer shapes to serve as supports, as in Figure 7.12.

Figure 7.11

The base now doesn't intersect the fan housing.

Figure 7.12

The finished high-resolution mesh

Creating the Low-Resolution Model

Now that you've finished the high-resolution mesh, you can begin to create the low-resolution mesh. Just as you have done in previous projects, you'll be duplicating the meshes and expanding the duplicates to encompass the higher detailed models.

Figure 7.13

The low-resolution meshes

1. Create a new layer in the Layer Bar and name it `Hi`. Assign all of your high-resolution meshes to it.

2. Create a new layer and name it `Lo`. As you begin to create your low-resolution meshes, assign them to this layer.

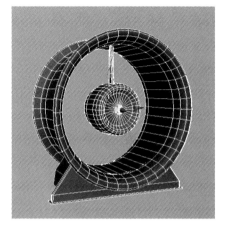

As with the other projects in this book, the main goal is to create low-resolution meshes for each unique piece of the model. This would include the base, the housing, the motor, and one of the fan blades (Figure 7.13).

Creating the UV Mapping

With the low-resolution meshes created and assigned to their own layer, it's time for UV mapping in preparation for texturing.

1. Select the outer ring of faces on the housing and apply a Cylindrical UV Map from the Create UVs menu. If yours is anything like mine, you'll probably need to rotate the mapping gizmo to correspond with the shape of the fan housing.

   You can do this by clicking the red hash mark on the corner of the mapping manipulator to activate the gizmo. The UV mapping manipulator gizmo is just like the gizmo used when extruding. By clicking the blue outer circle, it will toggle the cardinal direction manipulators, which will allow you to rotate the manipulator more easily. Rotate it to fit the shape (usually 90 degrees).

Figure 7.14

The UVs laid out in the UV Editor

2. In the UV Texture Editor (from the Window menu) you can see the UV shell that resulted from the cylindrical UV map. Reposition it to get it out of the way.

3. Select the rest of the housing's faces and perform another Cylindrical UV Map on the rest. Reposition the resulting shell in the UV Editor.

4. Continue to unwrap the UVs for the rest of the meshes using the techniques learned in the previous UV mapping sections of this book.

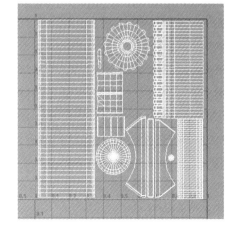

5. Once you have the UV shells in the UV Texture Editor, you can reposition them within the 0–1 space in the upper-right square of the editor's grid (Figure 7.14).

Completing the Model

Since we've now gone over this process six times in the last six chapters, I think it's safe to skip a little ahead. If you feel you need the rest of the process presented step-by-step, you can refer to the video reference included on the DVD.

Now that you have the low-resolution meshes, use the Transfer Maps command to bake 1024×1024 AO and normal maps for texture sources. You can also lower the resolution of the mesh further, deleting every other edge loop, but being careful to maintain your UV shell border edges. You should then have something similar to Figure 7.15.

Figure 7.15

The completed
low-resolution mesh

Creating the Textures

With your source textures baked, you can go into Photoshop and complete the texturing process, finishing your diffuse, normal, and specular maps.

1. In Photoshop, open your AO source image. Double-click its Background layer and click OK on the dialog window that opens, which converts it into a normal, editable layer. Rename the layer **AO**.

2. If you have some areas on the AO map that you don't want in your final, take some time to clean those areas up.

   For instance, in mine, you can see where each fan blade was near the fan housing along the interior of the housing mesh due to the black, shadowy lines that were created there.

   Using the Clone Stamp tool, you can fix these areas relatively easily. With the Clone Stamp tool active, hold down the Alt key and click in an area that you want to pull pixel details from. Let go of Alt and start clicking to brush down copies of those original pixels in a new location. You can see the result of this action in Figure 7.16.

3. The same can be done with the baked normal map. You may occasionally see areas that look strange and could require some manual cleanup.

In Figure 7.17, you can see the odd shading around the divots I carved into the fan blades. By using the Color Picker tool to pick out the color of the background, I just used my regular brush to paint around the holes, isolating them and removing the odd shading.

Once your cleanup is completed, you can start working on your diffuse texture. The texture for this fan is actually pretty simple. It'll be a silver-white metal look, mostly pretty clean, with some grunge here and there. Of course, you can texture your fan however you prefer.

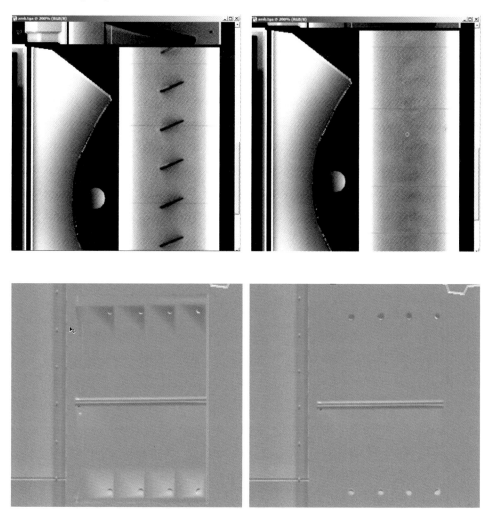

Figure 7.16

Cleaning up the AO map before (left) and after (right)

Figure 7.17

Cleaning up the baked normal map before (left) and after (right)

4. Open up a good metal texture (such as the `Alumox.jpg` image I've included on the DVD) and drag it into your AO file. If you need to, copy the metal image around to fill up your image and drag its layer to be below the AO layer. Set the AO layer's Blending Mode to Multiply, allowing the dark pixels of the AO map to be seen over the metal image.

5. Adjust the levels of your metal image to make it a bright colored metal—something like what you see in Figure 7.18.

6. Create two Hue/Saturation adjustment layers above your metal layer. In the first, lower its Brightness value down so that the image is much darker. Fill the layer mask (the white box next to the layer thumbnail) with black to hide the adjustment layer's effects. Then, take a white brush and start painting in the shadows.

   Shadows belong in places like in the middle of divots, inside the exhaust port, the underside of the frame and housing, and the interior of the housing as well.

7. In the second Hue/Saturation adjustment layer, increase the Brightness value, making the image much brighter, but again, hiding the effect by filling its layer mask with black.

   Then, with a white brush, paint in the highlights—the raised areas, the corners, the lips of metal plates, and so on. Continue to add highlights, shadows, and other details that you desire. Before too long, you should have something like Figure 7.19.

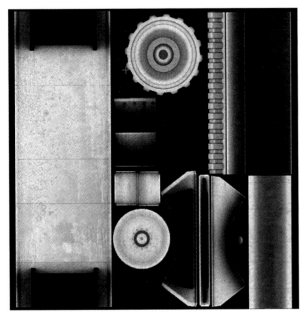

Figure 7.18

The diffuse texture coming together

Figure 7.19

Adding in shadows and highlights

8. Since, in my example, I don't want the surface of the fan to be too pockmarked, I'm going to leave my baked normal map alone, as I like the clean look it gives. Of course, you can continue to edit yours however you like to achieve the look you are going for.

9. For creating the specular map, you don't want to get too complicated with something that is made of the same material throughout. But you'll also want something that has relatively high contrast so that when the light hits the surface, it'll really pop out! To achieve this, hide all of your layers except the metal layer.

10. Select all (Ctrl+A), copy (Ctrl+C), create a new layer above all the rest, and paste (Ctrl+V). This pastes a copy of your metal layer so that you can make adjustments to it without affecting your original.

11. Simply adjust the levels (Ctrl+L) of the image until you have a high-contrast version of the metal, such as what I have in Figure 7.20.

    With your diffuse, normal, and specular maps all put together, you get your final result! Mine turned out as you see in Figure 7.21.

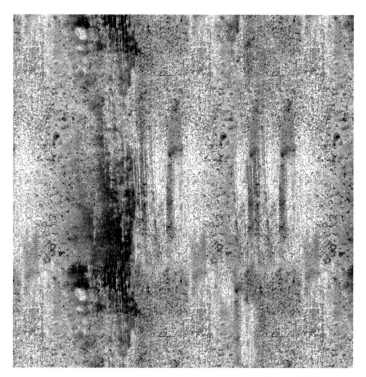

Figure 7.20

The final specular map

Figure 7.21

The final industrial fan model

Creating a Looping Animation

You're walking through a factory after hours. All of the workers are gone. You've tracked a serial killer to this location, and it's all up to you and your wits to find and put an end to the Curtain Call Killer once and for all! The only sound you hear is your own heartbeat and the constant churn of the industrial fans in the background.

Sounds like an exciting game! Adding even simple background movements (along with accompanying sound effects) can add a lot to an environment's ambiance and mood. It can also serve to tell little stories or give gameplay hints. What if, in our fictional detective game, the player notices that among all the fans in the factory, one has stopped turning near a long dark tunnel leading into blackness. Perhaps the killer has escaped that way? Giving level designers these types of options can give you a lot more input into a game's design than you might otherwise think.

But I digress. Let's make a looping animation for the industrial fan! It really depends on your game engine as to how animations are extracted from Maya and imported into the game itself. Some engines just allow you to animate normally and export them directly. Others may require that you animate things within the engine's specific editor. For this project, you'll just be using Maya to create the animation.

1. Switch to the Animation menu set, where all of your animation controls are. In the Front view, create a joint at the center of the fan. If you've been following along with me, that will be the origin of the scene and should be easy to grid-snap (hold X) to.

2. Press Enter after placing the joint. Rename the joint `Root`.

3. Select the fan blades, Shift-select the Root joint, and select Skin → Bind Skin → Smooth Bind → Options.

   In the options, there are several different settings and values. The main one you'll be looking at is the Bind To setting. Choose Selected Joints for the Bind To setting and click Apply.

   By choosing Selected Joints for your binding setting, it will bind the entire mesh to the Root joint. Since we only have one joint, it's not too big of a deal, but if you had an entire skeleton and you wanted the fan blades to only be bound to one joint, without any influence from another, choosing the Selected Joints setting would ensure that.

   Now that the fan blades are bound to the Root joint, you can begin setting keys. Before doing that, though, you need to make sure you are set to the correct *fps* (frames-per-second). Different kinds of animations require different fps settings. For instance, films run at 24 fps. Video games run at 30 fps.

4. Select Window → Settings/Preferences → Preferences (or click the Animation Preferences button at the far right of the Range slider). If your Playback Speed setting is at 30, you have the correct fps setting.

If not, click the Settings section on the left side of the Preferences window and change the Time setting to NTSC (30 fps). This should change the Playback Speed to 30 as well.

5. Go to Frame 1 in the Time slider. Select the Root joint and press Shift+E to set a key for its rotation channels (you'll see the rotation channels highlight orange in the Channel Box). In the Time slider, at Frame 1, a red hash mark will appear. This indicates a keyframe has been set.

6. Figure out how fast you want the fan to spin. I set mine to go at a rather slow pace. If you'd like to follow along, go to Frame 90 in the Time slider. Select the Root joint and, in the Channel Box, change the Rotate Z value to 356. This will spin the fan blades entirely around, minus 1 degree.

   You only spin it 356 degrees (and not a full 360) so that the first and last frames of your animation are not identical. If they were identical, you'd notice a small jerk as you run into two frames where the fan appears to stop. By using 356 degrees, the motion appears continuous when it loops.

7. Open the Graph Editor by selecting Window → Animation Editors → Graph Editor. Within this window, select the animation curves of the Root joint (make sure it's selected).

8. In the editor's menus, select Curves → Pre Infinity → Cycle. Then select Curves → Post Infinity → Cycle. These two options will make your animation loop continuously. Press Play!

Not Just a Level

Background animation is becoming more and more possible thanks to the advancements in game technology. Flowing grass, working machinery, waterfalls, and rumbling earthquakes are all possible now. But moving objects still require the hands of an artist to make the effect seamless within the game's world. To have a game character stand still and yet still have compelling visuals on the screen is the goal of the environment artist. Movement can make a game's world come alive so that it's no longer just a level, but rather a *place*!

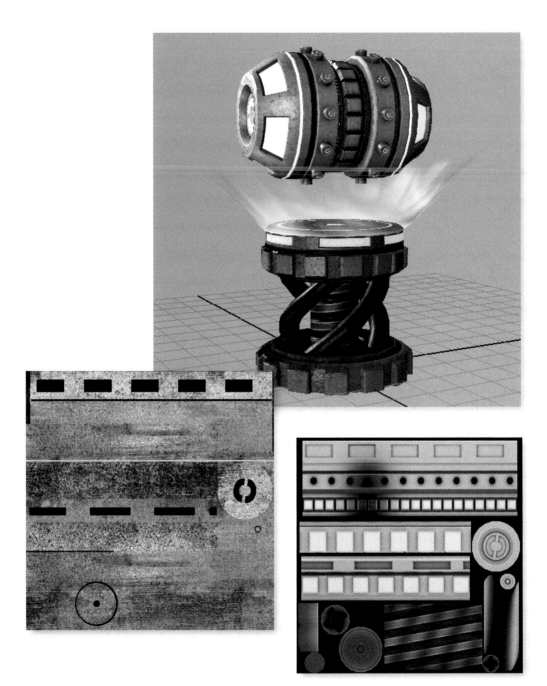

CHAPTER 8

Putting It All Together

Now that you've been through each of the major parts of a game model's creation—modeling, UV Mapping, texturing, and animating—you can start making your own game environments and props. For this chapter, let's combine the techniques you've learned so far and make something that you might consider more "gamey." Although every game will need vehicles, buildings, foliage, and even industrial fans (all of which can be very fun to make!), an environment artist might be a little extra enthusiastic about some items because they require a bit more imagination. In this chapter, you'll create a science-fiction . . . thing. I'm not sure exactly what it will be yet. Let's get started, and we'll see what comes out of it!

Project: Creating a Sci-Fi Prop

Here's the task: Create a science-fiction prop. It can look like anything you want, but it has to have certain requirements. It must be some sort of computer/machine, it must have some sort of glow effect (preferably blue), and it must move in some way. This really is the kind of task that an artist may receive on any given project. These kinds of tasks can be very exciting and really scary all at the same time.

It can be scary to create an object like this because you might come up with something that the boss doesn't like! Many artists (me included) prefer to have a bit more concrete direction, whether it is a concept sketch or some sort of reference to another prop or even another game to look at to get some sort of guideline. The best way to alleviate these kinds of concerns is to come up with several ideas and draw them out on paper or, if you aren't that good at drawing, even mock up your ideas in Maya using simple primitives to get the idea across. Then allow your boss to pick his favorite. This way, your boss can see what direction you are going in and can quickly change your thinking or, even better, praise your direction and tell you to continue.

This can be very exciting because it allows you to have some creative control. Sure, it's just a prop, but it's *your* prop. And if it is liked, you could get more such responsibility in the future and have more and more creative input. And even better, it more than likely means the boss has liked your work in the past and trusts your judgment to come up with something cool!

It's time to get started.

1. Create a short polygon cylinder and place it on the origin. Mine has about a 4 unit diameter with a height of about a half a unit. Lower the Subdivisions Caps to 0 to remove the pizza slicing faces.

2. Select the top face and bevel it slightly to round the edge. Select the top face again and apply an Extrude, scaling it inward to create an interior circular face on top of the cylinder.

3. Extrude again, bringing the extrusion up, and scale it inward slightly. Apply another Bevel to the topmost face to again round the edge. This creates a round pedestal shape like you see in Figure 8.1.

4. Around the circumference of the pedestal, select two adjacent faces, skip a face, select the next two faces, skip a face, and so on, until you have gone around the pedestal.

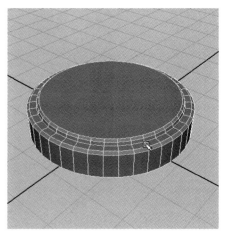

Figure 8.1
Creating the pedestal

5. Extrude the selection, pulling the faces outward to create a gear-like shape.

6. With the selection still active, go to the Side View. Press the R key to toggle the Scale Tool. Press the Insert key on the keyboard (usually near the Delete and Home keys). The scale gizmo will change, indicating that it's in Edit Pivot mode. Move the pivot handle down to be even with the base of the geometry.

7. Press Insert again to exit Edit Pivot mode. Be sure not to change your Scale Tool to a different tool or it will erase the pivot change. With the pivot change still active, scale down the faces, making them taper toward the base of the geometry (Figure 8.2).

8. Bevel the sides of the gear teeth to soften their edges. Continue to detail the pedestal however you see fit.

9. Once you have your pedestal detailed the way you like, duplicate it, move it up about 2.5 units, and flip it upside down.

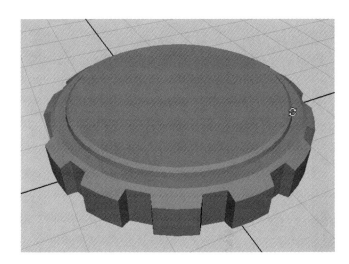

Figure 8.2

The pedestal gear teeth

10. Select the top face (what used to be the bottom) and raise it up slightly, making the gear teeth taper downward as the other side was tapered.

11. With the top face still selected, bevel it to get a rounded edge around the entire face. Maintaining your selection, apply an Extrude and scale the extrusion inward slightly to create an inner circular face.

Figure 8.3

The upper pedestal taking shape

12. Extrude again and pull upward about a quarter of a unit's distance. Extrude once again and scale it out, creating a lip that extends out beyond the previous face.

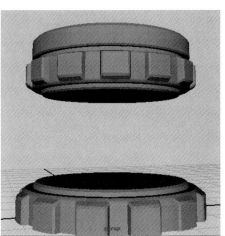

13. Extrude again, pulling up just slightly and scaling outward to round off the lip's edge. One final time, extrude and pull upward about a full unit's distance and bevel the top to round the resulting hard edge. After this series of Extrudes and Bevels, you should have something resembling Figure 8.3.

14. Next, you can add an indented circle around the top of the pedestal. Select the topmost face and apply an Extrude. Scale it inward, creating an inner circle on the top face. Extrude and scale inward again to create a ring around the top face, as in Figure 8.4.

Figure 8.4

Creating a ring
around the top face
of the pedestal

15. Select the faces of the ring. Do this by selecting the Select Edge Ring Tool from the Select menu. Double-click an edge within the ring of geometry on the pedestal and all of the edges should be selected within the loop. Go to Select → Convert Selection → To Faces (or press Ctrl+F11). This will, obviously, convert your edge selection to faces, allowing you to select the ring of faces very easily.

16. With the faces of the ring selected, apply an Extrude and push them down into the pedestal, creating a groove around the surface. Select the border edges of the groove and bevel them to soften their contours.

Connecting the Two Sides

Now that you have a top and bottom section for the pedestal you are creating, you can connect the two halves.

1. Create a cylinder that joins the bottom of the top half of the pedestal to the top of the bottom half of the pedestal. Decrease the Subdivisions Caps to 0 and increase the Subdivisions Axis to 40 to make the cylinder even more round.

2. Scale in the cylinder to make it approximately 1 unit in diameter, as you can see in Figure 8.5.

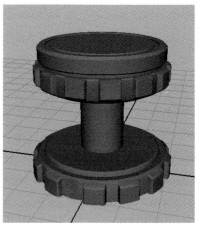

Figure 8.5

The cylinder connecting the two halves

3. To give this cylinder a more interesting shape, you can make it appear to have the grooves of a screw cut into it. This can easily be done using a Boolean Difference operation. Create a polygon helix with these settings:

Coils	8
Height	3.5
Width	1.5
Radius	0.12
Subdivisions Axis	16

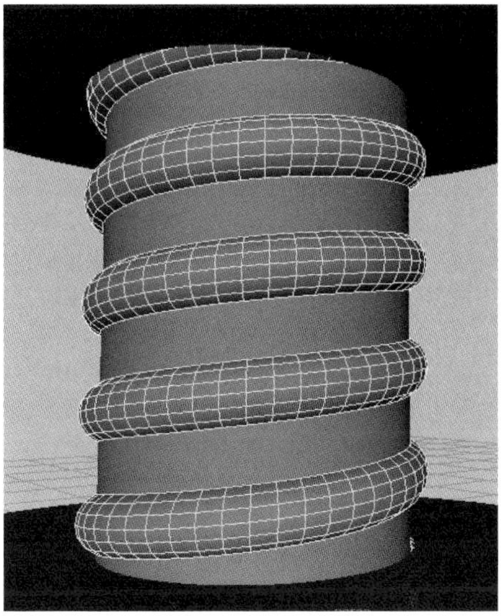

Figure 8.6

The helix positioned on the cylinder

Positioning the helix around the connecting cylinder should give you a result similar to Figure 8.6. Readjust the cylinder or helix shape if you need to make some changes to get it to look like this.

4. Select the cylinder and Shift-select the helix. Go to Polygons → Booleans → Difference. The result should give you screw-like grooves spiraling up the surface of the cylinder.

5. Using a combination of Extrudes and Bevels, create an indentation into the bottom half of the pedestal for the screw shape to fit into. Do the same for the bottom of the top half of the pedestal (Figure 8.7).

That helix shape was kind of interesting, wasn't it? Let's add some spiraling support structures to the pedestal to give it an otherworldly appearance.

Figure 8.7

Indentations for the screw shape to fit into

6. Create another polygonal helix primitive and adjust the following:

Coils	0.5
Height	3
Width	3
Radius	0.25
Subdivisions Axis	16

This creates a shape like what you see in Figure 8.8.

7. Position it as you see in the above figure and place its pivot point at the origin. Duplicate it and rotate it 90 degrees. Repeat this two more times to get four spirals arrayed around the pedestal.

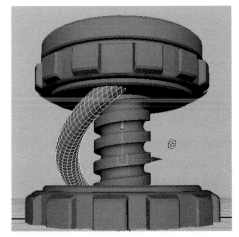

Figure 8.8

The first spiral support shape

I'm thinking this pedestal will act as a hover device with some sort of futuristic doodad hovering above it. To help sell this idea, let's add a small detail to the top of the pedestal to make it appear that some sort of lens device is creating a sort of propulsion above the pedestal.

8. Use a combination of Extrudes and Bevels to create an indention on top of the pedestal, which gives you a spot to place a lens-like device in a later step.

Building the Mysterious Device

Now you'll create the mysterious device that is hovering above the pedestal by means of some alien technology unheard of on Earth! Or something like that.

1. Create a cylinder that's about 2 units in diameter and about 3 units tall. Rotate it 90 degrees so that it's on its side and position it above the top of the pedestal by about 1 unit up. Decrease the Subdivisions Caps to 0.

2. Select the two cap faces and extrude them out about a full unit's length. Scale them inward to taper the sides of the capsule as in Figure 8.9.

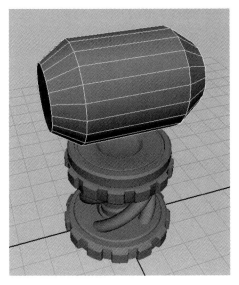

Figure 8.9

The beginnings of the strange object

3. Using the Select Edge Loop Tool from the Select menu, select both vertical edge loops at the base of the prior extrusions and bevel them slightly. Also bevel the two cap faces to round off their harder edges.

4. Select both cap faces again, if they aren't already selected. With a series of Extrudes and Bevels, create indentions on both ends of the capsule that look like the one in Figure 8.10—a rounded indentation with a small "shelf" raised inside. In a later step, you'll be adding a little window into the device on these surfaces.

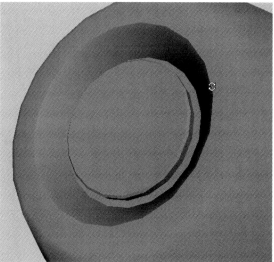

5. Select the center faces around the middle of the canister-like object and apply an Extrude. Scale it inward along the length of the canister about a quarter of a unit.

6. Extrude again and push inward slightly, scaling it in as well to create a small, beveled lip. Extrude again and push inward more, by another quarter unit or so.

Figure 8.10

The end caps of the cylinder with more details added

7. Extrude once again and scale in along the length of the canister. With another Extrude, pull back out, approaching the original surface depth. With a Bevel or another extrusion, round off the edges here. You should have something similar to Figure 8.11.

Figure 8.11

Adding two grooves around the canister object

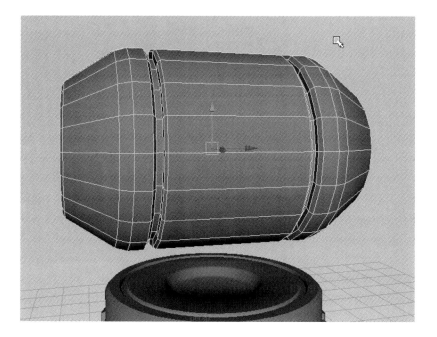

8. Determine what shape you want for the window that you place on either end cap of the object. In my case, I created a C-shaped object by using Booleans with a cylinder. I duplicated the cylinder and rotated the duplicate 180 degrees and combined the two together. I then duplicated the result to have two of them for each end of the canister. Your window object can look however you like.

9. With your window shape complete, use a Difference Boolean operation to cut the shape into the ends of the canister. You can see how mine turned out in Figure 8.12.

10. Select the center faces of the canister, between the two grooves you created earlier. Apply a series of Extrudes and Bevels to get a two-tiered groove running down the center of the canister, similar to the one in Figure 8.13.

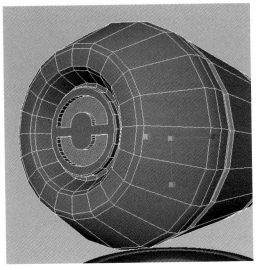

Figure 8.12
The window shape cut into the two ends of the canister

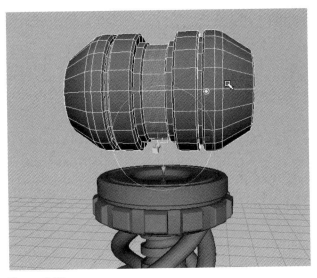

Figure 8.13
Creating a large two-tiered groove down the center of the canister

11. Select the innermost ring of faces of the canister at the center of the large groove you just created. Apply an Extrude and scale it in along the length of the canister to create a separation between the sides of the groove and the center ring of faces.

12. Apply another Extrude. This time, open the polyExtrudeFace Input node in the Channel Box on the right side of the screen that corresponds with the recent Extrude command. If you scroll down toward the bottom of the options and settings, you should find one called Keep Faces Together. Turn this setting off by typing the number 0 (or typing the word "off") in its entry field and pressing Enter.

13. Now, pull outward with the extrude handle and you should see that each face has extruded separately rather than all together like usual. Scale the Extrude inward

slightly to taper the ends. Apply a Bevel to soften the edges of the outward-facing polygons. You should end up with something similar to Figure 8.14.

14. You can continue to detail the main body of the canister however you wish. I proceeded to add some more windows into the canister along the outer tapered surface on either side of the object. I did this by selecting groups of three faces with an unselected face in between each selection. Then I applied a couple of extrusions to indent these groups inward, with a slight bevel to soften the edges.

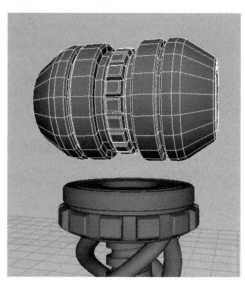

Figure 8.14

Creating a row of extruded faces around the center of the canister

15. You can also continue back over the pedestal and create any additional details you wish. I added a few more indented windows along the upper ring of the pedestal.

16. On top of the pedestal, you can add some lens-like shapes to give the implied hover technology a bit more believability. I did this simply by adding a few more extruded shapes in the middle, like you see in Figure 8.15.

Figure 8.15

Adding details to the pedestal and hovering canister

Adding Final Details

Although you could stop here and call the sci-fi prop's high-resolution model complete, you can still go back and add any details you may want. This isn't limited to cutting into the surface of the existing geometry. You can also create more bits and doodads for the prop if you like. Let's add another piece to the hovering canister to give a bit more visual pop to its silhouette.

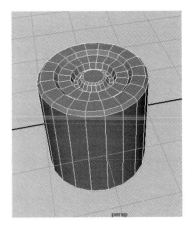

Figure 8.16
Adding some ringed details to the cap of the new cylinder

1. Create a cylinder and decrease its Subdivisions Caps to 0. Select the top cap face and, with a series of extrusions and bevels, create a pattern that you find interesting. Mine turned out like Figure 8.16.

2. Position the new cylinder along the left or right side ring near the base of the tapered sides. Position it so it is sticking up from the top of the canister like you see in Figure 8.17.

Figure 8.17
Positioning the cylinder along the top of the canister, near the tapered end

3. With the cylinder selected, press the Insert key to enter Edit Pivot mode. Hold the V key to enable Snap To Point and click and drag on the green y-axis handle, dragging it to a center point of the cylinder. The pivot should align to the center point of the canister.

4. Press Insert again to exit Edit Pivot mode. Duplicate the cylinder piece and rotate it about 30 degrees in either direction. Press Shift+D to Duplicate With Transform

to create another cylinder 30 degrees from the prior one. Continue to press Shift+D until the cylinders are arrayed in a ring around the canister.

5. Duplicate these cylinders to place another ring on the opposite end of the canister. The final result should look something like Figure 8.18.

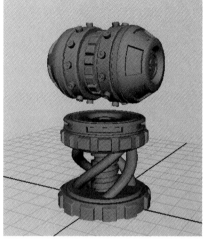

Figure 8.18

Adding the final details to the high-resolution mesh

Creating the Low-Resolution Mesh

As with all current-generation game props, you'll need to create a low-resolution mesh to use for the actual game asset. The low-resolution mesh has all the high-resolution details baked into its texture to allow for the game's technology to sell the illusion of a higher-detail mesh than there actually is. For this prop, the main thing to keep in mind is that simpler is better. Not every indentation and groove needs to be represented by geometry. In most cases, such details can be covered through the use of normal maps and such. The windows cut into the caps of the canister, for example, could be represented through the normal map. The larger windows cut into the tapered surfaces on either side of the canister, however, are large enough details that representing them within the low-resolution geometry could be better.

It comes down to what your final asset's polycount budget affords you. If the asset needs to be down to, for example, less than a thousand polygons, you'd have to choose your details very carefully. In such cases, only the largest of details would be wanted in the mesh, while all other details would remain in the texture.

Following the steps that have been gone over several times in this book, you can eventually come to the final low-resolution mesh shown in Figure 8.19. Don't forget that you can always check out the step-by-step explanation of how this particular mesh was created by watching the video supplement on the book's DVD.

Figure 8.19

The high (left) and low (right) resolution meshes

UV Mapping the Low-Res Mesh

Once you have your low-resolution mesh completed, you can begin UV mapping it to prepare the mesh for texturing. The most important aspect of UV mapping is efficiency—efficiency of space, to be exact. You want to make every pixel of your texture count, with as little unused space as possible. You also want each piece of the model to be represented by a proportional amount of texture space (large objects get more UV space than small objects). With that in mind, take a look at your model and study it to see if there are any possibilities for mirroring your texture.

Figure 8.20

The remainder after deleting mirrored geometry

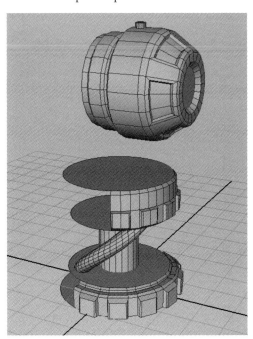

In other words, are there parts of the model that are identical and could share UV texture space? If there are, what I tend to do is to delete the duplicate sections of the model, UV map the remainder, and add back in the missing sides by duplicating the finished UV mapped portions.

For my model (which will be similar to yours if you are following along), I ended up with what you see in Figure 8.20. I deleted half of the pedestal rims, all but one of the small cylinder shapes and spiraling pedestal supports, and one end of the canister.

1. Select what is left of the canister and choose Create UVs → Cylindrical Mapping. You may need to rotate the mapping gizmo by clicking the small, red hash mark in one of its corners and clicking the blue rotation circle to enable the rotation controls. Adjust the cylindrical mapping gizmo until the UVs of the canister are laid out in a square in the UV Texture Editor (accessible from the Window menu).

2. Select the cap faces and choose Create UVs → Planar Mapping → Options. In the Planar Mapping options box that opens, change the Project From setting to the applicable axis direction you'll be projecting from. In my case, it's the x-axis. Click the Project button.

3. In the UV Editor, make any adjustments you may find necessary and lay out the UV shells as you see in Figure 8.21.

4. Continue to map and lay out the rest of the geometry in the same fashion. Apply cylindrical maps to the cylindrical shapes and planar maps to the caps and ends. Eventually, you should end up with something similar to Figure 8.22.

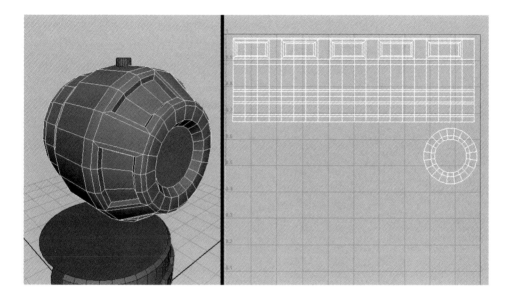

Figure 8.21

The canister UVs laid out in the UV Texture Editor

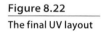

Figure 8.22

The final UV layout

5. Now you can generate your ambient occlusion and normal map sources. Just as you've done in the other projects within this book, create an AO and a normal map using the Transfer Maps command (found in the Rendering menu set under Lighting/Shading → Transfer Maps). Mine turned out like Figure 8.23.

6 Once your textures are generated, you can duplicate the remaining halves of the mesh and use them to fill in the gaps. Since the meshes you are duplicating are already mapped with UVs, the duplicates will share those same UV coordinates. The result will look like Figure 8.24.

Figure 8.23

The generated AO and normal maps

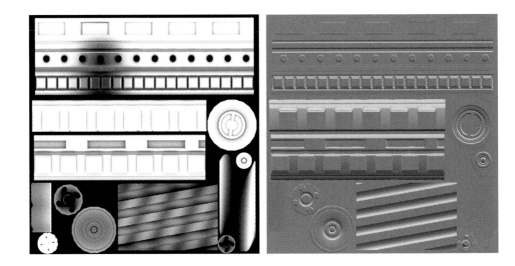

Figure 8.24

The final game prop with generated AO and normal map applied

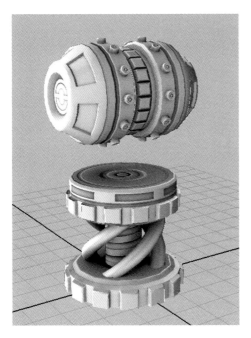

Creating the Final Textures

Now that the mesh is complete, you can focus on completing the prop's textures. For this prop, you'll need a diffuse map, a normal map, a specular map, and an emissive map for the glow effect.

1. The emissive map is rather quick, so you can tackle it first. Open your AO texture in Photoshop. Double-click the background layer and press OK to convert it to a normal layer. Rename it `AO`.

2. Create a new layer. Rename the new layer `Glow`.

3. Using the details found in your AO layer as a guide, select the areas that you want to glow. In your glow layer, fill these areas with a light blue color.

4. Create a new layer and place it below the Glow layer. Fill it with black. The result (Figure 8.25) is your emissive texture. Save it as `canister_emissive.tga` (or `canister_glow.tga`).

5. To begin the diffuse texture, open a metal texture source that doesn't have too much variation or contrast, such as the aluminum texture source that comes with this book's DVD. Drag it into your Photoshop file and place its layer below the AO layer. Fill the layer with the metal source, either by resizing it or copying it across the full image.

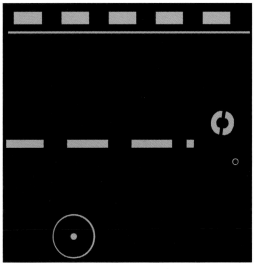

Figure 8.25

The relatively simple emissive texture

6. Adjust your metal image's saturation and contrast to make it have a blue tint with very low contrast. If you are using the textures provided in this book, you'll want to apply a Hue/Saturation adjustment layer and click the Colorize option in the lower-right corner of the Hue/Saturation dialog box.

   The Colorize setting will override the current hue values and apply a completely new hue value. Without Colorize checked, the hue adjustment is reliant on the image's original hue value. So, with Colorize checked, you can adjust the hue to be a blue color and lower the saturation down to around 12 or so to make the color more of a subtle tinting.

   > If you need to, you can apply a Brightness/Contrast adjustment layer to further adjust the source metal image to your preference.

7. Create a new Brightness/Contrast adjustment layer and drag the Brightness slider way down to, for example, -90. Increase the Contrast slider slightly to be around 10.

8. Select the adjustment layer's mask (the white box next to its layer image within the Layer palette) and fill with black, removing the adjustment layer's affect from the image.

9. With the mask still selected in the Layer palette, take a soft white brush and paint in the shadows in the low parts of the image. These would be the undersides of surfaces as well as the grooves and indentations.

10. Once the shadows are painted as you like, create a Hue/Saturation adjustment layer and increase the Lightness value to around 35 or so. Fill its mask with black and, with a white brush, paint in the extruded areas to brighten them. These would be, for example, the gear-like teeth around the rims of the pedestal. You should have something like Figure 8.26.

11. You can create additional Hue/Saturation adjustment layers and adjust the color values of the different sections of the prop to your liking. For example, I made the spiraling support bars a dark color and also darkened the pedestal overall so that the canister would stand out. In addition to making different areas brighter or darker, I also applied some color changes, making the ends of the canister a gold color.

12. To add more variation to certain elements of the prop, you can bring in other texture sources and blend them over the top of the existing metal. For example, you can bring in the Alumox metal source image from the DVD to apply a bit of surface variation. This texture source image has a splotchier metal look. Drag it into your Photoshop file and fill the image.

Figure 8.26

The diffuse texture so far

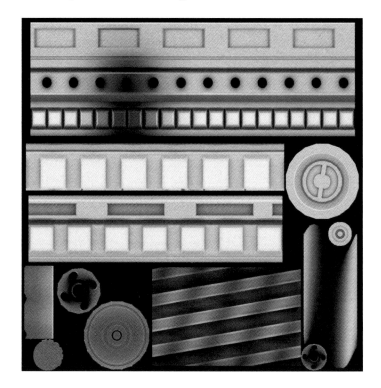

13. Adjust the layer's Blending Mode to Linear Light. This brightens the image and increases the contrast of the metal's splotches.

14. Apply a Hue/Saturation adjustment layer and decrease the Lightness value to darken the image, but maintain the contrast adjustment.

15. Although the contrast is pretty good, it's affecting the image more than I'd like. One way to have more control over the image blending is to adjust exactly how the images blend together.

    Right-click the splotchy metal layer and from the menu that appears, choose Blending Options. The Layer Style dialog box will open. At the bottom you should see two sliders. These two sliders adjust the blending of either the currently selected layer or the blending between the current layer and the rest of the image beneath it.

    Play with these two sliders until you get a look that you like. You can see how mine turned out in Figure 8.27.

Figure 8.27

Adding surface and color variation

    Save this image as `Canister_Diffuse.tga`.

16. Lastly, you'll create the specular map. Hide the AO layers and the shadow and highlight adjustment layers, leaving only the surface details and colors. Press Ctrl+A to select the entire canvas. Press Ctrl+Shift+C to copy the visible image. Create a new layer and paste.

17. You don't necessarily want the glowing portions of the prop to be highly specular since it could destroy the illusion of light being emitted from within the device. Find your Glow layer and Ctrl-click its thumbnail in the Layer palette. This will load it as a selection. Back in your specular layer, fill the selection with black.

18. One thing I like to do is punch up the saturation of the specular and contrast of the specular map. You can do this with adjustment layers. Once you have a specular map you like (such as Figure 8.28) save it as `Canister_Specular.tga`.

Figure 8.28

The final
specular map

Adding Geometry Glow Effects

If you recall from our initial job specifications, your boss wanted the prop to glow. You created an emissive map to cause certain parts of the prop to emanate a glowing blue color, but you could add a new piece of geometry to sell the prop's hovering effect.

These kinds of geometry effects are old fashioned, but still used a lot with certain environmental effects. To create beams of light or even falling drops of water, an environment artist may create a geometric shape representing the effect with an animated opacity texture to create the effect's look. You'll do something similar here.

1. Open Photoshop and create a blank image that is 512×512 resolution.

2. Select the Gradient Tool (G) and at the top-left of the interface and in the Options Bar, click the black-to-white gradient to access the Gradient Editor window.

3. In the Gradient Editor, adjust the colors to be a blue-to-white gradient like in Figure 8.29.

4. Once you have a gradient that you like, click the OK button to exit the Gradient Editor.

5. Back in the Options Bar, at the top of the interface, you'll see a series of buttons that change the type of gradient being used. Click the second one to toggle Radial Gradient. This will paint a gradient in a circular pattern with the colors blending from the center of the circle to the outer edge of the circle.

6. In your image, click in the approximate center (it doesn't have to be perfect) and drag out toward the side. This will paint in the circular gradient. The goal is to get a gradient that looks like Figure 8.30.

If your gradient is backward from your desired result, check the Reverse option in the Options Bar and draw the gradient again.

7. Rename this layer **Color** (you may need to double-click the layer to convert it from a background layer to a normal layer). Create a new layer and fill with black.

8. Create a third layer above the black layer. Choose a white color and a soft brush and paint a radiant glow outward from the approximate center of the image. It does not need to be perfect or even all that pretty. Paint it so that you get a nice radial pattern of white that is similar to Figure 8.31.

9. Save the white on black image as **Light_Opacity.tga**. Hide the top two layers and save the blue-to-white gradient image as **Light_Diffuse.tga**.

Figure 8.29

The blue-to-white gradient created in the Gradient Editor

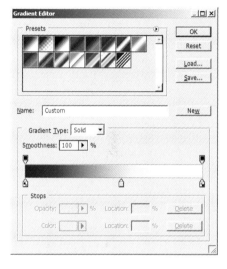

Figure 8.30
A blue-to-white radial gradient painted into your image

Figure 8.31
White strokes forming a radial glow from the center of a black canvass

10. Open your Maya canister scene. Create a polygonal cone primitive. Rotate it 90 degrees so that the point is pointing downward and reposition it on your model, as you see in Figure 8.32.

11. Select the cap face on the base of the cone and delete it. In the Front view, use the Cut Faces Tool (from the Edit Mesh menu) to cut a horizontal line across the cone where it meets the pedestal geometry. Delete the geometry below that line, leaving the remainder.

12. With the remaining cone geometry selected, select Create UVs → Planar Map → Options. In the options, choose the y-axis to project from and click the Project button.

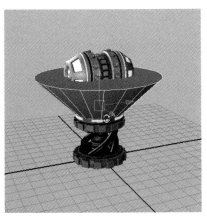

13. Apply a new material to the cone geometry and apply the Light_Diffuse.tga image to its Color attribute. Apply the Light_Opacity.tga image to its Transparency *and* Incandescence attribute. You should get a result similar to Figure 8.33.

Figure 8.32
The cone placed in the scene

Figure 8.33
The result after applying the light textures to the cone geometry's material

14. Feel free to add as many more glowing geometry shapes to your prop as you wish to get the look you desire.

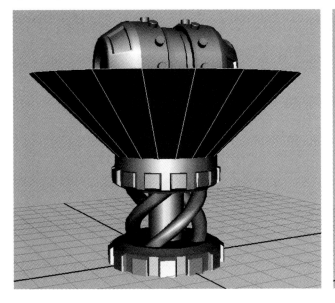

MANUALLY CONNECTING OPACITY

If your cone geometry's opacity texture is not displaying correctly, you may need to manually connect it to the material's Transparency attribute. Do this by opening the Hypershade (Window → Rendering Editors → Hypershade).

1. In the Hypershade, in the upper window, select the glow material that you applied to the cone. Click the Input And Output Connections button (indicated by a box with two arrows). You should see something like the below graphic:

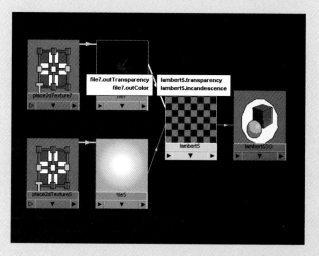

Hover your cursor over the connection between the Light_Opacity.tga and the material. You should see something like the above. What's happening is that the *transparency* of the opacity image is connected to the Transparency attribute of the material. What you actually want is for the *color* of the opacity image to be connected to the Transparency attribute of the material. You can fix this by following these steps.

2. Select the line connecting the Light_Opacity.tga image to the material and delete it by pressing the Delete key.

3. Middle-mouse click and drag the Light_Opacity.tga image onto the material. A list will appear. Choose the bottom option: Other.

    The Connection Editor will open. On the left side are all of the attributes of your image file and on the right side are all of the attributes of the material. Clicking an attribute on the left and the right links those attributes together.

4. In the left column, find and select the outColor attribute. In the right column, find and select the Transparency attribute. This will link the two and make the Transparency attribute display accurately in your scene. Click Close.

continues

MANUALLY CONNECTING OPACITY *(continued)*

5. However, you may notice that the transparency that is displayed is reversed from what you want! This can easily be fixed by double-clicking the image file node to open its attributes. Open the Effects section of the image's attributes and check the Invert checkbox. The transparency will display correctly.

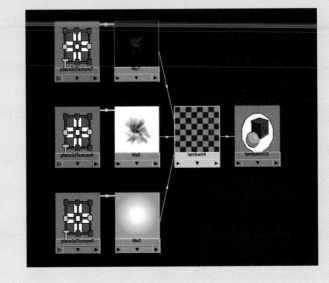

6. Don't forget to apply a new copy of the `Light_Opacity.tga` file to the Incandescence attribute!

Making It Move

You've essentially completed your prop at this point; however, one of the boss's stipulations at the beginning was that he wanted this thing to move. Since the canister is hovering above the glowing pedestal, you can focus on it.

1. First, make sure that your timeline is set correctly. Click the Animation Preferences button on the far right side of your Range Slider, below the playback controls.

2. Make sure your playback speed is set to 30 frames per second (fps). If your playback speed is set to 22 fps, you can change it under the Settings section of the Preferences window, in the Time setting.

3. Click Save and return to your scene.

4. Select the canister pieces and combine them together (Mesh → Combine). You can rename the combined objects `Canister`.

5. In the Time Slider, go to frame 1. Select the canister and press Shift+W and Shift+C. These are the keyboard shortcut commands for Key Transform and Key Rotation channels.

6. Go to frame 61. Rotate the canister **354** degrees in the y-axis and key the transform and rotation channels again.

7. Go to frame 30 and lower the canister slightly in the y-axis. Set a key for the transform channels.

   Press the Play button. You should see the canister spin on its axis and subtly bob up and down in space. If you'd like to add movement to the glowing light cone, you can do so using the same methods.

Project Complete!

After adding animation, you have completed your sci-fi prop to the "boss's" orders. Time for the next one!

I hope these projects have taught you how real game environments and props are created. The pipeline for asset creation is always in flux and advancing with new technology, and it's up to you to keep up. In the next chapter, you'll learn about some additional procedures and knowledge that an environment artist should be aware of before walking into a project.

CHAPTER 9

Pro Tips

This chapter will be somewhat free-flowing and will jump from one subject to another to convey additional information, concepts, methods, and terminology that I haven't covered in the previous projects of this book. These extras are important for any game artist to know. Many of these topics are techniques that you might use only every so often on certain projects, or perhaps never. But they are good tips that all good environment artists should be aware of.

Using Mudbox or ZBrush

Autodesk's Mudbox and Pixologic's ZBrush are two programs that have become extremely popular in the video game industry. They allow extremely high-resolution models to be made and can help create an exceptional amount of detail that just isn't possible in Maya alone. Although using these programs was not covered in this book (since this book is about Maya), I highly recommend trying one or both of them. You may also want to pick up *ZBrush Character Creation: Advanced Digital Sculpting* by Scott Spencer (Sybex, 2008) or *Introducing Mudbox* by Ara Kermanikian (Sybex, 2010). Both books do an excellent job covering their respective applications and can be great companion books for this one.

Creating Level of Detail

Many games will require you to create Level of Detail (or LOD) models for your environment props and assets, especially if the game features large vistas where the player is able to see for long distances. Creating LODs for your models enables the game to switch higher resolution models for lower resolution models as the player's vantage point gets farther away. This way, high detail meshes can be seen by players who are close to them and low detail meshes are seen from far away. If there were no differences in Level of Detail, you wouldn't be able to climb to the top of a tower in games such as *Assassin's Creed* and still be able to view the entire city below in all of its richness and splendor without the hardware or the game engine gasping and wheezing in protest.

You may think that such low-geometry models would detract from the look of the game, but they actually help. Take a game like *Crysis*, for example. It has a very elaborate LOD system to allow for large jungles with thousands of pieces of foliage. In that game, you can literally see a point from hundreds of yards away and run to that point without any load times slowing you down along the way. As the player gets closer to that distant point, the geometry that once was so far away gets closer as well. As it does, the game switches the low-resolution meshes with higher-resolution meshes. Meanwhile, the position that the player used to be in has been replaced with much lower-resolution geometry.

The farther away a prop is, the more LOD transitions may be needed. If a prop has only two LOD "steps," then the player could see the transition between the two LODs pop into view. If there are three or more LOD steps, the prop can transition between LODs as the player approaches, which allows for a smoother transition between low-resolution and high-resolution meshes.

Because the player was so far away, the low-resolution meshes looked just fine. If you were able to see the same geometry up close, it would have looked like a blocky, blurry mess! In the example (Figure 9.1), the building on the left is the high-resolution building. It is made with about 35,000 polygons. The building on the right is the low-resolution LOD mesh, which is meant to be viewed from a far distance. It is 16 polygons—much smaller in polycount and much less taxing on a game.

Figure 9.1

An example of using LODs

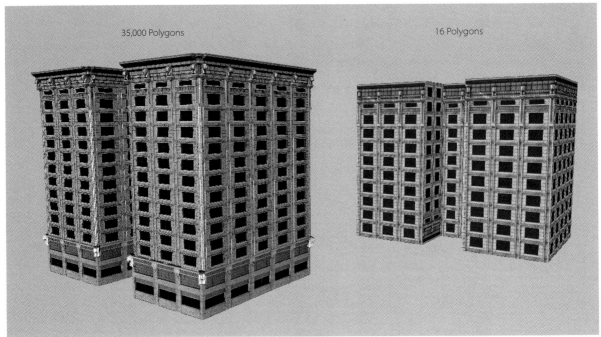

35,000 Polygons

16 Polygons

Mipmapping

Mipmapping is a form of LODs using textures. When a prop is close to the player, its texture will be the highest resolution available to be displayed, giving the prop crisp details with no blurriness. As the prop gets farther away from the player, the game engine will actually switch its texture to a lower resolution. This is due to a game engine's tendency to make normally crisp details look scratchy and dithered from a distance. By lowering the resolution to match the distance the prop is being viewed from, the scratchy dithering is diminished.

Most game engines are able to automatically create the different *mips* used in a mipmap, but in case you ever need to make your own, here's how:

1. In Photoshop, open your texture. In my case, I'll use a texture from Chapter 3's vehicle. My particular texture is 1024×1024 resolution. The next mip of this texture will be 512×512, as that is one power of two less than 1024×1024. The mip after that will be 256×256. The next will be 128×128, and so on.

2. Go to Image → Canvas Size and take a look at the options in the window that opens.

3. Change the Width and Height unit measurement from inches to pixels. Change the Width value to 2016. Change the Anchor point to the left-middle box (Figure 9.2).

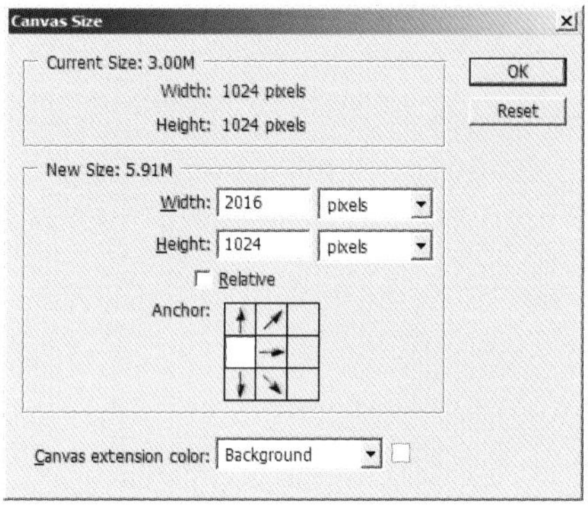

Figure 9.2

The Canvas Size options in Photoshop

> The value of 2,016 is derived by adding up the pixel width of each mip in the texture: 1,024 + 512 + 256 + 128 + 64 + 32 = 2,016. If your highest resolution was 512×512, then subtract 1,024 from 2,016 and you'd use 992.

4. Click OK to apply the changes. Your image's total area should expand to the right.

5. Duplicate the texture (by dragging its layer onto the New Layer button or by selecting its layer and pressing Ctrl+J). Use the Edit Transform command (Ctrl+T) to change the duplicate layer's size. Scale it down to 50 percent (use the percentage input boxes at the top of the screen if you need to). Position it directly to the right of the original texture, flush with the top of the image.

6. Do the same with the duplicate layer: Duplicate it again, scale this duplicate by 50 percent, and position it directly to the right. Eventually you get something like Figure 9.3.

7. Save the file.

Figure 9.3

The mipmapped texture with all of its mips in a row

Keep in mind that the exact specifications of a mipmap can vary per project. This one used six layers of mips. Some games may need only three or four. Your art director will be able to tell you more specifically what your project needs.

Using Multiple UV Channels

Some game engines, such as the popular Unreal Engine, make use of multiple UV channels (or sets) on meshes. Throughout the projects in this book, you created only a single UV channel—the one with the texture information that you can easily see. However, in the case of the Unreal Engine, a second UV channel can be used for lighting purposes. Other uses of a secondary UV channel may be for applying a decal image to a model or for the UV coordinates of a special detail texture. Secondary UV sets can have their own UV layout, meaning the textures that are applied with them do not have to match the layout of the textures from the primary UV set.

Follow these steps to create a new UV channel for a mesh in Maya:

1. Open any of your own projects or any of the projects on the book's companion DVD.

2. Select a low-resolution model and open the UV Texture Editor (found under the Window menu).

3. From the Create UVs menu, you have several options for creating new UV channels, depending on what you'd like to do:

- Create Empty UV Set will, as you'd expect, create a new UV channel for the model that has no pre-applied UVs. This means that while the new UV channel is active, you will need to remap all of the model's UVs.

- Copy UVs to UV Set will copy the currently active UVs to another UV channel or into a completely new UV channel. This is what I usually do so that I don't have to start from scratch in the new UV channel.

- Farther down the Create UVs menu, you can find the Delete Current UV Set command to remove the active UV channels from the model.

> You can change which UV set is currently active in the UV Texture Editor, under the UV Sets menu. The active UV set will be checked in the menu list that opens.

Creating Collision Meshes

It depends on the game engine being used, but many require the artist to create collision meshes for each prop she creates. These are generally very simple polygonal shapes—mostly cubes and cylinders. For example, the sci-fi prop that you created in Chapter 8 could very easily use a cube collision mesh, such as the one in Figure 9.4.

A collision mesh is an invisible object that does exactly what it sounds like: it creates a collision volume. If a prop is placed within a scene without a collision volume, the player (or other moving assets in the game) would be able to walk right through the prop. Using simple, geometric shapes for collision makes the mathematics involved in collision detection much simpler and faster to compute. There is nothing different about creating collision geometry from normal, visible geometry. It's simply a polygonal cube (or whatever shape the object may need).

The method used to get a game engine to recognize the collision geometry *as* collision geometry and not regular, visible geometry, however, can vary depending on the game engine. On one game I worked on, naming the collision mesh with the prefix "coll_" made the game engine automatically recognize and use the geometry as a collision mesh. In another game, the geometry needed to have a specific material applied to it. The specific requirements for this type of mesh can vary greatly

Figure 9.4

An example collision mesh (tinted blue)

between projects, so ask your art director if your game engine requires anything particular for such meshes and their use.

Although collision is the most widely used way of using invisible geometry to affect the game, other possible meshes include shadow meshes and, rarely, portal meshes. Shadow meshes are simple geometric shapes representing a more complex object. The game uses the invisible shadow mesh to compute shadow information, rather than the more complex, fully detailed version of the asset. This helps the game perform such effects faster and with less computational time. A portal mesh is similar to a window. When the player comes within view of a portal mesh, the level's contents that exist behind the portal mesh get loaded so the player can see through the portal mesh to the area on the other side. Having a level load in sections, rather than all at once, allows the levels to be more detailed and complex without slowing down the game.

Obviously, game programmers can invent any number of mesh objects to affect a game's creation. Make sure that you are aware of any such requirements for any project you work on.

Being Professional

The idea of being professional is a very broad topic and one that perhaps could be a book all unto itself. But in truth (and this applies to nearly every profession), being professional is the best thing any artist can do for his or her career. I thought I'd try to impress on you just a few ideas and concepts on this subject.

Learn to communicate well. Communication is vital in every field, but in a visual medium such as games, it is doubly so. Hours, days, weeks, and even months (dare I say, years?) of work can be wasted simply because of poor communication. If you have any question at all regarding an assignment that has been given to you, ask!—especially when you are first starting in your career. When sharing information or asking a question, attempt to convey your thoughts as clearly as possible. Try sketching it or even producing a small mockup to help make what you are saying as clear as possible.

Take direction and criticism. Beauty is in the eye of the beholder, but let's be clear—as an artist in the video game field, you are not creating art. You are creating *commercial* art. Yes, it can be beautiful, compelling, and have wonderful meaning, just as all good art does. But it is being produced for a client for their purpose and for their product. You could produce a piece of art that is a beauty to behold and the art director could ask for a change. You must be able to take direction and criticism. You must even *seek* it out from your peers! And take what they say seriously and with an open mind. And when your boss says, "Make it more purple," then more purple it will be!

Be creative on and off the clock. This is something that can be very difficult to do. Even I find it hard to make the time to create my own artwork after a hard week at the office. This was especially true while I was writing this book! But it's important that you do everything you can to further your own creativity and learning. Long after school, you can still be learning. I just started learning Pixologic's ZBrush this last year and am finding it to be a great tool that will further my skills as an artist in this industry, and that's after having done this job for seven years. I'm sure I'll have more to learn in the future. Do your best to make time to learn and to keep your creativity fresh. If you don't use it, after all, you'll lose it.

Do your best, regardless of the job. As a commercial artist, you *will* be tasked with an assignment that you don't like—maybe even something you hate. I know I have had such assignments. I worked on the game *SAW*, an adaptation of the horror films of the same name. I am not fan of the *SAW* films. Yet even though I was not the most enthusiastic about some of the work I was assigned, I still needed to do it and do it well. You have to be able to find your own fun sometimes. That can be easier said than done when you've just been given "rock duty" but, by golly, make each and every one of those rocks look good and you can be assured that your effort and good attitude will not go unnoticed by your superiors.

Have Fun!

I hope you have enjoyed this book and have found it useful. In these chapters, you've gone through the process of creating game environments and props several times. These processes are the essentials of nearly *every* asset you will ever make while in the game industry, so get used to them! And of course, always strive to learn more and more.

Have fun! After all, you *are* making games. It's a far cry from digging ditches or flipping burgers. (I can be the worst one at taking my own advice sometimes, and this one can be the hardest one of all.) It's so easy to become jaded in this industry. Do your best to keep a good attitude about what you're doing.

When I tell people what I do, I always hear the remark, "Wow! That must be fun." And you know what?

It is.

Title: Abandoned Colony

Artist: Bram Eulaers

Website: www.brameulaers.com

Info: Total scene polycount is approximately 100,000 polygons

"ABANDONED COLONY" - Beauty shot 1   bram.eulaers@gmail.com 😊

From the Artist: "Unearthly Challenge is an environment art competition organized by www.gameartisans.org and www.polycount.net. I won first prize in the 3D category and also won an extra honorary award. The scene is built in the Unreal Engine 3 with modular assets. I created all models, textures, effects, and lighting, and painted initial concepts before constructing the scene."

Image Gallery

Title: Medieval House

Artist: Jeff Parrott

Website: www.environmentartist.com

Info: 5,000 polygons

From the Artist: "I wanted to create a low polygon project that utilized hand-painted textures and vertex lighting in a painterly art style. As far as color scheme and lighting, I tried to keep it fun but simple."

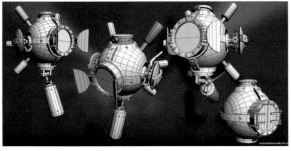

Title: Roberta: Depth Charge Drone

Artist: Adam Bromell

Website: www.adambromell.com

Info: Roberta model: 7,000 polygons; approximately 300,000 polygons for the entire scene

From the Artist: "I saw a concept for this robot-type thing by Feng Zhu, and after playing *Bioshock*, was inspired to take the design and come up with my own back story and setting for it. From there, *Roberta* was born."

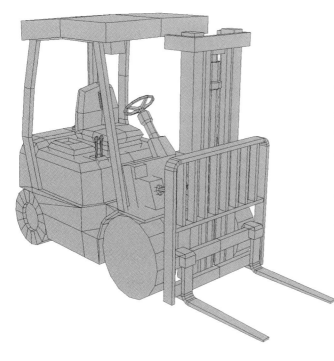

Title: Forklift

Artist: Tom Poon

Website: http://tompoon.com/

Info: 2,751 polygons

From the Artist: "It's not exactly a major prop, but I spent about 18 hours making this asset and had some fun with it. It's rendered using the Marmoset game engine."

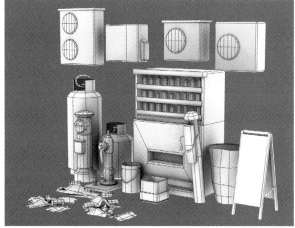

THIS PAGE AND OPPOSITE

Title: Asian City

Artist: Paul Presley

Website: www.3dpaul.com

From the Artist: "I've never been to Japan before, so trying to create a place where people can call she-nanigans on me if I got it wrong was a huge challenge. With tons of reference, I got to work on creating a city that would push me artistically and mentally. I worked on the piece whenever I had the free time, so when all was said and done, it was a huge relief and a great accomplishment to get something of this magnitude finished."

Title: Savannah Tree

Artist: Michael McKinley

Website: http://www.mtmckinley.net/

Info: 1,760 polygons

From the Artist: "The tree project was one of the first models I made for the book, and I wanted to do something a little bit different. Using a more cartoony style seemed to work well for it!"

Title: Number 77

Artist: Michael McKinley

Website: http://www.mtmckinley.net/

Info: 9,021 polygons

From the Artist: "I originally wanted to make a very realistic car for the book, but because of my lack of time, I had to go for a more stylized visual guideline for the vehicle, hence the lack of engine details. However, I think it worked pretty well in the end, and I could definitely see playing a racing game in this sort of style sometime in the future."

Title: The Office Building

Artist: Michael McKinley

Website: http://www.mtmckinley.net/

Info: Approximately 100 to 300 polygons per module

From the Artist: "One of the first jobs I had in the game industry relied heavily on modular assets because our team size was so small. But even with a small team, we managed to make large, varied levels using modular building."

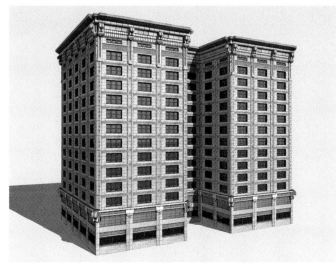

Title: The Mysterious Canister

Artist: Michael McKinley

Website: http://www.mtmckinley.net/

Info: 4,028 polygons

From the Artist: "This was a fun project for the book because I pretty much just allowed myself to make up stuff as I went along, using no guide or reference and just pulling ideas from the games I played in my youth, such as *Metroid* and *Contra*!"

About the Companion DVD

In this appendix:

- **What you'll find on the DVD**
- **System requirements**
- **Using the DVD**
- **Troubleshooting**

What You'll Find on the DVD

The DVD is divided into sections for your ease of use. These directories are Projects, Video, and Images. You will find all the files for completing the tutorials and understanding concepts in this book in the Projects directory. You can access the incrementally saved Maya scene files and textures for each project in the book in their respective chapter folders within the Projects directory.

In the Video directory you will find complete video captures of each project being created from start to finish. You can watch these in tandem with reading the lessons to help you follow along with any steps in the book where the example imagery may be hard to understand in print. The videos can also be very useful in showing you exactly what was done to create the projects, in the event that the explanation is difficult to grasp or understand.

In the Images directory are two folders: Textures and Gallery. The Textures directory contains texture sources that are generously donated from www.cgtextures.com as well as others from my personal collection. Some of these are used in the book as sources for project textures. Others are there simply for your own personal use.

In the Gallery folder are images from the book's gallery at high resolution for your viewing pleasure. There are also images that didn't make it into the printed gallery due to space constraints, but I wanted to share them anyway!

Don't work with Maya project files directly from the DVD. Maya scenes link to external files such as texture maps and dynamic caches, so it's better to copy the entire project for each chapter to your local drive, including the empty folders, to ensure that the example scenes function properly.

System Requirements

To fully use all the files on the DVD, you will need to be running Maya 2010 or Maya 2009 Unlimited (the software is *not* included on the DVD). Earlier versions of Maya should be capable of following along with the lessons in this book, but many of the menu commands and tools used may not be present or may be found in different menu locations. See the sidebar below for instructions on how to open the DVD's Maya files in earlier software iterations.

> There is no Maya software provided on the DVD. You need to already have a copy of Maya software to use the files on the DVD.

Make sure your computer meets the minimum system requirements shown in the following list. If your computer doesn't match up to these requirements, you may have problems using the files on the companion DVD.

- A PC running Microsoft Windows XP (SP2 or higher) or Windows Vista
- A Macintosh running Apple OS X 10.5.2 or later
- An Internet connection
- A CD/DVD-ROM drive
- Apple QuickTime 7.0 or later (download the latest version from www.quicktime.com)

For the latest information on system requirements for Maya, go to www.autodesk.com/maya. Although you can find specific hardware recommendations on these web pages, there is some general information that will help you determine if you're already set up to run Maya: You need a fast processor, a minimum 2GB of RAM, and a "workstation graphics card" for the best compatibility (rather than a consumer-grade gaming video card).

OPENING MAYA FILES IN EARLIER VERSIONS

You can save Maya files into two major formats that Maya understands—Maya binary files (.mb) and Maya ASCII files (.ma). If a file is saved in the binary format, it *must* be opened within the same version that it was saved or a later version. In other words, a Maya binary file saved in Maya 2010 can only be opened in Maya 2010 and later versions of the software. If you opened a .mb file within a text editor, such as Microsoft's native Notepad application, you would see something like this:

Looks pretty unintelligible, right? This is a file written in a coding language that Maya understands but that (more than likely) you and (definitely) I cannot make any sense of.

On the other hand, a Maya ASCII file opened in a text editor looks like this:

continues

OPENING MAYA FILES IN EARLIER VERSIONS *(continued)*

At first glance, this perhaps looks just as confusing. Upon closer inspection, however, you may notice that the words are actually written in English! That's because .ma files are written in ASCII language, which is much more intelligible to those with no programming knowledge (such as myself!).

In the first few paragraphs, you can see some entries like

```
requires maya "2010";
```

or

```
fileInfo "product" "Maya Unlimited 2010";
```

As you may infer from the wording, simply by changing these lines to read "2009" instead of "2010" allows Maya 2009 to open .ma files that were saved from Maya 2010! And this works for other versions of Maya as well.

Before you run off, a few words of warning. If a .ma file you are trying to open uses a feature that is not present in an earlier version of Maya, then this version-renaming trick will not work. Also, if you don't carefully look through the entire first page of the ASCII text document for *all* references to the software version and you miss one, the file may not open. And just to cover all the bases, even if you do everything right, there is no guarantee that the file will open correctly, just due to the finicky nature of manipulating code. With these caveats in mind, I recommend saving a copy of the .ma file you wish to adjust so that your original file isn't permanently mangled by your edits.

All of the Maya files on this book's DVD are saved in Maya ASCII format to allow you the opportunity to use the files in your version of the software. I hope they all work for you!

Using the DVD

To access the files from the DVD, follow these steps.

1. Insert the DVD into your computer's DVD-ROM drive. The license agreement appears.

Windows users: The interface won't launch if you have Autorun disabled. In that case, click Start → Run (for Windows Vista, Start → All Programs → Accessories → Run). In the dialog box that appears, type **D:\Start.exe**. (Replace *D* with the proper letter if your DVD drive uses a different letter. If you don't know the letter, see how your DVD drive is listed under My Computer.) Click OK.

2. Read through the license agreement, and then click the Accept button if you want to use the DVD.

The DVD interface appears. The interface allows you to access the content with just one or two clicks.

Alternately, you can access the files at the root directory of your computer and copy them to your hard drive from there.

> Mac users: The DVD icon will appear on your desktop; double-click the icon to open the DVD and then navigate to the files you want.

Troubleshooting

Wiley has attempted to provide programs that work on most computers with the minimum system requirements. Your computer may differ, and some programs may not work properly for some reason.

The two likeliest problems are that you don't have enough memory (RAM) for the programs you want to use, or you have other programs running that are affecting the installation or running of a program. If you get an error message such as "Not enough memory" or "Setup cannot continue," try one or more of the following suggestions and then try using the software again:

Turn off any antivirus software running on your computer. Installation programs sometimes mimic virus activity and may make your computer incorrectly believe that it's being infected by a virus.

Close all running programs. The more programs you have running, the less memory is available. Installation programs typically update files and programs, so if you keep other programs running, installation may not work properly.

Have your local computer store add more RAM to your computer. This is, admittedly, a drastic and somewhat expensive step. However, adding more memory can really help the speed of your computer and allow more programs to run at the same time.

Customer Care

If you have trouble with the book's companion DVD-ROM, please call the Wiley Product Technical Support phone number at (800) 762-2974. Outside the United States, call +1(317) 572-3994. You can also contact Wiley Product Technical Support at `http://sybex.custhelp` `.com`. John Wiley & Sons will provide technical support only for installation and other general quality control items. For technical support on the applications themselves, consult the program's vendor or author.

To place additional orders or to request information about other Wiley products, please call (877) 762-2974.

Please check the book's website www.sybex.com/go/mspgame, where we'll post additional content and updates that supplement this book should the need arise.

Index

Note to the reader: Throughout this index **boldfaced** page numbers indicate primary discussions of a topic. *Italicized* page numbers indicate illustrations.

A

Add Layer Mask, 43
Add Selected, 17
Adjustment Layer, 18
Adjustments, 28
alcove, roof, 164, *164*
Align, UV Texture Editor, 67, *68*
alpha channels, 16
    grayscale, 46
    ivy, 45–46, *47*
ambient lights, 184
ambient movement, **203–215**. *See also* industrial fan
Ambient Occlusion (AO), 21
    Blending Mode, 23, 212
    brick wall, 21–22
    diffuse maps, 22
    dune buggy, 137, 140
    industrial fan, 210, *211*
    ivy, 42–43, *43*
    low resolution, *177*
    mental ray, 22
    normal maps, 22
    revolver, *102*
    science-fiction prop, *230*
    skyscraper, 176, *177*
    Transfer Maps, 21–22, 176, 230
    wall sconce, 196, *197*
Ambient Shade, 20
[and], 44
Animation
    Create Deformers, 118
    deformation, 41
    industrial fan, 214–215
    revolver, 103–106
    wall sconce, 185
Animation Preferences, 103, 214, 238
Anti-aliasing Quality, 59
AO. *See* Ambient Occlusion
Append to Polygon tool, 40, 124, 130
Assign New Material, 13, 19, 193
Attach Curves, 112, 129
Attach Method, 112

Attribute Editor, 13, 129
AutoKey, 103
Automatic Mapping, 173, *173*
axle, dune buggy, *125*, **125–126**

B

backgrounds, **1–3**
Bake, 18
    dune buggy, 140
    industrial fan, 211, *211*
    ivy, 42–43
    wall sconce, 196–197
bark
    color, 66
    savannah tree, **62–66**
    texture, *65*
barrel
    low resolution, 95–96, *96*
    revolver, **80**
base
    corner column, *160*
    industrial fan, *207*, 207–208, *208*
    skyscraper, **168–171**, *169*
    wall sconce, *186*
base undercarriage, dune buggy, 128
Bend deformer, 118
Bevel, 4
    corner column, 159
    Edit Mesh, 39
    engine, 135
    hubcaps, *115*
    ivy, *39*
    roof, 163
    roof ledge, 157
    science-fiction prop, 219, 221, 224
    Segments, 150
    wall sconce, 185, 186
    windows, 145, 147
Bevel Offset, 150, 186
Bind Skin, 104, 214
Birail tool, 188, *188*
Blend, Attach Method, 112

Blending Mode
    AO, 23, 212
    color, 33
    Difference, 30
    industrial fan, 212
    ivy, 51
    Linear Dodge, 30, 180
    Linear Light, 233
    Multiply, 26, 177, 198
    Opacity, 25
    Overlay, 25, 66
    science-fiction prop, 233
    Screen, 199
    wall sconce, 198–199
Blending Options, 233
Blinn material, 12, 33
Blur, 43
BMP, 196
Boole, George, 74
Booleans, 73–76, *75. See also* Difference Boolean
    Intersection, 74
    science-fiction prop, 224
    Union, 74, 194, *194*
bracket, wall sconce, 185, **190–191**
branches
    leaves, *59*
    savannah tree, **56–60**, *57, 58*
    texture, 58–60
brick
    brick wall, 3–7
    corner column, 152, 159, *159, 160*
    corner roof ledge, 162
    skyscraper, 146, *146*
brick wall, **3–35**, *9, 11, 17, 34*
    AO, 21–22
    brick, 3–7
    diffuse maps, 12–16, *15, 27*
    grid lines, 4
    laying bricks in, 7–11
    normal maps, 17–21, *18*, 27–29
    texture, 12–15, *24*
Brick_Mask layer, 24
bricks, nooks and crannies in, 5–7
Bridge, Edit Mesh, 89
Brightness/Contrast, 23, 24, 26–27
    bark, 63
    ivy, 50
    science-fiction prop, 231
    skyscraper, 177
    specular maps, 33

buildings, **143–181**. *See also* skyscraper
bullets, revolver, 79, *79*
Bump Mapping, 12

C

Camera Settings, 59, *59*
cap
    corner column, *160*
    wall sconce, 187–190, *189*
ceilings, 1–34
Center Pivot
    Edit, 117
    Modify, 81
cgtexture s.com, 23
chairs, dune buggy, **128–130**, *130*
Chamfer Vertex, 163
Champions Online, 171
Change Offset, 4
Channel Box, 4
    Divisions, 55, 186
    Extrude, 186
    Inputs, 14, 145
    Layer Editor, 17
    polyBevel1 Inputs, 73
    polyCut1, 150
    polyCylinder1, 73, 78
    polyExtrudeFace1, 55, 83, 224
    Random, 5
    Shape, 41
    Subdivisions Width, 148
    Taper, 55
    Tessellate Input, 189
Circle, NURBS Primitives, 187, 191
Clone Stamp tool, 50, 210
cockpit, *123*
    dune buggy, *111*, **111**
coiled spring, shock absorbers, 122
collision meshes, *245*, 245–246
color
    bark, 66
    Blending Mode, 33
    diffuse maps, 12, 16–17
    leaves, 59
    normal maps, 29
    Opacity, 33, 237
    science-fiction prop, 236
    skyscraper, 178
Color Picker, 211

color variation
    brick wall, 25–27
    science-fiction prop, 233
ColorBase layer, 199
Combine, 74, 76, 116, 118
Common Output, 22, 197
Component Select mode, 55
Cone, Polygon Primitives, 99
Connect Output Maps, 15
Contrast Sensitive Production, 59
Convert Selection To Faces, 77
Copy Merged, 27, 32, 64
Corel Painter, 16
corner column
    base, *160*
    brick, 152, 159, *159*, *160*
    cap, *160*
    cylinder, 151, *151*
    large, **159–160**
    skyscraper, *150*, **150–152**, *151*, *152*, **159–160**
    small, **150–152**
    windows, *152*
corner roof ledge, *162*
    brick, 162
    dentil molding, 162
    skyscraper, **160–162**
Create Deformers, 54, 118, 185, 206
Create New Channel, 46
Create New Fill, 18
Create Polygon tool, 154, 160
    Mesh, 38, 58, 81, 86, 117, 147
    rear spoiler, 133
    roof, 163
    windows, 147
Create UVs
    Automatic Mapping, 173
    Cylindrical Mapping, 66, 209
    Mapping, 138
    Normalization Off, 42
    Planar Mapping, 228, 236
Cube, 7
Curve Points, 49
Cut Faces tool, 76, 90, *90*, 150
Cut Plan Center X, 150
Cut UV Edges, 138
CV Curve tool, 47
    branches, 57
    dune buggy, 120, 126
    revolver, 85

    savannah tree, 54, *55*, 56
    wall sconce, 189
cylinder, 78–79, *97*, 97–98, *98*
    corner column, 151, *151*
    engine, 135
    hubcaps, 119
    low resolution, 96–98
    Polygon Primitives, 72
    revolver, 72–79, *77*, *78*
    science-fiction prop, *220*, 220–221, *226*
    shock absorbers, 121, *121*
cylinder frame, *89*, *90*
    Cut Faces tool, 90, *90*
    revolver, *89*, **89–90**
Cylindrical Mapping, 66, 209

D

damage, weapons, 71–72
DDS, 196
deformation, 18, 41
Delete Edge/Vertex, 94–95, 96
dentil molding
    corner roof ledge, 162
    roof ledge, 156, *156*, *157*
    windows, 147, *147*, *148*
Desaturate, 28, 33
Diablo II, 1
Difference Boolean, 30, 74, 76, 78
    engine, 134
    industrial fan, 206
    roof, 164
    roof ledge, 156
    science-fiction prop, 221
Diffuse, Output Maps, 15
diffuse maps, 12, 22
    brick wall, 12–16, *15*, 27
    color, 12, 16–17
    industrial fan, *212*
    ivy, *51*, *52*
    science-fiction prop, *232*
directional lights, 19, 184
Divisions, Channel Box, 55, 186
dune buggy, **110–141**, *141*
    AO, 137, 140
    axle, *125*, 125–126
    base undercarriage, 128
    chairs, 128–130, *130*
    cockpit, 111, *111*

engine, 133–136, *136*
frame, 112, *112*, *113*, *114*
front grill, 136, *136*
headlights, 131, *131*
high resolution, *137*
hood, 113, *113*, 122–125, *123*, *125*
hubcaps, 115–116
low resolution, 137, *137*
normal maps, 137, 140
rear spoiler, 131–133, *132*, *133*
roll cage, *110*, 110–111
shock absorbers, 121–122, *122*
side panel, 126–127, *127*
steering wheel, 125–126, *126*
UV mapping, 138–140, *139*
wheels, *114*, 114–121, *116*
Duplicate Faces, 166
Duplicate With Transform, 8–9, 117, 155, 157, 159,
    226–227
    corner columns, 151
    windows, 147

E

Edge, UV Texture Editor, 67, 174
Edit
    Center Pivot, 117
    Ungroup, 151
Edit Curves, 112, 129
Edit Mesh, 5–6
    Append to Polygon tool, 40, 124
    Bevel, 39
    Bridge, 89
    Chamfer Vertex, 163
    Combine, 116
    Cut Faces tool, 76, 150
    Delete Edge/Vertex, 94–95, 96
    Duplicate Faces, 166
    Extrude, 39, 55, 159, 204
    Insert Edge Loop tool, 55–56, 60
    Merge, 39, 97, 116, 118
    Merge To Center, 49, 56
    Poke Face, 62
    Split Polygon tool, 39
Edit Pivot, 47, 58, 75, 218, 226
Edit Polygons, 39
emissive texture, 200–201, *201*, 231, *231*
End Angle, 206
engine, 135, *135*
    dune buggy, **133–136**, *136*
    platform, *134*

Extrude, 56, 113, 121, 128, 186, 191
    chairs, 128
    corner column, 159
    cylinder, 78–79
    cylinder frame, 90, *90*
    Edit Mesh, 39, 55, 159, 204
    engine, 134
    hood, 125
    hubcaps, *115*
    industrial fan, 204
    ivy vine, 48
    roof, 163
    round roof ledge, 167
    savannah tree, 55
    science-fiction prop, 219, 221, 224
    trigger frame, 87
    wall sconce, 185, 191
    windows, 145, 147

F

fan blade, industrial fan, *205*, 206, *206*
Feather, 50
ffd1LatticeShape:S Divisions, 41
Fill Hole, 5, 96, 116, 121, 191
    cylinder frame, 89
    revolver barrel, 96
    wall sconce, 191
Filter, 43, 52, 64
Final Fantasy, 71, 203
Final layer
    normal maps, 27–29
    specular maps, 32–33, *34*
Flare, 185, *185*
floors, 1–34
foliage, **37–69**
Foreground, 33
frame
    dune buggy, 112, *112*, *113*, *114*
    hood, *124*
    NURBS Primitives, 113
    UV mapping, 138, *140*
    wheels, *120*, *121*
Free Transform tool, 24, 66, 177
Freeze Transformations, 149
frieze, windows, *147*
front grill, dune buggy, **136**, *136*
Front view
    branch, 56
    brick, 4
    revolver, 72
    wall sconce, 189
    windows, 145

G

Gaussian Blur, 43
gear belt, engine, 135, *135*
GIMP. *See* GNU Image Manipulation Program
Glow layer, 199, 233
Glow_Falloff layer, 201, *201*
GNU Image Manipulation Program (GIMP), 16
Gradient Editor, 234, *235*
Gradient tool, 26
Gran Turismo, 109
Grand Theft Auto, 37, 71, 109, 143
grayscale, 33
    alpha channels, 46
    illuminators, 184
    layer mask, 43
    normal maps, 28
    specular maps, 32
grid lines, 4
Grime layer, 50
grip, revolver, **82–84**, *83*
groups, 167
GUN, 109
gun site, revolver, *80*

H

halved sphere, 5, *5*
hammer, revolver, **81–82**, *82*
headlights, dune buggy, *131*, **131**
Height2Normals, 28
High Quality Rendering, 12, 18, 33
high resolution, 137
    dune buggy, *137*
    revolver, *100*
    science-fiction prop, *227*
highlights
    industrial fan, *212*
    skyscraper, *178*
    wall sconce, *199*
HiLeaf mesh, 42
history
    deletion of, 13, 41, 167
    dune buggy, 115
hood, *123*, *124*
    dune buggy, 113, *113*, **122–125**, *123*, *125*
    UV mapping, *139*
HSV. *See* Hue, Saturation, and Value
hubcaps, *115*, 119, *119*, *120*
    dune buggy, **115–116**

hue, 45
Hue, Saturation, and Value (HSV), 19
Hue/Saturation, 24
    industrial fan, 212
    ivy, 50
    science-fiction prop, 231
    skyscraper, 177–178
    wall sconce, 199–200
    windows, 179

I

illuminators, **183–201**. *See also* wall sconce
Incandescence, 236
industrial fan, **204–215**, *211*
    Bake, 211, *211*
    base, *207*, 207–208, *208*
    diffuse maps, *212*
    fan blade, *205*, 206, *206*
    highlights, *212*
    housing, *204*
    looping animation, 214–215
    low resolution, 209, *209*, *210*
    motor, *205*
    normal maps, *211*
    shadows, *212*
    specular maps, *213*
    texture, 210–214
    UV mapping, 209, *209*
inFamous, 143
Input Levels, 29–30
Inputs, 14, 79, 145
Insert, Edit Pivot, 75
Insert Edge Loop tool, 55–56, 60
    cylinder frame, 90
    round roof ledge, 166
    wall sconce, *186*, 186–187
Intersection Booleans, 74
Introducing Mudbox (Kermanikian), 241
ivy, **38–53**, *39*
    alpha channels, 45–46, *47*
    AO, 42–43, *43*
    diffuse maps, *51*, *52*
    Hue/Saturation, 50
    layer mask, *44*
    normal maps, 43–44
    opacity maps, 45–46
    texture, 41–43, 49–53
    veins, *40*, 40–41
    vine, *47*, 47–49

J

Joint tool, 103–104

K

Keep Faces Together, 5
Kermanikian, Ara, 241
Key Rotation, 239
Key Transform, 239
keyframes, **105–106**

L

Lambert material, 13, 19, 73
    dune buggy, 137
    leaves, 59
Lattice, savannah tree, 54, *55*
lattice deforme, 41
Lattice Point, 41
Layer, 16
Layer Bar, 193
Layer Editor, 17
layer mask, ivy, 43–44, *44*
Layer Style, 233
leaves, *58, 61, 62. See also* ivy
    branches, *59*
    color, 59
    savannah tree, 58–62
    texture, 60–62
The Legend of Zelda: The Wind Waker, 58
Level of Detail (LOD), 241–242
Levels, 178–179
light arrays, 18–21, *21*
light source, 183
Lighting/Shading, 42, 230
Linear Dodge, 30, 180
Linear Gradient, 26
Linear Light, 233
LOD. *See* Level of Detail
Loft, 123, 126–127
looping animation, industrial fan, 214–215
low resolution
    AO, *177*
    cylinder, 96–98
    dune buggy, 137, *137*
    industrial fan, 209, *209*, *210*
    revolver, 93–100, *96*, *100*
    science-fiction prop, *227*, 227–230
    skyscraper, 171–174, *173*, *177*
    support strut, 165
    wall sconce, 193–195
    windows, *172*

lowlights, *178*
Low_Poly_Wall, 14, 17, 21
L-shaped polygon, 147, *147*, 154, *154*, 160

M

Madden NFL '09, 37
Magic Wand tool, 45
Mapping, 138
maps. *See specific map types*
Mental Ray, 22, 197
Menu Set, 3
Merge, 39, 97, 116, 118
Merge To Center, 49, 56
Mesh
    Booleans, 74
    Combine, 76, 118
    Create Polygon tool, 38, 58, 81, 86, 117, 147
    Fill Hole, 96, 116, 121, 191
    Mirror Geometry, 39
midmapping, 243–244, *244*
Mirror Direction, 39
Mirror Geometry, 39
mixing normal maps, *31*
Modify
    Center Pivot, 81
    Freeze Transformations, 149
Modify Curve, 185
modules, 143
Mortar layer, 23–24
motor, industrial fan, *205*
Move and Sew UV Edges, 174
Move Axis, 94, 157
Move tool, 75, 157, 193
Mudbox, 241
Multi-pixel Filter, 59
multiple UV channels, 244–245
Multiply, 26, 177, 198

N

negative-space objects, *6*
New Layer, 16, 198
nodes, 167
Nonlinear, 206
Normal Axis
    Move Axis, 157
    Move tool, 193
    revolver, *102*
normal maps, 12
    AO, 22

brick wall, 17–21, *18*, 27–29
dune buggy, 137, 140
industrial fan, *211*
ivy, 43–44
mixing, 29–31, *31*
science-fiction prop, *230*
Unreal Engine, 31
wall sconce, *197*
NormalAdd layer, 29–30
Normalization Off, 42, 60
Normal_Source, 29
NormalSubtract layer, 30
NURBS Primitives, 48, 113
Circle, 187, 191
wall sconce, 187, 191
nurbsTessellate Input, 204
nvidia.com, 28

O

object-space normals, 18
Offset, 64, 166, 186
Offset Curve, 129
Opacity, 25, 201
bark, 66
color, 33
science-fiction prop, 237–238
windows, 180
opacity maps, 37–38
ivy, 45–46
Open/Close Curves, 112, 129
Output Channel, 30
Output Levels, 28, 29–30
Output Maps, 15, 17, 21
Overlay, 25, 66

P

pedestal, science-fiction prop, *218*, *219*, *225*
Persp, 19
Perspective View, 76, 126
corner column, 151, 160
ivy, *39*, 42
revolver, 80, 81, 84, 85, 87
windows, 147
Photoshop, 13, 16, 32
Pipe, 145
Planar Mapping, 228, 236
platform, engine, **133–134**, *134*

Playback Speed, 214–215
point lights, 184
Poke Face, 62
polyBevel1, 4, 73
polyCut1, 150
polyCylinder1, 73, 78
polyExtrudeFace1, 55, 83
science-fiction prop, 224
Polygon Primitives, 5
Cone, 99
Cube, 7
cylinder, 72
Pipe, 145
Pyramid, 163
Polygonal Lasso, 50, 199
Polygons, 3, 14, 198
polySoftEdge1, 41
Post Infinity, 215
Pre Infinity, 215
Pyramid, 163

Q

quarter sphere, *89*

R

Radial Gradient, 234
Random, 5
randomness, 9–11
rear spoiler, dune buggy, **131–133**, *132*, *133*
Rebuild Curve, 129
Rectangular Marque tool, 26, 64
Red, Green, and Blue (RGB), 19, 29
Reference mode, 87
reflection, 32
Remove Map, 17
Render Current Frame, 59
Rendering, 14, 230
Resident Evil, 203
Resolution Gate, 59, *59*
Revolve, 189, 204
revolver, **72–106**, *91*, *102*
animation, 103–106
AO, *102*
barrel, 80
bullets, 79, *79*
cylinder, 72–79, *77*, *78*
cylinder frame, *89*, 89–90
grip, 82–84, *83*

gun site, *80*

hammer, 81–82, *82*

high resolution, *100*

low resolution, 93–100, *100*

screw, 92, *92*

texture, 102

trigger frame, *86*, 86–88, *87*, *88*

trigger guard, *84*, 84–85, *85*

RGB. *See* Red, Green, and Blue

roll cage, dune buggy, *110*, **110–111**

roof, *164*, 165, *165*

skyscraper, **163–165**

roof ledge. *See also* corner roof ledge; round roof
  ledge

dentil molding, 156, *156*, *157*

skyscraper, **155–158**, *158*, *162*

Root joint, 104

Rotate Clockwise, 174

Rotate Counterclockwise, 174

rotation, 18, 106

round roof ledge, skyscraper, *166*, **166–167**

S

Saint's Row, 109

savannah tree, **53–69**

bark, 62–66

branches, 56–60, *57*, *58*

CV Curve tool, 54, *55*, 56

Lattice, *55*

leaves, 58–62

SAW, 71

ScaleX, 111

science-fiction prop, **217–239**

AO, *230*

color, 236

cylinder, *220*, 220–221, *226*

diffuse maps, *232*

Edit Pivot, 226

emissive texture, 231, *231*

Glow layer, 233

Gradient Editor, 234, *235*

high resolution, *227*

Hue/Saturation, 231

low resolution, *227*, 227–230

normal maps, *230*

pedestal, *218*, 225

screw, 221, *221*

specular maps, 233, *234*

texture, 231–233

UV mapping, *229*

sconce. *See* wall sconce

Screen, Blending Mode, 199

screw

revolver, 92, *92*

science-fiction prop, 221, *221*

Search Envelope, 15

Segments, Bevel, 150

Select

Select Contiguous Edges, 76

Select Edge Loop tool, 130

Select Edge Ring tool, 77

Transform Selection, 64

Select Contiguous Edges, 76

Select Edge Loop tool, 40

dune buggy chairs, 130

revolver trigger guard, 85

wall sconce, 189

Select Edge Ring tool, 77

Select Mesh, 76

Select Surfaces, 56, 123

Loft, 126–127

Select Transform, 50

Sew UV Edges, 138

shadows, *212*

Shape, 41

Sharpen, 52

Shelf, 13

shock absorbers

cylinder, *121*

dune buggy, **121–122**, *122*

Split Polygon tool, 124

side panel, dune buggy, **126–127**, *127*

Side View

brick, 4, 10

Create Polygon tool, 160

dune buggy, 110

ivy, 38, 42

science-fiction prop, 218

Skeleton, Joint tool, 103–104

Skin, 104, 214

skyscraper, **144–181**, *171*, *181*

AO, 176, *177*

Automatic Mapping, 173, *173*

base, 168–171, *169*

brick, 146, *146*

color, 178

corner column, *150*, 150–152, *151*, *152*, 159–160

highlights, *178*

low resolution, 171–174, *173*, *177*

lowlights, *178*

roof, 163–165
roof ledge, 155–158, *158*, 160–162
round roof ledge, *166*, 166–167
support strut, 165
texture, *175*, 175–181, *180*
UV mapping, 173–174
windows, 144–149, *145*, *148*, *153*, 153–154,
154, *155*
Smooth Bind, 104, 214
SmoothDetails layer, 43
Smoothing Angle, 4
Snap To Curve, 47, 111, 188
Snap To Grid, 81
Snap To Point, 75, 97, *97*, 117, 119
corner column, 159
science-fiction prop, 226
windows, 145
Soft Light, 33, 51
Soften Edge, 41
Source Meshes, 14, 17, 21, 42, 196
Spec_Base layer, 32
Specular color, 12, 33
specular maps, 12, **32–33**
Final layer, *34*
grayscale, 32
industrial fan, *213*
Photoshop, 32
science-fiction prop, 233, *234*
wall sconce, 200
specularity, 32
Spencer, Scott, 241
Split Polygon tool
dune buggy hood, 123
Edit Mesh, 39
ivy veins, 40
revolver cylinder frame, 90
shock absorbers, 124
spot lights, 184
Start Angle, 206
Status Line, 59
steeple, roof, 165, *165*
steering wheel, dune buggy, **125–126**, *126*
storefront window, 170, *170*
Street Fighter, 109
Subdivisions Axis, 5, 54, 73, 121, 148
Subdivisions Caps, 73, 79, 82
science-fiction prop, 226
Subdivisions Depth, 205
Subdivisions Height, 5, 54, 73
cylinder frame, 89
Subdivisions Width, 148

support strut, 165
skyscraper, **165**
Surfaces, 48
Edit Curves, 112
Extrude, 113, 121, 128, 191
Revolve, 189, 204

T

T Divisions:, 41
Tangent Space Normals, 12, 18
Taper, 55
Targa (tga), 196
Target Meshes, 14, 15, 42
Template mode, 86
Tessellate Input, 189, 204
texture
backgrounds, 2
bark, *65*
branches, 58–60
brick wall, 12–15, *24*
emissive, 200–201, *201*, 231, *231*
industrial fan, 210–214
ivy, 41–43, 49–53
leaves, 60–62
library, 23
Photoshop, 13, 16
revolver, 102
science-fiction prop, 231–233
skyscraper, *175*, 175–181, *180*
wall sconce, 198–201, *199*
windows, 179–181
tga. *See* Targa
32 bits/pixel, 46
Time Slider, 103, 239
Tolerance, 45
Tomb Raider: Anniversary, 1
Toolbox, 75
Tools, 33
Transfer Maps, 14, 17, *21*
AO, 21–22, 176, 230
Lighting/Shading, 42
skyscraper, 176
Source Meshes, 196
Transform Selection, 64
Transparency
Lambert material, 73
Opacity, 237
science-fiction prop, 236
XRay mode, 73
tread, wheels, *117*, 117–119, *118*, *119*

trigger frame, revolver, *86*, **86–88**, *87, 88*
trigger guard, revolver, *84*, **84–85**, *85*
Trigger joint, Rotation, 106
24 bits/pixel, 46
Twist, 206

U

U Divisions:, 41
Underlying Layer, *25*, 25–26, *26*
Ungroup, 151
Union Boolean, 74, 194, *194*
Unreal Editor, 1
Unreal Engine, 31
Unsharp Mask filter, 27, 52
UV Editor, 67
    Cut UV Edges, 138
    UV mapping, *209*
UV mapping, 195, *196*
    dune buggy, 138–140, *139, 140*
    industrial fan, 209, *209*
    low resolution, 173–174
    science-fiction prop, 228–230, *229*
    skyscraper, 173–174
    wall sconce, 195
    windows, *174*
UV Normalization, 14
UV Snapshot, 198
UV Texture Editor
    Align, 67, *68*
    Edge, 67, 174
    industrial fan, 209
    multiple UV channels, 244–245
    revolver, 100–102
    savannah tree, 66–69
    science-fiction prop, *229*
    skyscraper, 173
    UV Snapshot, 198

V

V Number, 189, 204
vehicles, **109–141**. *See also* dune buggy
veins, ivy, *40*, **40–41**
vertices, cylinder, 97–98, *98*
View, Camera Settings, 59
vine, *49*
    ivy, *47*, **47–49**

W

wall sconce, **185–201**, *190, 192*
    Animation, 185
    AO, 196, *197*
    Assign New Material, 193
    Bake, 196–197
    base, *186*
    Bevel, 185, 186
    Birail tool, 188, *188*
    Blending Mode, 198–199
    bracket, 185, 190–191
    cap, 187–190, *189*
    CV Curve tool, 189
    Extrude, 185, 191
    Fill Hole, 191
    Flare, 185, *185*
    Front view, 189
    highlights, *199*
    Hue/Saturation, 199–200
    Insert Edge Loop tool, *186*, 186–187
    low resolution, 193–195
    Modify Curve, 185
    New Layer, 198
    normal maps, *197*
    NURBS Primitives, 187, 191
    Polygonal Lasso, 199
    Select Edge Loop tool, 189
    Snap To Curve, 188
    specular maps, 200
    texture, 198–201, *199*
    Union Boolean, 74, 194, *194*
    UV mapping, 195
walls, 1–34
weapons, **71–107**. *See also* revolver
    damage, 71–72
wheels
    dune buggy, *114*, **114–121**, *116*
    frame, *120, 121*
    hubcaps, *119, 120*
    tread, *117, 118, 119*
windows
    Bevel, 145, 147
    corner column, *152*
    Create Polygon tool, 147
    dentil molding, 147, *147, 148*
    Duplicate with Transform, 147
    Extrude, 145, 147
    frieze, *147*

Front view, 145
Hue/Saturation, 179
large, **144–149**
low resolution, *172*
L-shaped polygon, 147, *147*, 154, *154*, 160
Opacity, 180
Perspective View, 147
skyscraper, **144–149**, *145*, *148*, *153*, **153–154**,
    154, *155*
small, *153*, **153–154**, *154*, *155*
Snap To Point, 145
storefront, *170*
Subdivisions Axis, 148
texture, 179–181
UV mapping, *174*

Wireframe mode, 9
World Axis, Move tool, 157
World of Warcraft, 37, 54

X

xnormal.net, 28
XRay mode, 73, 96

Z

ZBrush, 241
*ZBrush Character Creation: Advanced Digital
    Sculpting* (Spencer), 241

Wiley Publishing, Inc.
End-User License Agreement